FISH-WATCHING AND PHOTOGRAPHY

FISH-WATCHING
AND PHOTOGRAPHY

KENDALL McDONALD
with
TONY BAVERSTOCK   COLIN DOEG
GEOFF HARWOOD   JOHN LYTHGOE
PETER SCOONES   PHILIP SMITH

No human being, however great, or powerful,
was ever so free as a fish.   JOHN RUSKIN

JOHN MURRAY

© Kendall McDonald 1972

Printed in Holland by
N.V. Grafische Industrie Haarlem

0 7195 2422 9

CONTENTS

I FISH-WATCHING

v

CONTENTS

II PHOTOGRAPHY

ILLUSTRATIONS

TROPICAL *pp. 134–135*

ASSOCIATED CREATURES *pp. 150–151*

ENDPAPERS: Pike (*Esox lucius*). (John Lythgoe)

PART ONE

Fish-Watching

IN SEARCH OF FISHES

The long chains of bubbles stream upward like white fizz. Somewhere down below, down deep, friends are already at work watching the fishes. From the concentration of the streams of bubbles, side by side, I know that the divers have stopped in one spot—that they have found something to photograph or something that interests them enough to make them concentrate on one tiny point in the vastness of the sea.

For a moment I hang there. Beside me the boat bobs comfortingly in a slight, but even swell. I notice that the paint on the boat's belly is flaking close to the keel and will need a lot of hard work at the end of the season. A stray bubble wobbles, trapped in the sharp angle between one of the clinkers, and then the boat rocks violently as Penny topples backward from the gunwale to join me in the water. She emerges from the cloud of disturbance, still holding her mask to prevent it being dislodged by her entry, and looks round, lost, until she sees me.

Still the bubbles stream upward from below and the two chains that mark the position of the divers meld together as they close in on whatever it is that they have found.

It is a beautiful sight. First the bubbles come from the darker black-green of the deep. Then they pass into the lighter mid-sea zone and finally, growing larger and larger, race through the bright blue just below the surface. Each one then takes on a quality and size of its own. Each looks like a mirror-reflection of a parachute's balloon of silk as it wells up towards the silver surface, changing shape and size in a last desperate rush for the freedom of air unlimited above.

I move slowly forward with a slight stroke of my fins and let the bubbles burst against me. It is a game—trying to catch the parachutes of air in my hands. But then Penny taps my arm and points downward. It is time to go. I feel that same old mixture of excitement, tinged with just a little fear, which comes at the start of each dive.

And then we tilt downward through the exhaust bubbles of our friends and out into the unsullied sea. Another dive has begun. We are going to join the fishes. . . .

Every dive is an adventure. Some, of course, are more adventurous than others. And though you may learn more about diving from one than another, it is impossible to recall any dive from which I have not learnt something about fishes and the life under the surface of the sea. On each dive you notice something—a fish in an unusual place perhaps—which means nothing to you at that time. But when you put together in your memory a mass of isolated observations, sometimes a pattern emerges. And you want to go on finding out more and more.

Beside me as I write is my diving logbook. Some of its pages are a little stained. Some, of course, are the stains of the sea. Others are the stains from the tables of the little bars in which we relaxed after a dive.

If the writing is not too good in some of the entries, it is not because of the wine, but because of the sun which bounced into my eyes from the pages where I noted it all down.

Some entries have been made in little Italian hotels where the beds were enormous and, in the morning, I wished I had not slept in them. Some in Spanish hotels of higher class where my money went further. Some in French pensions by the sea where after-dive relaxation was overshadowed by the worry that my francs might not last the holiday.

And many, many more entries were made in seaside British bed-and-breakfast establishments where the landladies would have had a fit if they had seen the rinsing out of equipment that took place secretly in their washbasins.

Some entries, of course, were written in the happiness that follows a good dive; others in the misery of a rainy evening after everything had gone wrong. But I have learned something about fish from them all.

I learned that fish are often easier to approach in the murkier waters around the coasts of Britain than in the clear-glass waters of the Mediterranean. Because of this, my wife Penny and I began to dive more and more in the waters not so far from home and found to our amazement that we could get so close to fish that we could touch them.

A particularly exciting example of this came when we dived one summer's day in Cornwall. We were exploring the wreckage of the *Andola* close inshore from the Manacle Rocks, which can lay ugly claim to have sunk more ships than any other reef in the South-West. The *Andola*, a 2,093-ton full-rigged steel sailing ship was wrecked on Shark's Fin Rock, near Porthoustock on the Lizard on January 29, 1895.

In the summer there is not much to be seen of the *Andola* and to find her plates you have to sink down through the great thick green and brown weed, mostly laminaria, that covers her grave. Finally, after you have let the slithery fronds close over your head, you find yourself among the thick stalks of the weed and on the steel plates which still resist the sea's corrosion. Under the plates are shallow caverns that hide crab and lobster, but little light penetrates and the search for fish or shellfish is a gloomy business.

One of the most expressive gestures that a diver can give underwater is an exaggerated shrug of indifference. Another diver seeing this knows exactly what is meant—that there is nothing of interest to see. It almost asks the question: what shall we do now? When I gave this signal to Penny she knew exactly what I meant and we finned upward through the weed to the lighter water above in the hope of seeing something of interest. But the misty blue sea above the carpet of weed that was brilliantly lit here and there by beams of sunlight seemed empty and uninteresting.

I looked at my contents gauge and judging that we had enough air left to dive another day if we cut short our time underwater now, signalled that we should head back to shore.

Penny slid on ahead while I probed the stringweed around a rock just in case there was something to photograph. As I rounded the curve of the rock I saw Penny making frantic signs to me to

5

hurry. I finned forward until I could see the reason for her excitement.

She had no need to point with her knife, though she did—she swims with her knife always in her hand, though she assures me it is for something to probe around with and not to beat off shark attacks—for I saw it at once.

There, hovering like a desert-camouflaged helicopter only a foot away from her, was a John Dory. His fins almost hummed as he manoeuvred a foot this way then a foot that. And all the time his brightly glowing sapphire eyes never left us. Then began one of those rare periods underwater when a fish behaves exactly as you want him to.

As I fumbled with the camera, adjusting focus, flash bulb and aperture, the John Dory behaved as though he knew he was having his picture taken. He swam through some stringweed slowly so that I could snap him emerging. He hung in the water at the right distance while Penny moved in behind shepherding him toward the camera. Against the blue, his markings stood out strongly. He was a photographer's dream fish.

Each time he filled my viewfinder I could see the great black spot dead centre on his side—these black 'thumbmarks' are said to be where St Peter held him while extracting the tribute money from his mouth. Then having posed, he would get a touch of temperament and dash away as hard as his fins would carry him. Penny and I swooped in pursuit. But he didn't go far.

Finally the film ran out and then, with Penny behind him and me in front, he seemed to surrender completely. I looked at him— thin end on—face to face. Slowly, not believing it possible, I reached out a hand and with a forefinger stroked him, not once but several times, down from his telescopic mouth which he shoots out to swallow smaller fish who mistake him face on for a thin blade of weed, down until my finger was under his belly. He stayed perfectly still, fins beating steadily to hold himself in that one place. But finally he had had enough. He made one more dart for freedom—and we let him go.

When we returned to shore and told Bernard and Colleen

Rogers—Bernard is the only diving farmer-fisherman I know, but then as his farm overlooks the Manacles that is only right—I don't think they really believed us (though on second thoughts they might have done because both have been snorkelling with seals).

The only really comparable fish behaviour to that of the John Dory comes when you dive on a sunken Mulberry unit some two miles out to sea from Bognor, Sussex.

The Mulberry, which was to have been part of the D-Day invasion harbour at Arromanches, broke its back and sank when starting the long tow to Occupied France. Today over the flat seabed around it swarm great shoals of banded pouting. They are so numerous and unafraid—other divers please keep it that way—that they swim all around and over you.

At times you even have to tap the youngsters out of the way of your camera lens, but even so, you will often find on developing the film an out-of-focus pouting face covering up the best of all you intended to be in the picture. These fish you can touch, but so far they will not let you stroke them like that John Dory.

Stroking fishes is all very well. That sort of experience tends to make you forget the true nature of life in the sea. A totally different impression comes from watching bass tear the guts out of a school of small pollack. Then the food chain of the sea becomes apparent. The fish that allows you to stroke it one day may be another fish's dinner the next.

The most vivid example of this sort of thing that I have seen when diving came one hot day when the Mediterranean was oily calm and the only breaks in the surface were the sploshing of tiny fish jumping. And even the ripples and rings they left soon died away.

Penny and I found it a relief to get in the water and out of the sun. We had anchored near an isolated rock not far from Punta Escalanya, near Aiguablava on Spain's Costa Brava. It was just another dive and I had no way of knowing that what I was going to see in the next twenty minutes would fill pages and pages of my logbook.

7

We had called the rock 'Lobster Rock' because one face of it—
the shadowed sheer one—was the home of at least a dozen young
spiny lobsters. In my hotel room that evening after the dive I
noted it down like this: 'Working along the South side of the rock
(mainly because I was using a negatively buoyant cylinder and too
much lead on my weightbelt, and the rock sloped gently there
compared with the sheer fall on the other) I was suddenly in the
middle of vast shoals of "whitebait"—transparent fry with
reddish intestines. They swooped this way and that, rather like a
curtain of net being pulled to and fro, in desperate attempts to
escape from something I could not yet see.

'Being careful to make sure that no sea urchins had chosen the
same ledge, I rested on the edge of a precipice and peered down
into the depths. Deep down—80 ft below me—in the almost royal
blue—silver flashed and tumbled. Suddenly the fry would well up,
completely cover me and make a sparkling cloud between me and
the mirror-white of the surface some 20 ft above.

'It was like sitting in a grandstand. From this position I was able
to watch what can only be described as a feeding frenzy. The fry
were being hunted all right. Closest in were sars of all kinds and at
first behind them I saw only one bass, a mere tiddler about a foot
long. His sides looked greenish in sharp contrast to the usual silver
sides of the adult bass.

'Whereas the sars seemed to be chasing the fry for pure sadistic
pleasure—first one way and then the other—splitting the little
fish into separate groups, the bass was quite clearly eating as he
cruised slowly past. Down below in the blue depths the same
thing was obviously happening judging by the flashes of fish sides
that showed every now and then.

'Suddenly a school of pilchards or sardines, little bigger than
the fry themselves, plunged down from far out and joined the fry
hunt. The curtain of fry swished this way and that, but though
their numbers appeared not the slightest bit diminished their losses
must have been enormous.

'Even farther out in front of me in the paler blue were millions
more fry and through this cloud of tiddlers came two majestic

fish. Silver, deep and huge, they cruised like Cadillacs among the
Minis. The larger one which led the way seemed at least 3 ft long.
Up came the camera and off went the flash, but they showed little
fear. Though the solitary small bass had fled twice, only to return
each time, these were a different mettle of fish. They were dentex
and they powered by me unconcerned, munching unhurriedly as
they went past.

'I just lay there and watched. The camera's film was exhausted.
The sea boiled and swayed. The sar swooped, the bass killed, the
dentex killed, and silver flashed all about from the surface white,
down through pale blue to the deep, deep blue-black of the
depths.'

And so I watched until my air ran out. But just before it did, I
suddenly noticed Penny only a few yards away to my right
transfixed on the rocks the same way that I was. I knew what I had
seen. I had seen the real sea. The sea of kill or be killed. And that
night over dinner, Penny suddenly said: 'There wasn't anything
very sentimental about that was there?' She had said exactly what
I was thinking. There is no place for sentiment in the sea—at least
there isn't when you see something like that.

But though there may be nothing sentimental about life in the
sea, divers do lapse unconsciously when talking about the fish
they meet, into words that have only human behaviour connections. They say such-and-such a fish is 'cheeky' or 'inquisitive'.
They talk of fishes playing 'hide-and-seek', being 'friendly', being
'frightened' or 'chasing one another'.

The scientists say that this is wrong—that one should never
ascribe human characteristics or behaviour to animals, birds or
fish. Few regular divers would agree with them. Perhaps we need
a whole new language to cope with the things that fish do underwater; perhaps there is some other explanation of marine creatures'
behaviour that is completely past our comprehension.

But anyone who has dived down on to an octopus as he or she
is spotted in the cleft of some Mediterranean rocks will have only
one explanation of the octopus's behaviour. That incredible
whitening of the entire body except for the area near the eyes can

9

only be compared with the surface expression of 'white with fear'. And who can blame the octopus for its reaction when a huge dark object with one great eye—the mask—in the centre of its head plunges swiftly down upon it?

How else can you explain, except in human terms, the red flush that will pervade the skin of the same octopus when poked and pushed by the same diver? If the scientists are right we cannot say that this is the red flush of anger—but it is the most remarkable imitation of it that anyone has ever seen.

But perhaps it is unfair to take the octopus as an example—for he shares with humans the best developed vision system or eyes that you will find in any underwater creature.

So let's take another example. What are those mullet doing, zooming and climbing and rolling from side to side in the sunlight? Yes, of course, they will snap up any trifle of food that comes their way in the course of such an aqua ballet—but the diver knows from watching them that they are indulging in the most obvious example of sheer joy of living that he can ever expect to see.

What brings the lobster out from the depths of his dark hole when the diver taps gently on the rock at its mouth? Hunger—or just plain curiosity?

What makes clouds of young pouting swim so close to the diver that he can push them aside with his hands? It must be curiosity. And when they are pushed out of the way, why do they come back again and again? What can it be—except that?

So, to the diver, the scientists appear to be wrong. Every diver knows that there are happy fish, sullen fish, inquisitive fish, frightened fish, intelligent fish and stupid fish. There are fish that kill for food and fish that seem to kill without reason. Perhaps that is the most human thing of all.

One thing is certain. It will take a great deal more diving and a great deal more underwater observation before we are able to draw any firm conclusions about the way fish behave under the surface of the sea. But that kind of diving has already started. . . .

KENDALL McDONALD

HOW TO GET CLOSE TO FISH

It is the diver-photographer who learns most about fish in their natural state. And it is precisely because he has got his camera with him underwater that he learns so much. If you see a diver in the water without a camera, you can be sure that he will hurry from rock to rock, perhaps searching for a tasty lobster, but by the very speed of his movement he will miss hundreds and thousands of interesting sights.

The underwater photographer, however, is intent on finding subjects for his pictures and so he studies the terrain and its population carefully. Fish respond to the gentle approach, the leisurely finning over the bottom, the quiet concentration on something else, such as a purple starfish or the waving fronds of a plumose anemone. It is because of this unhurried movement that the diver often looks up from his viewfinder and finds himself in turn being watched by some giant silvery bass or cloud of smaller fish.

And if we dare apply human instincts to fish for a moment the diver-photographer will tell you that most fish seem to have a 'sixth sense' about people underwater. They seem to know if harm is intended to them. It is difficult to understand how fish can tell the difference between a speargun's nozzle or a camera lens being pointed at them. But they certainly can.

Try focusing quietly on some large wrasse as he pokes his head out from a great clump of weed and within reason the fish will make only lazy movements. Do the same thing with a speargun and nine times out of ten you'll find yourself aiming at some weed that suddenly seems to be minus fish. Is it possible that we communicate our intent through the water to the fish? Is there something about the stance taken in the water by the spearfisherman that stirs something in the fish's memory about other predators? No one yet knows, but this aspect of fish behaviour has been observed by thousands of divers—both cameramen and spear-fishermen. They know, say the divers. And so they do.

Incidentally, few underwater photographers, however much they have suffered from the exploits of spearfishing colleagues—it is particularly infuriating to have the fish that you are about to photograph speared from under your very lens!—feel that the same thing will happen in British waters as it has in the Mediterranean.

In the more populated areas of the Mediterranean coastline there are few fish of certain species left. Spearfishermen, mostly tourists, outnumber decent-sized fish. Less than twenty years ago, to dive into the clear waters of the Med was to move into a watery wonderland. Big fish seemed to be under every rock and they did not slink away into cover at the sight of a snorkelling viewer.

Now, if you are equipped with mask and snorkel only, in those same areas you would be lucky to see anything but tiddlers. Spearfishermen of all nationalities have done that. Even in more remote areas the sight of a speargun is enough to frighten most fish well away.

But the reason that this was possible is that the waters of the Mediterranean are comparatively tideless and crystal clear on most days. Most important of all, the large species are mostly rock dwellers like the grouper, and could always be found in the same place. So the big fish have either been shot or have left the shallow inshore waters for much deeper homes.

It is impossible to believe that this could happen in murkier, tide-swept Northern waters, such as the seas around Britain, where so many fish roam freely. Added to this, spearfishing in our colder waters is unlikely ever to enjoy such a vogue as that experienced by the warm sunny waters of the Mediterranean.

Once having said that, it is obviously better to move among the fish with a camera than a speargun. If your pictures come out well, then you have a permanent record of the sights you saw, rather than a short-lived memory and a few bones on a plate.

The spearfisherman and the underwater photographer have, however, one main thing in common. Both have to get close to the fish. And this is where the approach is all important. All movements have to be leisurely and must appear unhurried even when the diver is finning desperately to hold himself in position against a racing tide. Few fish, however friendly, will take kindly to splashing and violent movement. Fish can be intensely curious about what divers are doing—but not curious enough to wait around something thrashing wildly about in the water.

To be a successful underwater photographer—or even to watch fish without a camera—you must have so much experience of diving with the aqualung that the equipment and use of it is second nature. So much so that during a dive you are not conscious of wearing it at all and all your attention can be given to the fish and to your camera.

You will not find out how to dive from reading this or any other book. There are, of course, many technical works that will teach you the theory, but the only way to learn is to take a course of diving instruction. Any branch of the British Sub-Aqua Club will teach you how to dive. And if you stick with that branch of the Club you will certainly reach the state of diving capability that you require to become an underwater photographer. You must be so familiar with the use of diving equipment that you are hardly aware that you are using it—yet you must be able to react in the correct manner if the slightest thing goes wrong.

As a trained diver you will still need to know how to approach the fish. There is usually a choice of two methods. One is the static dive approach—that is with the boat moored above some prominent feature, such as a wreck or an outcrop of rocks. The other is the drift dive—letting the currents carry the diver where they will.

The 'static approach' is really a term which bears no relation to the conditions that the diver is going to encounter beneath the boat. Though the boat may be anchored firmly in position, conditions down below will depend on the tide. Obviously one aims to dive when the tidal flow is minimal, but this may well not be the best time to observe fish.

At times of complete slack water, fish often seek shelter and are not seen at their best. Anyone who has watched a shoal of pollack sheltering behind wreckage or rocks in a tidal flow will know that the same fish have a totally different behaviour pattern when the water is not moving at all. In fact fish which like to keep head to tide during times of flow are much more approachable than at times of slack water.

Often the diver who approaches from behind—up tide—in such conditions when the tide is flowing strongly will find himself taking exactly the same precautions as the fish. The tide is pushing him strongly so he seeks shelter from it behind outcrops of rock or wreckage. He will find the fish doing exactly the same.

Though these conditions are an absolute joy for the fish-watcher —for he will find himself the 'Tail-End Charlie' of a shoal of fish with the tail fin of the last one only inches from his face mask—the diver-photographer will not be so happy. First of all the conditions of visibility will be lousy. All sorts of bits of gubbins will be flowing past him and his camera lens in the tide; and secondly the fish will insist on presenting him with tail views only.

You might think this state of affairs can easily be rectified by swimming against the tide ahead of the fish and letting the tide carry you down head-on to the fish. In practice this seldom works. On approaching the fish in this manner, the area that was one moment a solid mass of fish becomes a desert. It seems clear that the fish, seeing or sensing the diver's approach, let themselves slide away with the tide and positively refuse to be a head-on target.

The only possibility of approach in these tidal circumstances is to work up tide until parallel with the fish. This state of affairs they don't seem to mind though you can see many an apprehensive eye peeking over the flanks of others in the sheltering shoal.

There is obviously a great deal of research to be done on the behaviour of fish in tidal streams. Certainly fish such as the pollack rely on the tide to bring them the food that they enjoy. If a pollack can find a rock which shelters him from the tide and yet permits a tidal flow over the top, he has found the perfect self-service arrangement.

Behind such a rock the pollack will hang head up, tail down. In these circumstances the diver can enjoy the shelter too and watch the feeding behaviour of these fish. For a while the pollack will hang there and then suddenly dart upward, gobble at some tiny particle the tide has swept over the rock, and then drop back into the shelter of the obstruction once again. Such feeding rarely seems to take the fish into the full sweep of the current.

Divers who have seen this happening get the impression that the food is swept along in the full flow of the tide, but when it encounters the 'dead water' behind the obstruction, it sinks almost neatly into the fish's mouth. This seems logical if one examines the seabed behind such prominent rock features. Here the ground is a pile of empty shells, all of which obviously would flutter along in any really strong current.

When the tide is not in full flow, a large group of rocks or wreckage still provides shelter and the same fish are often present. But without the goodies brought along by the tide, the fish scene seems almost civilised. The same fish that hung in the current are now circulating without any pressure upon them. They don't feed, but they do seem much more suspicious. In fact the diver who visits a rock site at completely slack water will gain a completely different impression of the area to that of his colleague who, late perhaps in starting out, sees exactly the same site at half or even full tidal flow.

Diving in full tidal streams is, of course, a less comfortable method of watching fish and most divers seek slack water for their dives. The time of year that the diver visits a site also has a vast bearing on the fish population. In the spring, the water is more liable to be clear and the fish more wary. At the height of summer, the water is never so good from the point of view of visibility, but the fish are less cautious.

As summer mixes slowly into autumn, the shoals of pouting and pollack seem to grow in size. This is when the diver starts to see really large fish where before the fish in the schools were medium-sized or juvenile. It is the time too when the big bass seem to lose some of their caution and can be seen attacking such shoals in twos or threes. And then as autumn fades into winter, the water clears and caution returns once more to the fish population of our coastal waters.

So far we have dealt with the static situation—boat moored above rocks or wreck—but there is another way of watching fish throughout the year. This is the drift dive.

In some way it seems more hazardous and some divers don't like it at all. The idea of letting yourself drift wherever the tide cares to take you is, understandably, repugnant to some people. But, as you cover a much greater area than on the dive to a known fixed object, you are, in theory, more likely to see more of the life under the sea. Yet many a diver drifting through the foggy gloom over a grey seabed must be forgiven if he thinks at some stage on such a dive that he is likely to come face to face with something much bigger than he can handle!

Though the drift dive is an excellent idea if you are unable to get to the chosen spot at the exact moment of slack water, it is an extremely difficult method of taking underwater photographs.

True, you can watch fish for a certain length of time, but your period of observation is likely to be very short unless you can anchor yourself to some handy outcrop of rock and so stop yourself being carried right past some interesting section of seabed.

The purpose of a drift dive is obviously to carry you over a large area of seabed, and with a strong tide running it is amazing how much ground you can actually cover. Most underwater photographers tend to overweight themselves. This can be a positive disadvantage on a drift dive as it will inevitably result in contact with the seabed. The resultant cloud of stirred-up silt will only clear if you can stop and let it be carried away. Otherwise the silt will drift at the same rate as the diver and he will find himself continually enveloped in a cloud of his own making.

Before going into the technique of taking photographs on a drift dive any further it would probably be best to define exactly what is meant by such a dive.

On a drift dive the diver lets himself be carried by the tide wherever it wants to take him. Obviously, without boat cover this would be extremely dangerous. And it is also no use relying on some sharp-eyed lookout in a boat being able to follow the diver by his bubbles of expired air.

Anyone who has stayed in a boat and attempted to locate divers in any disturbed patch of water—the race over the Mixon Hole, Sussex, springs immediately to mind—will know that the slightest chop on the sea breaks up the exhaust bubbles to such an extent that it is impossible to say for certain exactly where a diver is.

Any diver on a drift dive, or in any waters that are anything more than glassy smooth, must be attached to a clearly recognisable buoy that the boat can follow easily. Such a buoy—large and unlikely to be pulled under—if attached to the diver by floating rope causes the minimum interference with his movements down below. A little fishing float will not do as it will certainly be lost by the lookout in the boat in even a slight chop. Nor can the divers on the seabed feel the slightest confidence that the boat will be close by when they surface if the buoy is not a really large affair.

Tides, contrary to fiction, do not flow due east or west or north or south. They curl, eddy and generally behave most strangely. And in accordance with such strange behaviour the divers do not follow any straight path. This makes the use of a marker buoy more than necessary. It makes its absence something close to suicidal.

But such diving does have its compensations. Drift diving over Luff Bucknell at Bognor—Luff Bucknell, despite the anglers' belief that it is a vast complex of huge rocks, is really a group of low rocks covered with laminaria weed—divers were amazed to find a school of large pollack—some looked over 3 ft long— being harassed by five even bigger bass. The bass would roar in, heavy, thick and silver, straight at the younger members of the school for all the world like a pack of snapping dogs. The larger pollack would take not the slightest notice. The divers hung there —desperately clinging on to the low rocks in a three to four-knot tide—in an attempt to photograph the action. In such a current it is almost impossible to clutch the rocks and sight and fire an underwater camera. Time after time the bass came in. Now they snapped at the pollack shoal in earnest. The water seemed to be shoved this way and that by the big fishes' attacks. But the pollack stayed remarkably calm.

The safest place for a pollack to be in such circumstances would seem to be the middle of the shoal. But the big fish seemed hardly concerned with that theory. Every now and then a big one would turn lazily from its position against the tide and curl round on the flank of the shoal before taking up a new and even more vulnerable position on the outside of the formation. Bass, they seemed to think, were a natural hazard that didn't really amount to much.

Suddenly the bass saw the divers or their bubbles and were gone. The pollack, however, stayed head to tide as though the divers didn't exist. At this moment one of the divers realised that he was all alone. But, as they were both well trained, he realised where his companion would be—following the basic safety rule which lays down that directly a diver loses sight of his companion he surfaces. So up through the misty green he went and had little answer to the shouted criticism—'Where the hell have you been? I've been waiting up here for ages!'

Drift diving is really no place for an underwater photographer unless you have a very patient companion who is prepared to swim by you at all times—even when you seem to be fiddling about with the camera near a barren rock. After all how can he know that you are preparing to take the underwater photograph of the year!

So the disadvantage of the drift dive is obviously that of staying in the same spot for any length of time. And it is only when you have done a great deal of drift diving that you will realise just how big the sea really is. And how difficult it is to relocate any special spot found on a drift dive.

It is essential for the diver who wants to observe fish properly that he should be able to return time and time again to the same spot. I have already said that the fish population changes from season to season. It does more. It changes from day to day. One day you will see a conger in a certain spot. The next the conger will be gone. But it is likely in this instance that the fish is not there because it is off hunting somewhere in the near neighbourhood.

So the diver who says 'Don't let's go there, there was nothing interesting there last time,' is probably missing out on the sight of a lifetime. We must, of course, exempt from this sort of generalisation the place that is obviously barren and quite clearly will almost always be so. Diving time is always limited and only a fool would keep diving in the same spot in the wild hope of seeing some free-swimming fish pass by.

For each fish has an ideal habitat. Each fish seems to conform to a certain set of circumstances, whether it be weed, mud, rock, sand or shingle. And it would be a foolish diver who said that it would be impossible to find one species of fish in one place and not in another.

It is true that water temperature and salinity set up certain impassable barriers but outside those, if you think about it, there is really nothing to stop one fish moving into another type of environment. The sea is a sort of all-embracing highway. A fish can, within the limits we have set, go anywhere there is enough water for it to swim through.

The diver is prepared to find any fish anywhere. No diver disbelieves another's story about the fish he has seen and where he has seen them. Size, like angler's tales, is another thing of course. The diver works in a world where magnification is the norm. But the more experienced a diver is, the more he is likely to tone down the size of the fish he saw rather than exaggerate it.

The sea is a big place—but it is only the diver who really knows what a big place it is. It is possible to know within half-a-mile where a wreck is, to find it once, and despite repeated dives, never to find it again.

But if you can relocate a likely spot, then regular visits will pay dividends. Take my favourite spot—that sunken Mulberry unit off the Sussex coast that never reached the D-Day beaches of Arromanches. Divers go there again and again—because they know that on each dive they will see something different.

In the spring they see the dark shapes of cod swimming low among the pouting schools. In the summer red mullet join the same schools in the same position, low down close to the sand, which they investigate with those twin barbels from their lower lip. In the autumn the pollack—big ones—form into huge shoals and move in close to the wreckage, whereas in the spring they were shy and swimming well out at the limits of visibility. And the stray big black bream swim solitarily, but close to other fish. In the winter the clarity comes back to the water and the life cycle returns to that of spring.

So only by diving again and again at the same spots can the fish-watcher or diving-photographer make any assessment of the value of the spot he has chosen.

It is the diver-photographer and the underwater fish-watcher who will provide the real answers to all the questions about the way fish behave when at home and alive.

But to answer any question about the life of fish the diver has still to get close. Visibility in the sea is such that even on the clearest days proper observations have to be made at close range. But this does not mean that he has to lie still on the seabed all the time. Some very fine pictures have been taken by the diver who is not using the aqualung with its cylinders of compressed air, but confines the length of his visits to the fish world by the amount of air he can hold in his lungs.

I am talking, of course, of the mask, fins and snorkel diver whose depth and stay is conditioned only by his fitness. On one single breath it is possible for a man to dive to depths in excess of 200 ft. But, of course, this superman is not the diver we have in mind.

Obviously the man who wants to watch fish and photograph them will be better off if he can stay quiet and still except for the gentle release of bubbles of exhausted air from his aqualung.

Some fish may be much more sensitive to sound than others. Species like haddock and whiting, for example, are rarely seen by divers, although a nearby rod-and-line or net fisherman can be hauling them up in dozens.

Dr 'Bill' Hemmings of the Government Fisheries Laboratory in Aberdeen has managed to lure a haddock into camera range by scattering the sea-bed with broken-up mussels. Haddock are known to be very sensitive to sound and it may be that they are scared away by the noise of the diver's demand valve as he breathes in and out. This would seem highly possible because Royal Navy divers who sometimes use acoustically silent gear do then see haddock.

For this sort of reason some of this country's finest underwater photographers have taken a number of their best shots in shallow water without the use of the aqualung. Some claim a more silent approach to fish without the aqualung's exhaust disturbing the stillness. And provided their equipment is not complicated, it is true that snorkel divers can take excellent pictures and see a great deal of the underwater world.

Taking this simple approach to marine life photography to its limits, it is possible to take some excellent pictures in rock pools by using a glass-bottomed box. You would be surprised how many photographs published in learned works on the sea-shore and its marine inhabitants have been taken by this method!

For this, a stout wooden box with strong waterproof sides— each made from one piece of wood of course—is fitted with a bottom of plate-glass. The connection between glass and wooden sides is waterproofed by means of one of the many excellent compounds in general use on car-bodies. The box is pushed down into the waters of some suitable rock pool and the camera is held inside the box and focused through the glass.

Take a correct exposure reading by meter from the position that will be occupied by the camera (make sure that no shadows fall on the glass) and a superb colour photograph of that beautiful anemone is yours. Of course this has its limitations, but unless you want to enter your picture for an underwater photography competition—the rules say that the photographer must be completely submerged—you could do worse!

KENDALL McDONALD

CHAPTER ONE

Northern Waters

ANGLERS, FLAT-FISH, CONGERS AND PORBEAGLE

There's no doubt about it—I have dived in clearer waters, like those off the West coast of Ireland. No doubt too that I have dived in warmer waters—the Red Sea and Mediterranean. But despite this there is also no doubt that I have found my main interest in the cold murky waters of the Sussex coast.

If this sounds strange it becomes even more so when you consider the condition of these home waters of mine between Beachy Head and Selsey Bill.

The sea is shallow and the bottom shelves very gently. The seabed is flat sand, shingle and mud all mixed up together, but there are occasional outcrops of rock and a sprinkling of wrecks. There are strong tides. Rivers feed into the sea and the area is frequently subject to bad weather. This all tends to make the conditions underwater unhelpful to the photographer. Visibility is more likely to be poor than good.

But all is not lost. Those rocks and wrecks attract fish. Pouting are always there. So are conger eels, crabs, lobsters and cod in season. So are bass. And away from the rocks on the plains are the flat-fish—if you can find them.

The poor visibility means that I usually have to use flash to get a decent photograph. But because flash means lighting up the particles in suspension in the water and a foggy effect on the final print, I do try to wait for those rare days when the visibility is good.

The odd thing is that fish appear to be far less wary in this area when the water is clear and the light good than when the water is cloudy and the light dull. Certainly I have found this always applies to the bottom-feeding fish such as gurnard and pouting. So the technique I have adopted is to go into the water with only one object—to find fish to photograph. It is so easy to go into the water and to be so anxious to miss nothing of any kind that, in fact, you end up by seeing none of the things you are looking for.

This concentration particularly applies to flat-fish. They are masters of camouflage and it requires a determined mind and a pair of sharp eyes to spot them. A sole in sand, or a plaice, a dab or a flounder on mud or shingle take some seeing. Very often all that can be seen is a 'water-mark' with the black dot of the eye showing at one end.

But it is not only the small fish that can fade into the background. There was a time on a British Sub-Aqua Club sea dive when the boat was making heavy work of very strong northerly off-shore winds. The original diving site was completely unsuitable so we anchored in shallow water under the cliffs to the East of Brighton.

There were eight divers in the group of which I was one. First opinion was that the dive was uninteresting—flat chalk rocks, sand patches and little else of note. Certainly I lugged my camera around and had found just a few sea anemones and whelks, which I photographed for lack of anything else.

However, when the last pair of divers surfaced they started calling for me—I was the only photographer in the boat—and they said they had found a large fish.

I went in again complete with camera and my last three flash bulbs. I didn't have to swim far. Following David Clark's directions I found the fish almost under the diving ladder from the boat.

The fish was a giant—an angler fish lying prone on both sand and rock. It was so beautifully camouflaged that I reckon that every one of us had swum over it without seeing anything.

This was quite a tribute to its camouflage as it was 6 ft long and 3 ft wide at the head. An uglier sight I have not seen—well, not in the sea anyway!

None of the earlier divers had seen it because the fish's outline was broken by irregular pieces of skin and the colour was a perfect match with the drab background. I took my photographs and the fish remained perfectly still. The only sign of life were the eyes, which watched every movement.

This co-operation gave me a little courage so I tried to get him to move by throwing a pebble. Throwing stones underwater just does not work and the pebble fell short. So I made a nervous approach to within arm's length and dropped a stone gently on to the massive head. The reaction of the fish was swift. The head turned, an enormous cavern of a mouth snapped open showing several rows of wicked teeth.

If the fish was swift, my actions were instantaneous. With a hop, skip and a jump I was up the ladder and on board the boat. I was safe, but still half-convinced that both legs had been secateured off!

Seconds later there was a boiling, frothy mass by the boat which turned out to be David Clark, who, unknown to me, had witnessed the whole performance. He was suffering from such an attack of near hysteria that he had to be hauled out. His version of the affair—when he stopped laughing—was that the fish raised itself leisurely off the bottom when I dropped the stone and then swam off in a dignified manner long after my hasty departure. My version is true.

The diver who wants to photograph flat-fish should swim above the bottom to avoid disturbing mud or sand and should head into the tide. Keep a good look out ahead and to each side. Once a fish is spotted, my method is then to rest on the bottom—any disturbance should be carried away behind you by the tide.

Check the camera. Make sure the flash bulb is properly in the holder. Check too that the camera is wound on and cocked. Then creep in very gently as close as possible. I like to take close-ups partly because the amount of water between lens and fish is minimised, reducing throwback from the flash, and partly because a close-up picture has greater impact.

For flat-fish, a head-on view with the camera at an angle of $45°$ to horizontal seems to give a good effect.

Unfortunately, the fish is not always placed so that the head is pointing towards you if you approach from down tide. So you may have to creep round the side, trying to control your breathing so that great gobs of expired air do not disturb the fish. Avoid contact with the seabed as much as possible because sediment will well up immediately you do.

This method of photographing flatfish is really quite an obvious approach. It works well and repeated shots of the same fish can be taken with the subject quite undisturbed by the one-eyed monster with the bright flashing light. I have often been able to take shot after shot with a close-up lens only 7 in. away from the fish.

Whiting and most members of the cod family are fairly easy to photograph. Certainly pouting and channel whiting found around wrecks and rocks, where there is a mixture of light and shade, are inquisitive. If the photographer rests on rock, wreck or in mid-water near them, they will swim in a circle round him. They get closer and closer and really can be a bit of a nuisance—particularly if you are trying to focus on something else.

Cod make extremely good subjects, particularly if they are feeding, but they do tend to be shy. It is not easy to get more than one shot of a cod, especially if you use flash.

Bass are difficult to photograph. It always seems to me that the best time to catch them is when the tide is strong. At slack water they tend to stay very much out of the picture. Making a fixed point dive in a strong current is not a practice to be encouraged.

It is, however, possible to plan such a dive using a line to rocks or wreck, and from the line get into the shelter of the leeside of the obstruction. In these circumstances bass will sometimes come very close indeed. But the real trouble with photographing bass is their silvery colour. Against a water background they tend to look transparent.

Conger eels on the other hand are easy to photograph. A gentle approach to a known conger hole will not make them withdraw their head—which is normally poking out of their chosen hide-away. Not so frequently—usually near dawn or dusk—they can be found swimming free and on dull days you will sometimes come upon them in the same state. But they can be swift and I have never got a good photograph of a free swimming conger in its entirety. Because of their length, for anything but a head-on shot you would need an ultra wide-angle lens.

Nothing I am told about congers can surprise me any more—except, perhaps, real evidence of their legendary ferocity.

While diving to recover an inshore fisherman's lost trawl, we found an uncharted wreck about four miles off Shoreham. It looked like a First World War trawler and, for the Sussex coast, was in a remarkably good state, sitting upright on the seabed in 70 ft of water.

There was a deep scouring of the seabed due to the tides on one side of the hull and a build-up of sand on the other. We cleared the trawl and visited the wreck again for another dive. This time a very, very large conger was found in the companionway leading to the engine room. We decided on a group basis that capturing the giant alive and bringing it back intact as a specimen for Brighton Aquarium would be a most satisfactory exercise—especially if it were landed on the end of one of Brighton's piers and borne to the Aquarium in triumph amid the full glare of unwanted (but not ignored) publicity!

Well, conger eels are conger eels and though we had never met an angry one, we decided that a really safe plan for the giant's capture was needed.

But divers tend to be individualists and among the team there soon appeared two factions. One decided that the only way to effect the capture was to fill a pouting with tranquilliser pills and feed it to the conger. The other band, led by a farmer, duly appeared with a large veterinary hypodermic syringe mounted on a pole and loaded with tranquilliser normally used for quieting cows needing repairs to torn udders.

So we set off. The wreck was located and anchor dropped. A large net was ready in which to roll the doped conger—and a supply of damp sacks made ready to ease his journey back to Brighton.

Now pouting are rather the marine equivalent of urban sparrows and are always present on wrecks. But on this particular day they defied all attempts to be caught. So the hypodermic lance party took advantage of the delay to put their plan into operation. Unfortunately the giant conger was not in the expected place.

As a consolation prize, however, a medium-sized, respectable-looking specimen was found under the stern in the space between the curve of the wreck's bilge and the seabed. And without much trouble the hypodermic was pushed in behind the head and enough drug to put a heifer to sleep was injected.

Now the instructions said: Allow ten minutes for the drug to take effect. In a warm-blooded mammal that is. So twenty minutes were allowed to elapse before the recovery party, plus net, descended to haul out the recumbent body. Unfortunately, there were now two congers in the space—and no one knew which was which! Sadly, the conger's reputation won and the Aquarium did not get its monster.

It seems a shame about the conger's reputation for ferocity. It all seems to stem from anglers unfortunate enough to be bitten after landing a conger. I must say if I were a conger and had a good set of teeth, I would do the same.

Yet once we found three young congers lying out in the open in shallow water on a sunny day. They were in a gully in the chalk. We tickled them, at first with a snorkel and then with a finger. They rolled on their backs and it only wanted a few purrs for the comparison with drowsy kittens to be complete.

In contrast to this, on another occasion a conger under a rock was being teased by two divers. I was at the head end and a friend was down at the tail. Finally the conger got fed up, grabbed the metal snorkel I was holding and gave it a good shake. It dented badly. But there was no doubt that the conger had been provoked into retaliation.

It does seem that unless teased or tormented the conger is inclined to the peaceful life. Once I was diving to recover a trawl snagged on the wreck of the Belgian trawler, *Celtic*. The visibility underwater was bad, but I felt very confident as I knew the wreck well, due to a period of unsuccessful salvage on her.

The trawl was hooked around the after area and considerable effort was needed to free it piece by piece. However, the mizzen mast was very close to me and I leaned against it to rest from my efforts. It swam away! What I had taken for the mast was a conger, vertical and motionless.

In general I would say that photographing fish is far easier than photographing land- and air-based forms of wild life. The reason I say this is because it seems to me that fish and marine life are not usually afraid of divers; the reverse may not be true.

Certainly the actual business of taking photographs in my local Sussex waters is simplicity itself. All you have to do is to wait for reasonably clear conditions, use flash, do not try to exceed 5 ft in range, and use $1/125$ and $f/8$. For close-ups try $1/125$ at $f/22$.

The biggest snag of the lot in my experience is the flash unit. It must be exquisitely clean with all contacts, including those on the bulb, checked by rubbing with fine emery paper before each dive. Do this and then all you have to do is dive.

All you have to do is dive—I say this and then think about sharks. Sharks evoke all sorts of emotions in all sorts of people. Fear comes first and fascination follows a close second. Most divers know—though most trippers don't—that there are sharks in the seas around the coasts of Britain. But, so far as the safety of the average British bather is concerned, the sharks that visit our shores are harmless.

No one has ever been bitten by a shark while swimming around this country.

So when a leading British game fisherman, John Holmes, asked me to join him on his boat for a porbeagle shark fishing expedition off the Isle of Wight, I readily accepted.

The expedition was to fish an area to the South of St Catherine's Point. And, relying on the non-existent British records of shark attacks, I asked if I could bring aqualung and camera equipment along.

The chosen day was overcast. Sea calm. Poor visibility both above and below water. We caught mackerel for bait. These were cut up and placed in a mesh bag and hung over the stern. This bag of 'rubby-dubby' was banged against the hull every minute or so and a slick of flesh and oil spread out behind the drifting boat. Rods and reels were rigged.

John Holmes has fished for sharks and big fish in many parts of the world and held the record for porbeagle (199 lb) since 1953. His stories of mako, hammerhead, thresher and other sharks, of manta rays and big game fish, made the time pass quickly. I was so absorbed in his experiences that it came as a shock when a shark suddenly appeared near the boat and just as suddenly disappeared.

I was probably more shocked than the others. I realised that I had come to photograph shark. What had seemed a jolly idea on shore was no longer so appealing.

John assured me that porbeagle only eat fish. But the shark I had just seen seemed to have a mouthful of teeth that could cope with something larger!

I wondered if it was possible to invent a quick cold, a blocked sinus, or whether I should just admit to cowardice. But neither seemed to match the loss of face I was bound to suffer.

So I got into the water. And there was nothing to see. I kept near to the boat, however, and fiddled with the camera. I told myself that I was trying to decide how to photograph the creature if and when it appeared. Something touched me! Now no diver likes being touched underwater and I was no exception. My jump took me nearly back into the boat. Then I realised that it was an old diving friend, Vic Wheele, who had given me a prod with the shark gaff.

Nothing seemed around. So I climbed aboard again. Suddenly things started to happen. An unseen porbeagle took the bait on one line and the fight began. Dramatically the rod bowed into a semi-circle, the reel really screamed and the fish sounded. My interest in what was happening underwater was too intense for my fear and back into the water I went. It *was* interesting. A large porbeagle is obviously very cross when hooked and the nearer the boat it is pulled the more unpredictable its rushes become. Several times I found rapid retracting of my legs an essential of this kind of underwater photography.

I took one roll of film in natural light and then reloaded the camera. Another shark was soon hooked and I had another go—this time using flash bulbs as the light was poor. A lot seemed to be happening all at once. It is bad enough trying to use a camera underwater with flash in ideal conditions, but when your subject is maddened and seems intent on making repeated rushes between your legs, the situation does tend to become confused.

For the record, they—those safely in the boat—they caught and landed two porbeagle. One weighed 183 lb and the other 150. I took two rolls of film, 24 exposures and most of them got away. One or two were reasonable.

Two out of 24. Well, in my area that's a reasonable day's underwater photography, that is.

TONY BAVERSTOCK

NIGHT-DIVING AND A BASKING SHARK

The faded orange-yellow torch beam scratched a signal in the wet black night and the other divers began poling themselves back over the seabed with their straight sticks of light until they were clustered together. The rays from their torches showed a John Dory hovering in mid-water, the slab-sided body as big as a soup-plate and the long, spiky fins shimmering in the glare. The fish's sapphire-blue eyes peered blindly at the beams that stabbed at him from the darkness and his fins quivered uncertainly as we gazed at him.

Puddles of bright white illumination splashed over the fish as we took our pictures, the harsh, brief salvos from the electronic flash guns and the lazier, more reddish blazes of intensity from the flash bulbs etched his strange shape against the indigo backdrop.

The John Dory was a perfect model. It posed while we tried one camera angle after another until, finally, we were satisfied and moved off again, ranging the seabed in search of other subjects.

Night is often the best time to photograph many of the more wary or timid creatures which you find in the sea.

Night is the time when conger eels docilely wait to be stroked and when you will find great shoals of fish asleep among the ghostly forests of weed, whole platoons of them swaying rhythmically backwards and forwards in their slumbers.

Night is the time when even the wary limpet unlocks its shell and wanders over the rocks in search of food.

It is an exciting experience to swim stealthily through the gleaming darkness, your world concentrated in the small patch of light shed by your waterproof torch. But you need strong nerves and the determination to ignore what might lie outside that small area of illumination especially when sand eels rain on your wet suit and hurtle off into the darkness.

One of the thrills of night diving lies in the possibility of seeing fish that you never could by day. This is why enthusiasts with marine aquaria collect their specimens at night. They can fill their tanks with creatures I have yet to see on a daylight dive. Fish that would explode into flight at the slightest hint of a diver during daylight wait placidly to be coaxed into a plastic bag or net and will even allow you to touch them.

But, when you are diving at night, make sure that you have a reliable companion, a good torch apiece, a compass and depth gauge with which to monitor your position. Also make sure there is some means of quickly identifying where your base is on shore —some sort of light is best.

It is extremely easy to become confused underwater and find you are confidently heading out into the English Channel at the moment you expect to touch the bottom and be able to wade safely ashore. Also, arrange some sort of torch signals between you because you can't give many hand signals that can be seen. Those that you do give must all be made with one hand in the beam of light from your torch.

If you are planning your first night dive it is also a good idea to begin in an area which you know well by daylight. You won't be bored because you will be surprised how completely different it will seem at night. But don't be lulled into thinking you know the area so well that you don't need a buddy diver.

There are occasions when I prefer to dive on my own. But night time is not one of them. However, I do believe that there are times when you will get a better picture of particular fish if you are on your own. Bass and mullet are both wary of divers but, when diving on my own, I have been able to get within focusing distance of them. With other fish such as dragonets, pouting and many of the wrasse family it doesn't seem to matter if there are two of you provided you move slowly and don't crowd in on each other.

On the other hand there are times when it is absolutely fool-hardy even to dip a fin in the water without some reliable companions around. When I photographed a 16 ft basking shark I was jolly glad to have two other highly experienced divers in the sea with me—Brian Booth and Alex Double.

It all started quite quietly. There were over a dozen of us in a substantial diving boat which was working its way against the tide about a mile or more off the Devon coast. It was a dream of a day —azure sky, no clouds and a calm sea.

I was lolling against the cabin, out of the breeze but in the hot sunshine. Suddenly someone said, 'Great Scott, . . . look at that!' I don't know what I expected to find as I scrambled to my feet, but I certainly never bargained on seeing a basking shark wallowing alongside our boat and looking as big as a midget submarine.

Being the stuff that heroes are made of, I grabbed my Nikonos . . . and tried leaning over the side to get a few shots, but the gunwales were so high up I couldn't even get the camera under water.

This was a chance in a lifetime, I kept telling myself as I dithered by the rail trying to think of a thoroughly convincing reason to stay safely on board.

The skipper, who couldn't swim and had never been nearer to a shark than the end of a heavy fishing line, assured me the creature was harmless. But ringing away in the back of my mind was a remark made by Kendall McDonald with such calculated casualness that you needed anti-freeze in your bloodstream for ever afterwards. 'Basking sharks,' he had solemnly assured me once, 'are harmless. That is unless they leap on top of you. And then it is like having a double-decker bus land on you.'

Every time I see a bus I still think of basking sharks. And, right there, as the boat rode the waves out in the English Channel, all I could see were big red double-decker buses before the eyes.

With a reluctance I tried not to show, I tugged on my wet suit, loaded the Nikonos with a fresh cassette of Tri-X to ensure I would have 36 exposures, and jumped over the side. For the record I was first in the water. But as everyone knows, it is always important to have a human figure in photographs of large fish such as sharks because it gives an idea of scale . . . and also increases the photographer's chances of survival by two to one. As I let Brian and Alex fin ahead of me I reasoned that, apart from increasing the photographic possibilities, I had also improved my survival ratio to three to one.

Anyway, there were now three of us in the water, excluding the shark. We had a high speed inflatable with a 30-h.p. outboard as a diving tender and this was now circling about with Roy Howkins at the tiller. The main diving boat hove-to a short distance away and all those with enough sense to remain on board lined the rails and waited for developments like expectant spectators at a bull fight.

The water was thick with plankton. Clouds of it hung everywhere, bright green and yellow in the dark water. We fanned out in the shark's path and waited, bobbing up and down on the surface. It was so quiet you could imagine you could hear the rumble of fleets of huge, red double-decker buses from as far away as London.

The shark never deviated. It just came straight for us. Every time you looked up you could see the triangular fin slashing through the wave-crests and getting nearer and bigger. How big would it be? I kept wondering as I looked up to check its position and then dunked my facemask beneath the waves and stared through the thick clouds of plankton.

Suddenly it was within camera range. I don't know what I had expected to see, but I didn't bargain for the huge, pallid white mouth with the gaping jaws that loomed out of the curtain of plankton. The maw seemed big enough to park a car in . . . perhaps even a double-decker bus! It swung ominously from side to side as the shark sieved its lunch out of the water.

It came nearer and nearer, the tall tail fin weaving from side to side in muscled might and the jaws straining open. It seemed all mouth and tail.

I hoped I had remembered to set the camera correctly—I was by now swimming backwards out of its path, big fins flailing while I worked the Nikonos like a sequence camera. The mighty mouth swung nearer, seeming to be seeking me out. It looked near enough to suck me in as it pointed my way. But only for an instant. Then the huge length of the shark was sliding by in the viewfinder.

Detail registered in fragments. The tiny eyes and the gills pushed wide open by the power of the water funnelling through the mouth. The tapered length of the body with the remoras dangling beneath it and the great fin sculling backwards and forwards. The dark, wrinkled skin. And then the clouds of plankton closed in again and only the sight of the tall fin flopping over at the top and sailing on through the waves told me it had all happened.

We all sat there in the water for a moment, with the waves lapping against our facemasks and then, excitedly we began finning towards the Zodiac inflatable. One by one we scrambled aboard and then Roy Howkins sent it leaping along to head off the shark. Feeling more confident, we rolled off in its path once more. Even so, the sight of the great gaping mouth weaving from side to side in search of food was still a sight which made my heart miss a couple of beats.

But now I wanted to take more shots from various angles and at various camera settings in order to make sure that at least some of them would come out. The Zodiac roared in to pick us up again and the shark plunged down into deeper water. We clambered aboard and waited. Perhaps we had had our chance and the shark was off to a less crowded and less noisy 'restaurant'.

But no. The triangular fin broke surface some way off and the business of plankton gathering continued. 'He doesn't like the sound of the motor,' someone shouted above the noise of the snarling exhaust. 'He doesn't like it. We can herd him with the noise. Get back in the water and the noise will drive him towards you.'

So back we went and the Zodiac creamed a wide white wake as it zoomed off to round up the shark.

The idea worked like a charm. We sat there leisurely treading water and checking our camera settings and even chatting while Roy herded the big fellow towards us. At last we were able to introduce a measure of control into the situation.

1 TOMPOT BLENNY [*Blennius gattorugine*] Swanage, Dorset
Depth 7 ft Bronica Flash *f*11 Ektacolor S (*Peter Scoones*)

2 PLAICE [*Pleuronectes platessa*] Newhaven, Sussex
Depth 25 ft Rolleimarin + close-up Flash (PF5) *f*22/125
Kodacolor X (*Tony Baverstock*)

3 CUCKOO WRASSE [*Labrus mixtus*]   The Bowes, Isle of Man   (*Ron Hook*)
Depth 70 ft   Calypsophot   Electronic flash   *f*4/30   Kodachrome II

4 CORKWING WRASSE [*Crenilabrus melops*]   Swanage Bay, Dorset
Depth 20 ft   Rolleimarin   Flash   Ektachrome-X (*Philip Smith*)

5 CONGER EEL [*Conger conger*] Bournemouth Bay, Hampshire (*Philip Smith*)
Depth 30 ft Rolleimarin Flash (PF1B) *f*16/125 Ektachrome-X

6 SOLE [*Solea solea*] Brighton, Sussex (*Tony Baverstock*)
Depth 30 ft Rolleimarin Flash *f*22/125 High Speed Ektachrome

7 RAY [*Raja* sp.] Swanage, Dorset
Depth 30 ft Exa *f*5·6/60 Ektachrome-X (*Geoff Harwood*)

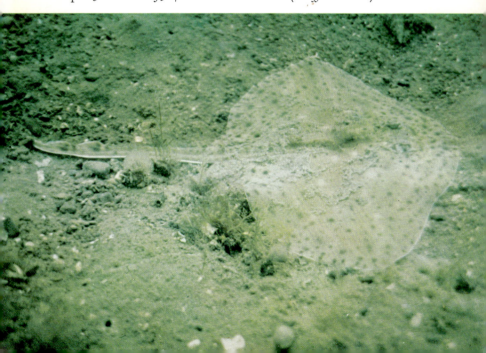

8 COD [*Gadus morhua*] Shoreham, Sussex (*Tony Baverstock*)
Depth 40 ft Rolleimarin Flash $f5 \cdot 6/125$ Ektacolor

9 LEOPARD-SPOTTED GOBIES [*Thorogobius ephippiatus*] Mousehole, Cornwall
Depth 40 ft Exa Elec. flash $f16/60$ Ektachrome-X (*Geoff Harwood*)

10 JOHN DORY [*Zeus faber*] The Manacles, Cornwall (*Kendall McDonald*)
Depth 40 ft Nikonos *f* 8/60 High Speed Ektachrome

11 POUTING [*Gadus luscus*] Bognor, Sussex
Depth 35 ft Nikonos Flash (PF1B) *f* 11/60 High Speed
Ektachrome (*Kendall McDonald*)

12 POLLACK [*Gadus pollachius*] Kimmeridge Bay, Dorset
Depth 10 ft Rolleimarin + supp. lens $f5\cdot6/100$ High Speed
Ektachrome   (*Colin Doeg*)

13 BASS [*Morone labrax*] Worthing, Sussex (*Tony Baverstock*)
Depth 30 ft Rolleimarin $f8/125$ High Speed Ektachrome

14 PORBEAGLE SHARK [*Lamna nasus*] St Catherine's, Isle of Wight
Depth 15 ft Rolleimarin *f*5·6/250 High Speed Ektachrome
(*Tony Baverstock*)
Note: This fish was later captured and was weighed at 193 lb

15 LESSER-SPOTTED DOGFISH [*Scyliorhinus canicula*] Abereiddy, S. Wales
Depth 30 ft Agfa Flexilette + close-up Elec. flash *f*11/125
Ektachrome-X (*Geoff Harwood*)

16 ANGLER FISH [*Lophias piscatorius*] Black Rock, Brighton
Depth 20 ft Calypsophot Flash (PF24) *f*8/125 High Speed
Ektachrome (*Tony Baverstock*)

17 PLAICE [*Pleuronectes platessa*] Newhaven, Sussex (*Tony Baverstock*)
Depth 25 ft Calypsophot + close-up lens Flash *f*22/125 Tri-X

18 EEL [*Anguilla anguilla*] Pagham, Sussex
Depth 10 ft Exa Elec. flash Plus-X (*Geoff Harwood*)

19 PIPEFISH [*Entelurus aequorus*] Swanage, Dorset
Depth 30 ft Exa Elec. flash *f*16/60 Plus-X (*Geoff Harwood*)

20 LONG-SPINED SEA SCORPION [*Taurulus bubalis*] Swanage, Dorset
Depth 6 ft Bronica Flash *f*11 Tri-X (*Peter Scoones*)

21, 22 THICK-LIPPED GREY MULLET [*Mugil labrosus*] Swanage, Dorset
Depth 10 ft Calypsophot *f*5·6/500 Tri-X (*Colin Doeg*)

23 CUCKOO WRASSE [*Labrus mixtus*] Eddystone Light, Cornwall
Depth 100 ft   Exa   Elec. flash   *f*16/60   Plus-X   (*Geoff Harwood*)

24 BLENNY [*Blennius* sp.] Bournemouth Bay, Hampshire (*Philip Smith*)
Depth 30 ft Rolleimarin + close-up Flash *f*16/125 Ektachrome-X

25 DRAGONET [*Callionymus lyra*] Swanage, Dorset (*Colin Doeg*)
Depth 10 ft Calypsophot + 20 cm close-up *f*5·6/125 Tri-X

26 BASS [*Morone labrax*] Kimmeridge, Dorset
Depth 15 ft Nikonos *f*5·6/500 Tri-X (*Colin Doeg*)

27 BALLAN WRASSE [*Labrus bergylta*] Kimmeridge, Dorset
Depth 6 ft Calypsophot *f*11/125 Tri-X (*Colin Doeg*)

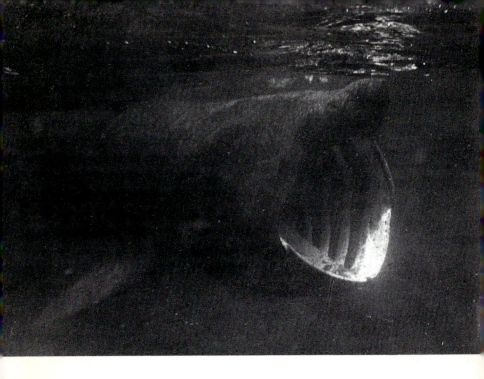

28, 29 BASKING SHARK [*Cetorhinus maximus*] Prawle Point, Devon
Depth 3 ft Nikonos *f*11/125 Tri-X (*Colin Doeg*)

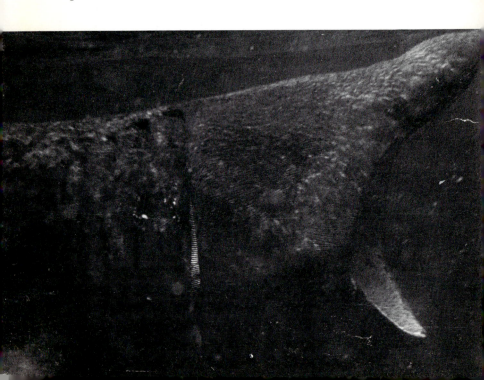

When you are photographing fish you have got to have luck on your side. Sometimes it is genuine luck. But most of the time, to be sure it will happen, it is better to try to manufacture some of your own. And our shark round-up technique was doing just that.

Now we could work at getting that terrifying maw properly illuminated by driving the fish into the sun. Also we were able to get it out of the really tasty plankton clouds and into some water that was a lot clearer but still murky by exacting standards.

In no time, the cassette of Tri-X was used up. I scrambled back on board the main diving boat, re-loaded and went in again, this time taking a Rolleimarin as well.

The spectators still weren't bored. They remained in their ring-side seats. Perhaps they thought someone might still be needed to tell the Coroner exactly how it all happened.

But by now I was beginning to feel happier. I had forgotten temporarily about double-decker buses. One roll of Tri-X was exposed and another was ready for use. Also, there was a chance of underpinning the black and white shots with some alternatives in colour.

The odds of something worthwhile being produced were beginning to increase. And perhaps this time I would dare to plant myself square on to that mouth and sink down out of its path at the last moment. (Memo to Coroner and double-decker buses: I didn't.)

After about an hour it was all over. The Zodiac was once more trailing astern of the larger boat and we were out of the water, cold, but far too excited to notice. I was as content as anyone can be until they have seen their prints.

I had got off some extra shots on the Nikonos and I would develop them first in order to ensure that my normal development technique was adequate. If not I could alter it for the first cassette, on which I thought I had some better pictures.

This is a 'dodge' that is well worth using when you photograph something that may never be repeated. As you begin to take pictures of it get off a few quick shots in the general conditions of the situation before you start to work in close and take the really telling photographs. Then, if there are any doubts in your mind, process those few throw-away frames first. If your normal processing isn't suitable you can modify it before you develop the rest of the film.

That night I practised what I preach. I buried myself in the bedclothes and loaded that second film into a developing tank. The processing in D.76 was fine. With fingers crossed I developed the original cassette of Tri-X and hung it up to dry. The scenes were there in the negatives—the awe-inspiring mouth and both Brian and Alex swimming closer to the shark than I dared to do. Even now I look at them once in a while to reassure myself that the encounter with the basking shark really did happen and wasn't just a dream . . . along with double-decker buses.

COLIN DOEG

GUIDE TO THE
FISHES OF NORTHERN WATERS

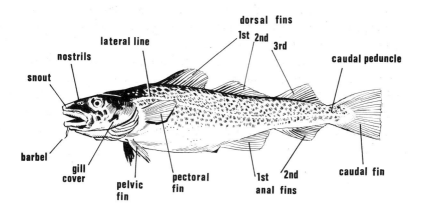

In this section we are dealing with the fish of the North Sea, the Channel, the Irish Sea and the Atlantic. All these seas border on the coasts of Great Britain. But they lap or crash on the shores of many other countries too. And there is no reason to believe that what the divers see in the waters around Britain is greatly different from what divers see if they penetrate the shores of any other North European country.

The information about fish which follows in this section—and indeed in all the chapters of this book—is the result of many years' diving experience in the sea and not on observation of fish trapped in the unreal confines of some aquarium. Information not obtained directly from underwater observation has its source clearly stated.

The whole object of the chapters on fish is to report on the way that fishes have been seen to behave in their natural surroundings, not to repeat old information, much of it based on dubious study and copied from one book to another.

The colours given in the descriptions of fish are the colours that appear to the diver underwater, not those of dead specimens or aquarium prisoners.

The names of the fish are given in the languages of the countries surrounding the seas in which the fish are found. To these languages have been added those most used by tourist visitors.

Note: Fish that are common to many seas will only be found in one of the three chapters of descriptions. But details of that fish's behaviour in other seas, where it differs or is of great interest, will be found in a special sub-section. For example, the stingray is described in the chapter on Northern waters, but its behaviour in the Mediterranean will also be found under the same heading.

ROCKS, WEEDS AND WRECKS

Bib [*Gadus luscus*]   PLATE II

(*Or* pout, pouting, whiting pout.)

Da: Skaegtorsk. *Du*: Steenbokk. *Fr*: Tacaud. *G*: Franzosendorsch.
Norw: Skjeggtorsk.

A very common fish. Reference books will describe this barbelled
fish as having a light coppery colour with dark cross bands, but the
diver knows that this is wrong. This is basically a dark fish with
light bands that disappear until the older specimens are completely
dark brown in colour. Where there are rocks you will find this
fish in schools that can number over 100 at a time. Certainly the
fish is rarely alone. Where there is one there are bound to be more.
The fish looks soft underwater—and is soft when brought to the
surface. One barbel sprouts underneath the chin. The pelvic fins
are forked and quite soft.

A diver is never alone with a bib. It is only when you find bib
away from the low rock inshore that you appreciate how many of
them there must be in the sea.

Around a wreck or rocky outcrop well out to sea, vast
schools of more than 200 will circulate around the diver. They do
not even wait for the diver to pass to shoot in and snatch any
spare bits of food from the point where the diver has disturbed
the seabed. Divers all get the impression that the bib is a
friendly fish. At times they get in so close that the underwater
photographer has to push them away with his hand. And even
a smart smack on the fish's side will not deter the bolder ones
from returning too close to the camera to allow the diver to
focus.

The pelvic fins are used like little hands. And these appendages
are obviously a sense organ, like the barbel, because not only will
they be used to locate food on the seabed, but divers have watched

43

them use their pelvics to measure distance from other fish beneath them in the school.

This is the behaviour of young fish. The older bib seems less puppy-like and seeks the shelter of the dark places which abound in the remnants of a wreck. Early in the year it is only in these dark caverns that you find the really big bib. Reference books mark the bib as having a maximum length of 16 in., but divers know that this is more the norm for the older fish than the extraordinary.

The big fish are, to the diver, more like 2 ft long. And they are very different from their cheekier, banded, children. They have no reaction, unlike the pollack, to the explosion of a flash-bulb in their dark hiding places. These big fish are completely brown in colour and only confirm the idea that the older the fish becomes, the darker its colouration tends to be.

Divers watching bib have been concerned to note that adult fish are sometimes to be seen swimming with their mouths wide open and that these fish have a white fungus-like growth around their mouths. Some divers suspect that this fungus is the result of man's pollution of the sea, though the white fungus has been observed in bib colonies in many places, some of which appear to be well away from effluent outlets.

It is unusual to witness the actual death of a fish (apart from the violent end that comes with one fish eating another), but Kendall McDonald did see one of these unwounded fungus-marked bib die. At first it swam slightly out of true as though leaning into a tight turn, then the list became more apparent, and finally the fish—an adult of about 18 in. in length—started swimming completely on its side in a great shuddering circle, bumping into rocks and weed until it finally flopped with white belly up twitching to the seabed.

Black Bream [*Spondyliosoma cantharus*]
(*Often called* the 'Old Wife')

Da: Havrude. *Du*: Zeekarper. *Fr*: Griset. *G*: Streifenbrassen. *Norw*: Havkaruss.

Probably the most fish-shaped fish of all the North European fishes. Though the fish shows a number of dark bars and black markings when caught by anglers, underwater it appears to the diver as a totally grey fish.

They come into the coasts of Southern England to spawn in May, dependent on whether the spring is advanced or not. Bream, when seen by divers, often swim in lines of three or four fish. These lines are usually led by a large and obviously older fish. Many of these older fish appear to have light scars on their flanks at spawning time. These, however, may not be scars from fighting, but part of the males' breeding dress.

Though most observation by divers has been made at places like Bognor and Littlehampton, Sussex, when the fish come in to spawn, single specimens have been observed much later in the year. Underwater these fish look absolutely enormous for a bream—about 2 ft long—and are impossible to mistake for any other fish.

The difficulty the diver finds with these big specimen fish is in approaching them closely. They seem extremely shy. They are impossible to mistake for any other fish for the simple reason that their outline underwater is exactly the sort of basic representation of a fish that children first draw—an oval with a big forked tail at the back and eye at the front. This great grey oval body, when seen underwater, is a marvellous sight. The crescent fork of the tail is particularly striking.

When moving close to a pollack shoal the diver sometimes sees these big fish standing out like a sore thumb from the sleeker lines of the pollack. Sneaking around rocks and through thick laminaria cover will rarely ensure that the diver can get closer than 10 or 12 ft. Holding your breath helps, but when you are finally forced to breathe and the bubbles leap from the demand valve, the bream will take off at an incredible rate and disappear in the misty distance.

Blennies [Blenniidae] PLATES I, 24

Da: Tangkvabbe. *Du*: Slijmvisch. *Fr*: Blennie. *G*: Seeschmetterling. *Norw*: Tangkvabbe.

Slimy-looking, rather menacing small fish found almost everywhere around the British and French coasts, but not so common farther North. The blennies are completely harmless—it is just their sinuous swimming that tends to give the diver a sense of revulsion.

Blennies of all kinds are very common. The diver sees them so often that he gets to a state where he hardly notices them—and then gets a shock when a tompot blenny (he is the fellow with the fringed tentacles over his eyes) suddenly peers into the diver's mask from no distance at all. The blenny is undoubtedly a fish with a strong sense of curiosity and large numbers will gather round the diver taking pictures in a rocky area.

MEDITERRANEAN PLATE 35

Most of the Northern waters blennies are to be found in the Mediterranean. In particular, the tompot blenny is always well to the fore round any group of rocks.

Two striking species found in Mediterranean waters are *Tripterygion tripteronotus* (PLATES 40, 41) and *Tripterygion minor*.

Fr: Tripterygion à bec. *G*: Tripterygion. *It*: Bavosa peparuolo. *Serb-Cr*: Pjevcic ostronosic. *Sp*: Moma nariguda.

Most common is the first named. He has a scarlet body with yellowish spots and a dark purple head with mottled lighter markings.

The less common variety of this blenny (*Tripterygion minor*) is yellow-bodied, but still retains the purple marking on the head. This variety seems more likely to be found at depth.

Both varieties rest on rocks and move over short distances to 'peck' at algae. They rotate their eyes in an obvious check for intruders. For a fish only about 3 in. long they are extremely interested in divers and with patience can be photographed in real close-up. When viewed extremely closely, the most noticeable feature, apart from their colouring, is the wedge-shaped head. Keep an eye open for them when looking up at overhangs and the roofs of caves.

Cod [*Gadus morhua*]   PLATE 8

Da: Torsk. *Du*: Kabeljauw. *Fr*: Morue. *G*: Kabeljau. *Norw*: Torsk.

Dark powerful fish. Three dorsal fins, two anal. Head rather like a grouper (*see* Mediterranean fish), but lower jaw is shorter. Barbels are long. Whole impression is of a fish full of power. Lateral line is white. Colour varies from dark green, to brown, to black.

Large solitary specimens are common in the early part of the year. Large head makes them unmistakable together with their habit of hanging in mid-water like a Mediterranean grouper with much fanning of fins. Often found swimming underneath big schools of pouting, they are attracted to big rocks and wrecks and can be stalked to close proximity if care is taken. Young cod are much more orange-brown in colour.

Cod have changed their pattern of movements quite considerably in the past four or five years. Divers off the Sussex coast report seeing more and more of these fine fish, whereas before a cod was something of a rarity. Line fishermen in the area are now taking big catches of cod.

Tony Baverstock likes to compare cod to cows. 'The cod I have seen in Sussex waters,' he says, 'are usually in twos and are always around rocks or wreckage. They really do remind me of cows, the way they graze on the growth on rocks. They chomp at the growth and then spit the bits of weed out.

'What they are after are the little crabs hiding in the growths. You can get quite close to them when they are grazing like this. I think they are very pretty—trout-like in colour, all speckly greens and greys. Mind you, when disturbed they can move very fast.'

47

Conger [*Conger conger*] PLATE 5

Da: Haval. *Du*: Zeepaling. *Fr*: Congre. *G*: Congeraale. *It*: Grongo.
Norw: Haval. *Serbo-Cr*: Ugor. *Sp*: Congrio.

Is the source of more monster stories than practically any other
cold-water fish. Big fish are described by non-divers as creatures
of unparalleled ferocity. Most of this nonsense can probably be
attributed to anglers' stories of the way boated fish will bite at
anything that comes near the powerful jaws—hardly, one would
have thought, an unexpected reaction. Adding fuel to these stories
is the size of some congers caught by professional fishermen. A
monster—and this time the word is probably justified—of 252 lbs
was trawled up by a Belgian ship off Iceland. No skin diver would,
of course, treat such a monster lightly, but the experience of most
divers is that the conger is a pretty shy and remarkably placid
fellow. Colouration varies from slate-blue to brown.

The first view a diver has of a conger is usually of just the head.
The cold gold-rimmed eye and snake-like movement do nothing
to undo their reputation. Add a pair of gaping jaws and you have
got a fish that does look pretty terrifying.

Of course, the surroundings in which the conger is found do
little to ease its ferocious looks. A black hole in a wreck, a
rusting ship's boiler, broken sewer pipes, a jungle of broken iron
beneath a pier or harbour wall, any dark hole in a group of rocks
—these are home to the conger.

Phil Smith knows one place in Poole Bay, Dorset, where
broken blocks of granite support a sewer pipe. Here there are
literally dozens of congers in residence, their heads poking out
from every cranny. It was here, too, that another diver had a fin
pulled off his foot by a large conger which swam out from a hole
behind him and bit it. But even in this case the diver is charitable
enough to say that the conger probably mistook a fluttering fin
for a fish in difficulties.

Obviously the conger is not a fellow to provoke, though Geoff
Harwood reports trying to get a fair-sized fish into a more photographic position by employing a colleague to prod it in the tail—

without result. The conger is strong and his strength can be judged by the fact that one pierced by spearfisherman John Messent bent a steel spear in two as though it was a piece of soft wire. That fish weighed 23 lbs.

But, in complete contrast to this fearsome display of strength, Tony Baverstock has tickled young conger with his finger and found that they behaved like kittens, rolling over on their backs to have their tummies stroked (*see* Northern Waters).

Conger are generally to be found during the day in holes with only their heads sticking out. They feed at night but are not averse to snapping up any trifle which comes within range at any time of the day. The conger should not be rated as stupid. One off the Sussex coast was tempted into snapping at a steel rod waved in front of his nose. On a subsequent visit to his home a week later he positively refused to ruin his teeth on the same rod however much provocation and rod-waving in front of his nose took place.

Divers do find conger out in the open at odd times, however. At dawn and dusk they are well away from their holes and this also happens at slack water if the visibility is poor and the weather dull.

Photographing a whole conger is difficult for this reason, but many excellent pictures have been taken of congers at home with only the head and neck showing.

The breeding habits of conger is a field in which the diver could help a great deal. Aquarium studies suggest that congers only breed once and then die. In unnatural aquarium conditions at mating time their teeth drop out, their bones turn to jelly and the fish stop feeding. Death follows shortly afterwards, so the mating act has never been observed. Spawning areas have been located near the Azores and in the Mediterranean, but no one has yet reported seeing the actual event.

MEDITERRANEAN

Conger are often seen in the Mediterranean, but seem to prefer deeper water than their Northern colleagues. This is probably due to the increased penetration of the light in the clearer Mediterranean. They often take on a much bluer colouration.

The conger's behaviour does not differ from that of his colleagues in colder waters.

Dogfish [*Scyliorhinus stellaris* and *S. caniculus*] PLATE 15

Da: Rodhaj. *Du*: Hondshaai. *Fr*: Grande Roussette. (Greater Spotted); Petite Roussette (Lesser Spotted). *G*: Katzenhaie. *Norw*: Rodha.

From the point of view of the diver, these observations have been confined to the two kinds of dogfish he is most likely to meet— these are the Greater Spotted and the Lesser Spotted. Dogfish have many names. In one part of the country they will be called nurse hounds, in another smooth hounds, bull huss, catfish, sandy dogs, rough hounds. But in the fish-and-chip shop they will all be lumped together as 'huss' and 'rock salmon'.

Underwater there is little likelihood of mistaking a dogfish for anything else. Even the big ones cannot be confused with the true sharks. And the reason, as any diver will tell you, is the way that a dogfish behaves. They are usually seen swimming lazily just off the bottom with a side-to-side snakelike motion. The fact that they lack a swim bladder means that they have to keep swimming to stay off the bottom. The Greater Spotted dogfish, as its name implies, has large blotches (not spots) on its basic brown skin. Some have very orange blotches which make them visible for a long distance. The Lesser Spotted has a large number of dark brown spots covering its body on a lighter basic ground.

The diver finds the dogfish moving slowly through laminaria weed or resting on the bottom near vertical cliff faces. Though they swim with a lazy action, it is often difficult for the diver— even when flat out—to keep up with one that seems to have taken a decision to travel. Then they cruise over the short weed on an otherwise flat seabed until lost in the mist at the limit of visibility.

Usually they are not the slightest bit disturbed by the presence of divers and can be touched without difficulty. One diver unkindly decided that they were like the taxmen in the world above—'they go about their business without the slightest interest in their surroundings'. The cine photographer finds them very good for his kind of work, but the stills man will really only get the best pictures if the fish can be spotted coming towards him. But dogfish lying on the bottom asleep—and there seems little doubt that this is the explanation of the state the diver often finds these fish—are a gift to any photographer.

In this state, if you find one in an awkward gully—from the photographer's point of view—a gentle poke will move him forward a yard or so and then he'll settle down again. Flash bulbs or cameras shoved in really close don't seem to worry the fish at all. And if you really have great trouble posing your dogfish, they can easily be caught by a quick grab at the tail. Take care—they can turn round and bite as they are very supple. They will even bite themselves and stay in this position for some time. Anglers believe that a dogfish bites itself like this before it dies, but divers have no evidence to support this.

Fifteen-spined stickleback [*Spinachia spinachia*]

Da: Tangsnarre. *Du*: Zeestekelbaars. *Fr*: Epinoche de mer. *G*: Seestichling. *Norw*: Tangstikling.

The only stickleback that lives wholly in the sea—though it is worth noting that the common tiddler, the stickleback with three spines, can exist in estuaries where the water is almost completely salt and in Scotland lives in pure sea water.

Looks very like a pipefish—except for those spines of course—and comes in both green and brown.

One to keep an eye open for when expecting to see pipefish among the weed. Though the fin area doesn't look large or powerful, these thin fellows can move very smartly.

Like their freshwater cousins, they build a nest too. You'll find it among clumps of weed and your best clue to its situation will be the determined 'buzzing' by the male whose job it is to guard the nest.

Gobies [Gobiidae] PLATE 9

Da: Lerkutling. *Du*: Grondel. *Fr*: Gobie. *G*: Strandkuling. *Norw*: Kutling.

Gobies tend to behave the same way as blennies, but are slightly more inclined than blennies to sit out in the open. To tell a goby from a blenny, look at the dorsal fin arrangement. The gobies have two clearly separate dorsal fins—the blennies have virtually one fin running along the back with just a dip between the spiny rays in front and the soft rays behind.

There are many species of goby. All are difficult to identify without doubt.

Gobies tend to roll their eyes apprehensively at the diver's approach, but can, in fact, be lured easily into camera range by hand feeding.

John Dory [*Zeus faber*] PLATE 10

Da: St Petersfisk. *Du*: Zonnevissen. *Fr*: Saint-Pierre. *G*: Heringskonige. *Norw*: St Petersfisk.

Has the most exotic looks of all the North European fish. The Dory is, according to legend, the fish from which St Peter took the tribute money and so it bears his thumbprint on its side for evermore. Belly is white, sides marked with yellowish brown or yellow-green whirls rather like the old wartime desert camouflage. The distinctive black spot is circled by a yellowy band. Eyes are a bright sapphire blue.

Lurks just above or among all kinds of weed and moves like a helicopter slowly about in them. From head-on, it is so thin that it looks just like a piece of weed. The sapphire eyes at times add to this illusion, looking like the sunlight reflecting on the shiny weed surface.

The John Dory swims slowly with all fins working away like mad—giving it the effect of being a child's toy whirring away. But this is no toy. It can swim fast for short distances, but relies on stalking its prey quietly until really close—then the telescopic mouth is flung forward and a small fish is taken in one gulp.

Photographers will find that it is fond of presenting its tail to the camera, but all the time the protruding blue eyes are studying the diver backwards down the sides of its slim body. The Dory can be easily herded with the help of another diver and after a while of this will surrender completely. Then it may hover only a few inches from the diver's mask and can be stroked gently with a finger.

Lumpsucker [*Cyclopterus lumpus*]

Da: Stenbider. *Du*: Snotdolf. *Fr*: Lompe. *G*: Seehase. *Norw*: Rognkjeks.

At first sight a most unpleasant fish. Yet when observed close-to it has a certain beauty. Females in most cases are grey, but the male in season is often a bright red all over. Head-on view is the best with the fins spread outwards, framing a not unintelligent face.

Divers usually find this fish stationary on the rocks and attached by the extraordinary sucker which is a combination of fin and flesh. Well camouflaged on top, this fish seems to rely on keeping very still rather than making violent movements that the thick head and strong body would indicate as a likely method of escape. The face is warty, but, divers say, likeable. One seen many times by divers lives inside the hollow mast of a wreck and will retreat slowly down this when caught in the open.

Pipefish [Syngnathidae] PLATE 19

Da: Tangnal. *Du*: Zeenaald. *Fr*: Aiguille de mer. *G*: Seenadel. *Norw*: Kantnaal.

At least five kinds of pipefish are seen in Northern European waters. They are really like a sea-horse straightened out and share many of the same habits—an example is the use of the tail to curl round weed and hold on. And the males of each species incubate the eggs.

The most commonly seen by divers is the Great Pipefish. Its brown body has darker bands around it. In the water it often has a sheen not unlike the sheen seen on weed—which, of course, helps it with its camouflage.

Divers usually find the pipefish among weed in fairly shallow water. And once a diver has spotted one, he can usually spot them more easily in future. Their camouflage is extremely good as they tend to lie up in weed and adopt the angle the weed is pushed into by the tide. When disturbed, they delve deeper into the weed without any real sign of fear. Divers have been known to pick them up and move them to more photogenic locations, but although most swim slowly, others can move off in mid-water at a faster rate than a diver can swim. Their movements then are side-to-side like a snake travelling on land. At night they are to be seen lying on their side as though asleep and will move only with great reluctance.

Have been seen by divers to stretch to 24 in. When not actually in the weed they seem to spend a lot of their life lying amid broken and rotting weed fragments that carpet the seabed in shallow areas. In this situation it needs a keen eye to pick the fish out especially as they lie in a curved position just like all the rest of the broken weed.

Pollack [*Gadus pollachius*]   PLATE 12

Da: Lubbe. *Du*: Witte koolvis. *Fr*: Lieu jaune. *G*: Pollack. *Norw*: Lyr.

Pollack and coalfish (or saithe) can be discussed together. The pollack is common in all the North European waters, but the saithe takes over as the really common variety in the North. The saithe has both jaws about equal; the pollack's lower jaw is longer. A minute barbel on the lower jaw in immature fish is probably the best way to tell the saithe from the pollack. A green-backed fish with white-silver sides.

Underwater the pollack is unmistakable. His jaw juts, his eyes look the size of pennies, and his silver flanks make such a stream-lined shape that there can be no confusion. The pollack can grow into a big fellow—29-lb fish have been taken on trot lines in the Plymouth area. They love wrecks and rocky areas. Some like deep gullies, shaded by the long fronds of laminaria, but most prefer to keep on the move, circling wrecks or waiting behind shelter for anything the tide may bring.

When in shelter, pollack never seem to rest horizontally—they hang in the water at about 45°, head down or up, but the typical feeding 'stance' of the pollack is to hang tail down behind the shelter of a rock or wreck and to wait for the 'goodies' the tide brings as it sweeps over the top of such shelter.

As something is brought over the top by the tide, the pollack spurt upward, dropping down to shelter again as soon as the food is taken. One diver, seeking pollack, capitalised on this habit by letting go a handful of silver paper fragments into the tide. It worked—and pollack rose up from their hiding places to strike at the sparkling fragments.

Flash bulbs released near them seem to give the fish some sort of shock. When the bulb goes off, the fish break away from the school in something approaching panic.

Colin Doeg, when diving in Cornwall, watched a group of nine or ten pollack herd a shoal of small fry into a rock corral. While the rest of the 'cowboys' rode herd on the fry, each pollack in turn would move in, take his lunch and then move out, allowing another pollack to take his place to eat.

Wrasse [Labridae]   PLATES 3, 4, 23, 27

Da: Berggylt. *Du*: Lipvissen. *Fr*: Labres. *G*: Lippfische. *Norw*: Leppefisker.

There are five species which the diver sees. First the **ballan wrasse**, which is the most common sight to a diver around rocks and weed. Mainly green in colour (but brown ones are quite common). Sometimes spotted around the front of the belly. Builds a nest and can often be seen carrying weed in its mouth for this collection of weed stuffed into a hole in rocks or clay.

The **goldsinny** is another wrasse commonly seen by divers. Colouring varies from reddish-brown to pinky-gold and there is always a black spot on the top edge of the tail stalk. Small lively fish, they are often found in the vicinity of piers and rocks.

The **cuckoo wrasse** is one of the most colourful of the species. Males are bright light blue and yellow and the female is duller—a brown or orange with dark spots on the back. Will defend their nesting spot with great persistence even making rushes at divers— which would be suicidal if the diver was a predatory fish.

The **corkwing**. Small and olive-green with some red and blue markings. Small black spot on tail stalk.

The **rock cock**. Greeny-brown, some blue flecking. Has a black band on the tail. Usually very small.

The first fish any diver sees on his first dive is bound to be a wrasse—and it is a rare inshore dive in which one or other of these fish is not seen. The diver gets so used to them that it is only a really big fish that attracts his attention. All wrasse seem slow-moving—until alarmed—and often come curling out of the weed to meet the diver. The thick lips and inquisitive manner gives them a distinctively friendly look. Strangely enough such a harmless creature possesses an alarming set of teeth. These the wrasse puts to good use by crushing small crustaceans and molluscs in the daily hunt for food. This food hunt leaves many traces behind. Limpets on rocks in a very 'wrassey' area can be seen with white wet scars where the tops have been gnawed off. The wrasse bites off the top of the limpet and then sucks out the flesh. The fine bits of shell are then blown out in little clouds, like puffs from an aerosol spray.

The lazy movements of the wrasse hide a fine turn of speed when the fish is really disturbed. Then they go with a fine tizzy of fins in a series of darting movements changing direction several times before diving into cover. The bouncy jerking motion of their swimming is due to the use of pectoral fins, the main source of propulsion.

The wrasse is an expert at sliding through weed. If you lift the weed at the exact spot that you saw a wrasse take cover, you will never find the fish there. The wrasse will travel along under cover of the weed for many feet finally emerging in a totally different spot to the one in which he entered. Only when really cornered will the wrasse stay still and then he flattens into the background relying on his camouflage to prevent discovery. This 'lying up' is repeated at night for wrasse only swim in the daytime. The size of wrasse is a matter of great dispute. The rod-and-line record for the ballan wrasse is said to be 12 lb 12 oz, but in most areas a 3–4 lb fish is considered a good one. But in the West Country only a 7–8 lb fish is considered large. Divers on wrecks however have reported fish considerably in excess of that weight. In a sheltered overhang in such places it is common to see really big fish sheltering at the back of dark holes and sliding away through colonies of deadmen's fingers (Plate 104) at the diver's approach.

Divers, too, have seen females at breeding time with round distended egg-sacs still attached to their bodies. When young, wrasse do congregate, but not in schools, rather in small groups around rocks. The larger the fish, the more likely it is to be alone.

MEDITERRANEAN   PLATES 36, 37, 50

The wrasse of Mediterranean waters include many of the species found in more Northern waters. But in the Med there is a confusing mass of others to add to the family. Many are so alike that it takes a careful out-of-water count of rays and markings to fully identify each one.

To find out just how many wrasse inhabit one spot, try breaking up a sea-urchin at the foot of some rocks where the weed banks begin. Only one or two are distinctive enough to remain in the diver's mind. One in particular—the Mediterranean **rainbow wrasse** [*Coris julis. Fr:* Girelle. *G:* Meerjunker. *It:* Girella. *Serb-Cr:* Knez. *Sp:* Julia] has particularly striking markings when the male of the species is on view. He is green-backed with a bright red stripe running along his side and he is always one of the first on the scene when there is any food about.

Not all wrasse seek out publicity like *Coris julis.* Some lie in impossible cracks any way up and will not flee until actually touched. Easy to photograph but look dead.

There is another lesson for the diving-photographer when taking pictures of wrasse. Though they look easy to photograph, these fish are extremely mobile from about half-way down their body and turn abruptly. Many a wrasse picture comes out looking as though there was only half a fish swimming about!

SAND, MUD AND SHINGLE

Angler fish   [*Lophius piscatorius*]   PLATE 16

Da: Havtaske. *Du*: Zeeduivel. *Fr*: Baudroie. *G*: Seeteufel. *It*: Rana
pescatrice. *Norw*: Breiflabb. *Serb-Cr*: Grdobina mrkulja. *Sp*: Rape.

Without doubt the most unattractive of all inshore fishes. Colour
varies with the ground on which it is found. Has great ability to
camouflage, but is usually brown or greenish with mottled top-
side and white underparts.

When you see this one underwater you can't mistake it. The
head is enormous and seems to be all teeth. It can grow to over
100 lb in weight and divers who have seen a really big one are
not ashamed of reporting that they were frightened by the sight—
especially as the camouflage is so good that one is almost on top of
the fish before spotting it.

Is equipped with its own fishing tackle—a thin, fleshy antenna
protruding from the head. This is moved up and down in front of
the fish's mouth. Any small fish foolish enough to investigate has
made his last move. The mouth opens and the victim seems to be
sucked in.

The angler can be met with anywhere over sand, shingle, weed
or rock. It is an alarming sight when first spotted—the irregular
pieces of skin which break up the outline and aid the camouflage
merely add to the 'sea monster' effect.

MEDITERRANEAN   PLATE 51

No difference in appearance from those found in Northern waters.

In most Mediterranean countries this is a prized food fish. It is
said that special instructions are given to chefs in tourist hotels
never to allow their clients to see the hideous head which is often
cut off long before the fish reaches the hotels. This is said to have
come about as a result of an elderly Englishwoman dying of a

heart attack after being shown by an enthusiastic cook a whole fish of the same kind that she had just eaten for dinner.

The angler moves into shallow water at the height of Mediterranean summer heat and is reliably reported to have bitten a small child unfortunate enough to step into the mouth while paddling.

Brill [*Scophthalmus rhombus*]

> *Da*: Slethvarre. *Du*: Griet. *Fr*: Barbue. *G*: Glattbutt. *Norw*: Slettvar.

When searching over sandy or shingle bottoms this is a fellow to look out for. Has all the camouflage instincts of the rest of the flatfish, but differs in colouration in that the back is darkish brown and is decorated with darker brown freckles or starring.

Grows up to 10 or 12 lbs, but a diver spotting an 8-lb fish will think he's found a whopping turbot. Another look will show a more oval shape than that of the turbot. Small emerald-green eyes are another distinguishing feature. Skin is smooth.

Dragonet [*Callionymus lyra*]   PLATE 25

> *Da*: Stribet Flojfisk. *Du*: Pitvisch. *Fr*: Lavandiere. *G*: Leierfische. *Norw*: Flojfisk.

A fun fish. Dragonets have enormous fins—especially the dorsal, the first of which leans backwards over the second. General impression is of a brown fish, but mature males carry a number of blue markings, particularly on the second dorsal where long blue stripes stand out on the yellow ground of the fin.

Dragonets sit on the bottom, sometimes alone and sometimes in large groups. Any sand patch seems to suit. A good example of the terrain that they like is the sand at the foot of Swanage Pier, Dorset. But this may well be chosen because of the food supply present in the sand. Dragonets feed by eating mouthfuls of sand and then squirting the unwanted basic material out of the top of the gills. Because of this they leave little clouds of dust behind them as they move over the seabed using this feeding technique.

Not a big fish, the common variety—there is also the spotted dragonet which looks exactly as its name implies—rarely grows to over 12 in. in length.

Diving photographers have tried to tempt these photogenic fish away from areas where they are half-buried in the sand into more suitable surroundings. One method tried was hand-feeding ragworms to them. But the dragonets took such tasty morsels on the run at high speed without stopping for the photograph. Add to this the fact that they can swivel their eyes independently and you have a fish which is difficult to photograph. They have a spectacular display of fins when courting so photographers consider it worth while going to extreme lengths for a good picture—even getting the camera down to their level by digging a hole in the sand for it.

Flounder [*Platichthys flesus*]

Da: Skrubbe. *Du*: Bot. *Fr*: Flet. *G*: Flunder. *Norw*: Skrubbe.

Flounders are found in much the same sort of situations as plaice, but prefer the cloudier waters of estuaries and harbours. And they revel in mud, real mud, the muddier the better. A grey-brown back sometimes has reddish spots on it.

Not a fish that the diver sees much of—unless he is a regular muddy water diver. The flounder is a much more wary fish than the plaice, but its shape—much slimmer—makes it instantly recognisable. The best way to tell a flounder is by looking for the row of little knobs at the base of the fin rays.

Gurnards [Triglidae]   PLATE 46

Da: Knurhaner. *Du*: Poonen. *Fr*: Grondins. *G*: Knurrhahne. *Norw*: Knurrfisker.

The grey, red and tub (or sapphire) gurnards are the ones most often seen by divers in Northern waters. There is no difficulty in identifying the gurnard from other fish, though there may be in telling one gurnard from another. In all species the pectoral fins have been modified into legs on which they walk about the bottom, feeling with these 'legs' for food. Shining green or sapphire blue eyes add to their beauty.

This fish is a delight to an underwater photographer. They are not only beautiful, but can also usually be approached very closely. If really frightened however they can swim like greased lightning. Do not always expect to find your gurnard raised up on his 'legs'. They can be found at rest lying on the bottom.

Plaice [*Pleuronectes platessa*]   PLATES 2, 17

Da: Rodspaette. *Du*: Schol. *Fr*: Carrelet. *G*: Scholle. *Norw*: Rodspette.

A funny fish. Not in the sense that it makes you laugh, but in the sense that its camouflage is often completely hopeless. So much so that at times this flatfish will catch the eye purely because its camouflage arrangements have gone wildly wrong.

The mouth is to the right of the eyes, the brown back is spotted with large orange or yellow blobs, and the underside is very white.

Plaice travel amazing distances from their breeding grounds in the North Sea and millions migrate each year to the shallows of the Heligoland Bight and the coast of Denmark to spawn. Fish tagged and then released in Poole Bay, Dorset, have been recovered well into the North Sea and off the German coast.

Spawning grounds occur in many similar places but the North Sea 20-fathom line is the most important. The eggs and larvae float and drift into shallow water. Very young plaice tend to live in shallow water and move offshore as they get bigger. However, as a complete contradiction to this rule, exceptionally large fish are sometimes found inshore.

Plaice are common all round the coasts of Britain with the South, South-West and East Coasts recording more consistent quantities than any other.

The diver knows that sandy areas are the best place to spot plaice. Their eyes and gill flap are the most obvious give-away when the fish is lying half-buried on sand. The first sign to a diver of the presence of these fish is their outline, because the plaice can shuffle down into the sand so that it covers their back. And they can alter their colouration to fit the bottom on which they are lying. A plaice half on sand and half on shingle can do a half-and-half colouration trick. Yet at other times the diver will find it lying on sand or mud or among weed completely uncamouflaged—so much so that its orange or yellow spots are a complete give-away. In fact the diver would certainly not have spotted the fish without its bright spots.

Once the plaice is in what it considers a properly camouflaged position, the underwater photographer can approach very close indeed. So close in fact that a really close-up lens can be used. All this is, of course, conditional on the diver making only slow movements.

In this situation some plaice will allow the diver to feed them worms or smashed-up mussels (mussel beds are a favourite feeding place). When the plaice has had enough and is about to move off it signals its intent by a slight arching of the back. Flight follows within seconds. Often a disturbed plaice will swim right out of vision, but sometimes they settle down again within a short distance of the original resting spot. But on this second settling the fish is much more wary than it was on the first occasion.

Watching a plaice bury itself is quite fascinating. Large specimens throw sand over themselves by means of the frilled fins running down their sides. Watch out when taking pictures that you don't end up with a boss-eyed fish—the eyes can swivel independently.

We have a lot more to learn about the behaviour of plaice underwater. For though plaice are usually found lying on the bottom, they can be met in mid-water free-swimming. One, recently, was watched, and followed, swimming up the sides of a wreck, out over the exposed compartments until disappearing from view in mid-water.

Sand eels [Ammodytidae]

Da: Tobis. *Du*: Zandaal. *Fr*: Lancons. *G*: Sandaale. *Norw*: Tobiser.

There are, according to Wheeler (see Bibliography) five species of sand eels in Northern European waters. Underwater, all look like tiny silver eels with forked tails. They are greatly in demand for bait by bass fishermen. Are often called lance or launce.

Sometimes the diver will find himself surrounded by clouds of these little creatures. Most seem about 2–3 in. long though they do grow to well over 10 in. in length. When first seen underwater they are like silver streaks swimming in groups five or ten strong about 3 ft above a sandy bottom. They are difficult in this situation to approach much closer than 6 ft.

When chased they are most uncooperative and can accelerate very quickly. As a last resort they will disappear into the sand. Their speed of burrowing has to be seen to be believed. Diver observation shows that their burrowing into the sand is done tail-first. Other divers report that before this manoeuvre takes place, the whole school swims head-down as though looking for a likely place in which to burrow.

Certainly the schools all move in the same direction at the same time, turn all at once, and never bump into each other. At night this sense of coordination and direction seems lost and, at the approach of a diver, they will burst out of the sand and zoom in all directions—even raining off the diver's body.

Sole *[Solea solea]*   PLATE 6

Da: Tunger. *Du*: Tong. *Fr*: Sole. *G*: Seezungen. *Norw*: Tunger.

Of the sole family the common sole, or Dover sole, is more frequently seen than any other. If anything, the sole's camouflage is better than that of the plaice. Dark blotches on a brown ground make the back distinctive, but the colour can vary to an astonishing degree. Some soles are much much lighter than others.

The diver looking for sole should investigate any patch of sand among rocks. And his inspection will have to be close for only a close look will show the sole's tiny beady eyes, which are set well down in the head. Otherwise only its gill flap and pectoral fin will give its resting place away. Sole are strong for their size and twist and curl with surprising power as they shoot off from the seabed leaving only a puff of sand behind.

Yet for all this the sole sometimes makes even more incredible camouflage mistakes than the plaice. At times they lie flat on the sides of boulders and only move a few inches sideways before settling down again. On other occasions they can be found lying so obviously on the flat fronds of laminaria that their white underside can be seen clearly from several feet away.

In this exposed position, when the sun is out, the diver can see a succession of ripple movements passing through the fins around their sides. This presumably is so that the fish can retain its precarious perch on the weed. Some divers suspect that these out-in-the-open fish are females who have 'lost their way' and are resting after depositing their eggs.

Stingray [Dasyatis pastinaca]   PLATE 7

> Da: Pigrokke. Du: Stekelroggen. Fr: Pastenague. G: Stechrochen. It: Pastinaca. Norw: Pil-skater. Serb-Cr: Zutulja. Sp: Pastinaca.

Black, grey, brown, sometimes spotted—that's the stingray. They come inshore in high summer and are found lying on the sand near rocks. They appear to be sunning themselves, but it is probable that their entry into shallow warm water is for spawning purposes. Identification is usually the long tail and the 'sting' which is raised in offence or defence from the tail near the junction with the body.

Until the advent of diving these were thought to be rare visitors to North European shores, but it now seems that they are relatively common. The sting is dangerous and is covered with spiny mucus which seems to inflame the wound and cause festering. Big fish can be seen in very shallow water. A stingray of 44 lb has been caught in the Solent by spearfishermen.

At Bognor in Sussex, fishermen had always blamed tope for

damage to their nets until divers Kendall McDonald and Malcolm Todd found large (6-ft) stingrays lying in sand between reef and shore in only 10 ft of water.

At first sight these stingrays looked to the divers like crumpled pieces of corrugated iron. But on closer inspection, it was clear that their approach was being carefully followed—and the eyes moved round to watch them. The fact that the tail with its sting was buried in the sand merely added to the any-old-iron impression. This illusion is quickly dispelled when the ray takes flight and the sand is beaten into turmoil by the take-off beat of the 'wings'. Once 'airborne', the stingray, like the thornback, is a wonderful sight, the 'wings' move lazily up and down and at times curl to meet over the back.

MEDITERRANEAN

No different from the fish found in more Northern waters, but much more often seen in the Mediterranean.

Can often be found foraging over the sand in search of small shellfish. When resting they seem to prefer to get out of the sun and under rock shelves. One of the authors has seen up to five rays of considerable size—up to 6 ft across—piled up on top of one another under rocks off the coast of Libya. Often the long whip-like tail curled outside the rock is the only sign of the fish's presence.

This gregarious behaviour is not only seen in adult fish. One of the most beautiful sights in Mediterranean waters is to see a 'family' of sting rays flapping their wings in slow motion as they 'fly' through the blue water. First the adult pair and then, scurrying behind, one or two tiny 'children'.

The sting near the base of the tail is not the only danger to the unwary swimmer—though this can cause a severe wound and the venom if spiked into a main vein could kill—for the tail itself can cut.

Some Mediterranean divers have found thin razor slashes in the hard rubber compound of their fins after getting too close to the whipping action of the tail.

The stingray is not an easy fish to photograph satisfactorily. Best shot is from the front and below when the full thickness of the fish can be seen.

Thornback ray [*Raja clavata*]

Da: Somrokke. *Du*: Stekelrog. *Fr*: Raie bouclée. *G*: Nagelroche. *Norw*: Piggskate.

There are many rays and they are generally confused with each other. It does not help that thornbacks are marketed in the United Kingdom under the name of skate, ray and roker. The thornback is brown, grey or something in between in colour. Thorns on the back from which the fish takes its name all point aft. Has a short nose and this is one point of identification when trying to tell a thornback from a skate (which has a dark underside and much more pointed nose).

The diver usually finds the thornback or skate lying on a sandy bottom among rocks. It is often so buried in the sand that only the eyes and breathing holes are showing with a thin line marking the line of back and the tail. When disturbed they will swim a short distance and then settle in a more photogenic state for they either don't have time or don't bother to bury themselves again. When swimming they make a magnificent cine subject; the sinuous movements of the wings are one of the most graceful sights in nature.

Some daring divers reckon that a big thornback is a ticket to an exciting ride. Thick gloves are a necessity—not because of the thorns, but to get a good grip as rays are much more slippery than dogfish. Very large fish, both thornbacks and skate, come into quite shallow water to spawn. One of over a hundredweight was seen and later caught in Studland Bay, Dorset. Generally fish of about 15 lb are found over rough ground in inshore bays. Please take care to avoid the base of the tail—the sharp projections can cause a painful wound if you indulge in careless driving or towing!

Turbot [*Scophthalmus maximus*]

Da: Pighvarre. *Du*: Tarbot. *Fr*: Turbot. *G*: Steinbutt. *Norw*: Piggvar.

A big fish which can grow to over 50 lb. Usually has a sand colouration overall with dark brown starring as though a fountain pen loaded with brown ink had been flicked onto a wet surface. Very slimy skin. Mouth is enormous when extended and is to the left of the eyes. A thick fish—and of course a valuable one.

The turbot is much more common than most divers give it credit for. There are many known turbot haunts such as the Skerries Banks off Dartmouth, but any diver moving over a sandy bottom should be looking for flatfish and the turbot is one that he is likely to find. In most cases the turbot is well concealed, but the very thickness of its body usually gives it away. Divers should therefore spare a moment or two to look at any humps in an otherwise flat seabed. Large turbot (over 10 lb) have been seen off the Sussex coast. All that can be seen of this fish at this time, usually late autumn, is a hump in the otherwise flat shingle-sand seafloor, but on closer inspection it is possible to make out the full outline of the fish including the give-away eyes.

Weevers [Trachinidae]

Da: Fjaesing. *Du*: Pieterman. *Fr*: Vive. *G*: Petermann. *Norw*: Fjesing.

Lesser and Greater. Both are yellowy-brown on the back and the only real difference is in size. A nasty stinger producing intense pain.

The weevers—the lesser is more likely to be found in shallow water—lie on clean sand. The diver is unlikely to see one until it breaks cover. Then it swims with the black dorsal fin erect over its sand-camouflaged body. When the fish settles it wriggles into the sand until only its eyes and dorsal fin are above sand level. At rest the fin is folded back, but at the approach of a diver—or the foot of an unwary paddler—the fin erects and the poison spines are ready for action. (For treatment of stings *see* Dangers.)

OPEN WATER

Basking shark [*Cetorhinus maximus*] PLATES 28, 29

Da: Brugde. *Du*: Reuzenhaai. *Fr*: Pelerins. *G*: Riesenhaie. *Norw*: Brugde.

The largest fish to be encountered by divers in Northern European waters. Its size makes identification (even if the diver stays in the water!) easy. All shades of brown to black. Can grow to over 40 ft. From the surface, the great dorsal fin travelling through the water followed yards afterwards by the tail fin is enough to give any diver pause to wonder why he dives at all!

A plankton feeder, it is often in schools. Will not harm the diver BUT there is evidence that if this shark has young, its method of defence is to leap out of the water and fall flat on its attacker. This method of defence has been observed when the basking shark is under attack by its more vicious relatives.

Divers should remember this though there are no reports of aggressive action against man. Boats bump into these monsters and divers cadge lifts on the dorsal fin without any harm coming to them—yet in Scotland and Ireland, divers have reported apparent attempts to overturn boats.

Underwater observation of these monsters relies in Britain to a large extent on the reports of Colin Doeg, Brian Booth, a National Coach of the British Sub-Aqua Club, and Alex Double. All have swum with a basking shark (a lone specimen) and found no aggressive action from the shark despite numerous contacts with the dorsal fin and other parts of the fish.

Part of the difficulty in determining the intention of such sharks is the fact that they are usually met with in water thick with plankton. Colin Doeg is one of the few men to have photographed these fish underwater—the first to have done so in British waters. He is convinced that their eyesight is extremely poor and that they bump into boats simply because they haven't seen them. His observation, backed by fantastic into-mouth photographs, is that the sharks are only interested in the collection of their planktonic food. They swim close to the surface when feeding, he says, and have small eyes right at the front of their noses. The mouth, in the feeding position, is open extremely wide, and the shark swims forward slowly moving its head from side to side as it strains its food from the sea.

Certainly engine noise upsets them and Doeg made use of the 30-h.p. engine on the diving boat to herd the shark into clearer water. Apart from this, it is difficult to make the shark deviate from its course and the underwater photographer can be certain that if he drops into the water ahead of the shark it will soon loom up in his viewfinder.

Bass [*Dicentrarchus labrax*] PLATE 26

> *Da*: Bars. *Du*: Zeebaars. *Fr*: Bar (commercially); more commonly, Loup. *G*: Wolfsbarsch. *It*: Spigola. *Norw*: Havabor. *Serb-Cr*: Lubanz. *Sp*: Lubina.

Once seen never forgotten. The total impression is of power and rapacity. A bright silver, heavy-looking fish whose flanks will often stand out, in shadow, as a startling blue. Belly is white.

Often called the wolf of the sea—and anyone who has seen a pack of bass attacking other fish will not quarrel with the name. Nor will any diver quarrel with the impression—and demonstration—of power that this fish gives. When it takes fright, it does not zigzag away, but literally streaks out of sight. Though it would be fair to describe the fish as shy, it does not give the impression of being frightened. Yet this contrasts with what experienced spearfishermen say about it. They report that curiosity is often its downfall. Bubbles and glinting objects will often attract them close to the diver—which only confirms what every angler knows, that bass will take a polished spinner more often than a dull one.

Photographically they can be a bit of a handful. Their speed makes life difficult for the photographer, so does their colour.

Some photographers say that trying to photograph bass is like trying to outline a silver coin against a white sheet. Some say that flash only adds to this camouflage. Others that the only way to photograph bass is to use flash.

Their unexpected arrival in front of the camera does not help. For you can find bass almost anywhere. They will venture some way into brackish water and can often be found swimming with schools of mullet. Bass of 14 lb and over will suddenly swim in from the mist of visibility to a wreck or isolated group of rocks and will just as quickly fade out again. These rushes into such areas seem more in the nature of a raid on the sheltering fish life than a liking for this kind of territory.

In poor visibility the bass suddenly looms out of the haze and is gone again just as quickly. But they can be found in crystal-clear water. At the Eddystone Light, for example, divers report enormous schools of large bass milling around in an almost solid mass between the surface and the rocky bottom some 20 ft down. These are not school bass, which are sometimes found by divers in tight formations below mackerel shoals. The school bass seem to be snapping up the mackerel's discarded kills as well as young mackerel.

The bass is a handsome fish—perhaps a trifle too thick-bodied to be super-streamlined, but this does not seem to slow him down. When attacking groups of fish, like pollack, he really gives the impression of being a wolf. And his swirling, swinging approaches and abrupt changes of direction make the diver almost duck as though expecting a wave of water to follow such thumping action.

Divers have reported seeing fish that, allowing for underwater magnification, would easily tip the rod-and-line record of 18 lb 2 oz. In fact the size of fish seen by divers would lead one to think that the head and shoulders of a fish found on a beach in Pembrokeshire—this part alone weighed over 20 lb—might well be nothing out of the ordinary.

Some divers say that underwater the bass can be confused with the mullet, but they are in a minority. The bass has a larger head and mouth (the mouth of an eight pounder can easily take a man's fist). The eye is also larger and more prominent than that of the mullet. The mullet's sides are striped—the bass's are not and are covered with bright silver scales shading through deep-blue to a deep slate grey on the back.

But the bass, like the mullet, does seem fond of brackish waters and can be found in the shallow waters of harbours, estuaries and rivers. Though you can find the bass everywhere, there are places that are famous for them, such as the Splaugh Rocks in Southern Ireland.

The rays of the large dorsal fin of a bass are tipped with needle-sharp spines and though no photographer-diver is likely to run the risk of getting cut, the spearfisherman knows this to his cost. When in a school, the bass run to about 3 lb, but the larger the fish grows the more solitary it seems to become. Big specimens are usually seen by divers alone or in pairs and it is interesting to note that these pairs are not of equal size. There is always a larger one who leads the way with a smaller one trailing in attendance. Divers, of course, suspect that the smaller one is the female. But bass do group into packs of five or six really big ones. Whether this is intentional or whether they only group when finding some defenceless 'herd' of fish, there is no way of knowing.

Bass are virtually unknown to divers on the East Coast above Yorkshire and most reported sightings—and pictures—are from the South and South-West.

The photographer's approach to bass is one of stealth. Quiet fin movements are of the utmost importance and controlled breathing may help. Some indication of the power of a bass's tail, the main motive power, comes from divers who have reported hearing an actual thump in the water when a bass takes off in flight.

Bass are, of course, predators, and feed greedily on fish fry and small fish when available. They are particularly partial to sand eels, 'whitebait', soft crabs—so much so that any diver who swims into a cloud of sand eels will almost certainly see bass. High water seems to be the best time to encounter bass as they swim in over the rocks in search of their food. They work their way up sandy channels between rocks. But there is no infallible rule for bass. In places like the Kimmeridge Ledges, near Poole, Dorset, bass of 10 lb and over can be seen feeding at low water springs.

Bass seem to favour sand patches in rocky areas and weed which shelters shrimp and prawn. They sometimes become so engrossed in their feeding in these areas that a close approach is possible.

MEDITERRANEAN

The Mediterranean bass undoubtedly look like and indeed are the same fish that the diver meets in Northern waters, but their behaviour seems to differ drastically.

In Northern waters it would be a rare bass that would hide underneath a rock, but in the Mediterranean this behaviour seems by no means uncommon. Even bass that could make the straight-line-for-the-open-sea sort of escape that is usual with their cold-water cousins, have been seen to dive under a rock—and leave their tails sticking out to mark the spot for all to see. This hiding habit might seem sensible if the fish was trapped in a narrow gully with its exit to the open sea blocked by a diver, but in the instances where this habit has been observed, such was not the case.

On one occasion, for example, a bass had apparently made its getaway when surprised near the shore and the diver–photographer gloomily reflected that his high-speed snap of the fish was likely to show nothing but a disappearing tail. The diver swam on over the ridge of rocks in the direction of which the bass had disappeared.

But there at the foot of the other side of the ridge was undoubtedly the same bass—under a rock with his tail sticking out! Only once has similar behaviour been seen by the authors in British waters—and on that occasion the fish was using thick weed as a hiding place.

Garfish [*Belone belone*]

Da: Hornfisk. *Du*: Geep. *Fr*: Orphie. *G*: Hornhecht. *Norw*: Horngjel.

An incredibly fast-moving fish with a great long beak, and a great long thin body. Back is dark-green or dark-blue and the sides silver that shades to white on the belly. Moves in large schools and, to the angler's amazement, will walk on the water with its tail just touching when hooked. Seems to eat anything of a reasonable size that swims.

Is a difficult fish for the diver to spot when swimming as, like the mackerel, it is extremely well camouflaged. When resting, which appears to be rare, the garfish hangs in the water like a great question mark. On one occasion a garfish was observed in this position examining a diver who was having trouble clearing his ears. The fish hung in the water apparently fascinated by what was going on as the diver struggled to equalise the pressure. The streams of bubbles pouring from the aqualung demand valve seemed to fascinate the garfish and so great was its curiosity that in the end it appeared to be peering intently into the diver's mask.

Mackerel [*Scomber scombrus*]

Da: Makrel. *Du*: Makreel. *Fr*: Maquereaux. *G*: Makrelen. *Norw*: Makrell.

Who doesn't know what a mackerel looks like? The answer would seem to be the diver. For however pretty the fish looks when just caught by the angler with its brilliant blue or green back with black lines curving across it and its silvery sides—the divers report that this is one of the best camouflaged fish in the sea.

The mackerel is one of the most elusive fish from the point of view of the diver-photographer. Even diving from a fishing boat into the middle of a known mackerel school does not produce the pictures one would expect. They appear almost invisible side on. Then their presence is only betrayed by flashes of light in the water. They always seem to be at the limit of visibility but are obviously milling around in all directions—and only show up as a sparkle when a fish turns and catches the light.

In attempts to get pictures, divers have gone into the water when anglers in the boat above were catching masses of fish on feathers. Reports Peter Scoones, one of the divers concerned: 'I was in the middle of the shoal—there was no doubt about that. But it was impossible to see the fish until they struck at the feathers and became impaled on the hooks. When this happened they were only five or six feet in front of me—and the visibility was in the region of 15 to 10 ft.'

Flash from below seems to be the only way to take pictures of these fish, though other divers report that they can be seen from above when descending into a shoal.

Mullet [Mugilidae]   PLATES 21, 22

Da: Multe. *Du*: Harder aaldoe. *Fr*: Muges or Mulets. *G*: Meeraschen. *It*: Muggine chelone. *Norw*: Multer. *Serb-Cr*: Skocac putnik. *Sp*: Lisa.

There are over 100 species of mullet in the world—and even the experts have difficulty in telling them apart. Fortunately for the mullet observer's peace of mind, only three are common to Northern waters. These are the thick-lipped grey mullet, the thin-lipped grey mullet and the golden mullet.

The first of these is by far the most numerous. The golden mullet is something of a rarity, but be careful in identifying your mullet—a large thick-lipped specimen will have a golden sheen on its flanks. The rod-caught grey mullet record is just over 10 lb, but larger specimens have been netted and 15-lb fish have been found dead in Ireland.

The adult grey mullet is a handsome fish with dark blue-grey back and silvery sides with thick pronounced scales. Beware of the dorsal fin, which is tipped with sharp spines. Lateral stripes run the length of the body from behind the gill plates to the tail and this is a first-class recognition aid underwater. The flick of a V-shaped tail and a streamlined striped body mean mullet to every diver.

Mullet are friendly fish and collect together in the shallow waters and estuaries of Northern Europe. In Britain, however, they don't seem to be very keen on the North Sea and East Coast.

They obviously like brackish water and can survive for a long time in almost completely land-locked lagoons. One diver, for example reports schools of mullet in the Dorset Stour over ten miles from the river mouth and the sea.

Mullet are not predators and their main source of food is the minute crustaceans which live on weed. They favour the thin weed that grows on jetties and under boats and can often be seen from the surface nosing around such places.

If approached quietly their white telescopic lips can be clearly seen sucking at the green fronds in the search for such delicacies. It is fascinating to see them start on a particular piece of weed at its base and move right up to the tip like a living vacuum cleaner. Seen head-on, their lips appear heart-shaped. But you will not always find the vacuum cleaner technique being used on weed. They can work a sandy patch just as well and leave puffs of disturbed sand behind them as they go.

Divers are divided about the action of mullet when frightened. Some describe something like a seabed explosion when these very shy, elusive fish take flight. Others say that if the diver remains still the fish will approach him quite closely. All are agreed that if really disturbed they will disappear with great haste, but will also sometimes return to the same feeding spot within ten minutes. Spearfishermen also say that after they have fired at a mullet and missed the same fish will turn round and swim right up to them.

Certainly mullet in boat-frequented waters are not so shy as those found further out to sea. The best place for anyone who wants to find mullet is close in to the white water around rocks. Mullet move in with the advancing tide feeding on sand hoppers and other tiny marine life. In deeper water the long thin weed seems to be a particular favourite. Yet mullet seem completely unpredictable—divers sometimes come upon great schools of them in deep gullies or even caves. Then the sea around the diver becomes a whirl of flashing bodies and twisting fins as the mullet try desperately to escape to the open sea.

MEDITERRANEAN

Exactly similar in looks to the thick-lipped mullet of Northern waters, but behaves differently.

The main difference in behaviour is that the Mediterranean mullet seems to love the surf which breaks around rocks. In particular the smaller, younger fish delight in moving in and out of the broken water in rocky clefts. If you approach close to the surface on one of those days when the Med is not the lake that everyone likes to pretend it is, you will soon spot the young mullet darting here and there among the bubbles in the white water as it washes back off the rocks.

These young fish can make very attractive photographs because the fish are being lit by the blue water beneath them, despite the fact that they are swimming against a background of dark rocks. In these circumstances a high shutter speed is, of course, essential.

Porbeagle shark [*Lamna nasus*]   PLATE 14

> *Da*: Sildehaj. *Du*: Haringhaai. *Fr*: Lamie. *G*: Heringshai. *Norw*: Haabrand.

Dark-blue running into grey and then white belly. This is the porbeagle shark, which has only recently been photographed underwater off the British Isles by Tony Baverstock. Identification of this shark is never in doubt underwater for the porbeagle is a really shark-like shark! Main dorsal fin is exactly above the pectoral.

Baverstock entered the water while 'rubby-dubby' (crushed fish food) was being trailed from a shark-fishing boat off the Isle of Wight. When the porbeagle took the bait, it went berserk rushing hither and thither at considerable speed. The fish taken while Baverstock was filming were of over 100 lbs, some nearer 200. The fish can go to over 10 ft in length and weigh nearly 400 lb according to Wheeler. (*See* Bibliography in Appendix 4.)

Salmon   [*Salmo salar*]

Da: Laks. *Du*: Zalm. *Fr*: Saumon. *G*: Lachse. *Norw*: Lax.

Not a fish often seen by divers, but the recent furore about the discovery of their breeding grounds off Greenland and subsequent heavy fishing makes divers' observations important. Most divers who have seen this fish describe them as 'silver', but Wheeler (see Bibliography) says that the salmon's colour depends on whether it is in the sea or fresh water. At sea, says Wheeler, the back is a silvery blue-green, the sides silvery and the belly white, with small black X-shaped and round spots above the lateral line. On entering fresh water it loses its silvery pigment and becomes greenish or brown mottled with red or orange and has large dark spots edged with a lighter colour.

Both Geoff Harwood and Roger Bruce have observed salmon underwater. Both had totally different experiences. Geoff Harwood was in Ireland and found in North Donegal that a small river, which runs through Bunbeg Harbour, was the route used by salmon on their way inland. Each tide brought the salmon in and they could be seen jumping on their run up the river. Water visibility from the surface looked good, but Harwood found, once he was in the water, horizontal visibility of less than one foot.

Once he reached the seabed the reason became obvious. Brown peaty river water was flowing over the clear sea water in a sharply defined layer only a few inches thick. The salmon were travelling in this thick layer and not in the clearer water below. Salmon flashed overhead, but Harwood got no opportunity to photograph them.

Roger Bruce in Scotland diving in a salmon river had the opposite experience. He found that the salmon were intensely curious and crowded round him to such an extent that he found it extremely difficult to obtain more than a blurred close-up of the fish.

CHAPTER TWO

Mediterranean

DIVING IN THE MEDITERRANEAN

There are divers who describe the Mediterranean as 'barren'. But they don't really mean it. What they are drawing attention to is the fact that they miss the luxuriant weed forests and life that they have become accustomed to in colder waters. They are also saying, 'In the place that I dived in the Med, I didn't see as many big fish as I do on dives of similar duration in Northern waters.'

But they don't mean that it is barren, not in the sense of absence of fish and other life. The trouble is often that tourist divers have to dive near tourist spots and in those areas the Mediterranean is sometimes very short of sizeable marine life.

No one could complain about the clarity of the water in the Mediterranean. Though this is a joy for the diver because he can often see over 100 ft in any direction, it does work both ways. If he can see that far, so can some of the fish. And there is no reason for them to hang around and wait for this new monster to chase them. The wide-ranging fish seek the shelter of the open sea and the rock-dwellers shrink deeper into cover. And the diver who expects all fish to come to him will see none of them.

But the diving photographer once again is the man who will make the most of the marvellous clarity of these waters. He will look under every rock, will move unhurriedly from underwater crag to cave and back again. And all the time he will be conscious of the marvellous blue around him and the shining silver screen of the surface.

Another kind of underwater worker is the man who should be blamed for the lack of large-sized fish close to tourist areas. I mean, of course, the spearfisherman, whose activities are referred to in other places in this book. But it would be foolish to assume that because of spearfishing it is impossible to find reasonably-sized fish within easy reach of holiday resorts.

Just off Conca Beach, near Playa de Aro, on the Costa Brava, I have seen huge sars swimming in and out of the legs of the paddlers, snapping up the delicacies that unwitting feet have stirred up from the sand.

And, in a rocky outcrop only feet from the main bathing beach at Ste Maxime in the South of France, I spotted a huge scorpion fish that would well have delighted any French cook looking for such a delicacy for his bouillabaisse.

Fish are where you find them. And even if the seabed in your particular piece of the Mediterranean looks extremely unfruitful, you would be well-advised not to abandon the area without a thorough search.

Don't be put off by the veterans' tales of the days when every sizeable rock housed a giant grouper and every stone concealed a huge corb, a-swirl with glorious fins just like a Spanish senorita with her mantilla and fan. True, in well-dived areas the grouper is not easy to find, but then neither is the traditional senorita. She's in a near-miss of a mini-skirt and you'll have to search deep in a night-club for a close imitation of the original.

Near tourist areas too, you'll have to go deep to find a grouper. But take care. Deep in the Mediterranean can mean very deep indeed. And though no Lorelei calls the diver down to the depths, it is easy to press on down and not realise how deep you are.

Sometimes you can still see the surface from amazing depths. I can remember cruising happily along for what seemed like ages at 30 ft (according to my depth gauge). I remember too look-ing up at the surface and thinking how far away it seemed. It was only on the return to the boat and in the course of general dis-cussion about the dive that I realised that my depth gauge had stuck at 30 ft. In reality we had been moving over the seabed between 60 and 80 ft and both the other divers' depth gauges had agreed about this.

Some divers talk about their experiences being 'like diving in a giant aquarium'. This fairly describes Mediterranean diving. And that sort of clarity tends to lead the diver into abusing safety rules. In fact, one of the main problems that instructors have in countries that border on the Mediterranean is in restraining their trainee divers once they have had their first lesson from plunging in and hurtling down to the 100-ft depths.

But if clarity brings its own problems to the diver, so does the tourist boom to the fish.

Groupers, for example, have the totally English trait of regarding their home as their castle. They develop an almost fanatical devotion to the hole, cleft, cave, or tunnel that they have decided to call home. A particularly good illustration of this was given by the grouper that made his home in a cave directly in front of what is now a complex of flats and a swimming pool-cum-night-club at Port Salvi on the headland overlooking the harbour of San Feliu de Guixols, capital of the Costa Brava.

When I say that his home was directly in front of this entertainment complex I mean, of course, that it was in the sea 60 ft down and at that time it was right underneath the site of a new block of cliff-top flats. Divers visited him regularly because Pat Harrison, who ran a diving school there, would take divers down to see the fish on the strict understanding that they did not interfere with him in any way.

Unless the divers became too pressing, the fish would not take fright. When he did, he slid carefully away from a back exit and the divers made it a rule not to station themselves there to block his escape route.

The trouble was that rubble jettisoned from the building work rolled down the steep slope underwater and came closer and closer to the grouper's home.

The fish stuck it out and only finally evacuated his home when rubble completely blocked the front entrance.

All this talk of rubble in the water tends to make it sound as though the Mediterranean is completely finished. Yet a diver like Peter Scoones, who has worked the North African coastline with his camera, will tell you that this sea is far from finished. That fish there are just as prolific as ever they were along the coastline that has now been built up into a tourist's playground.

It would be wrong, however, to suggest that only the North African coast is suitable for the man who wishes to see fishes.

The Mediterranean has more moods than many other waters. And the moods affect the fish.

In Spain when the tramontana blows treacherously—and anybody who thinks of the Mediterranean as some kind of playboy's lake made for mindless idiots to sail upon would do well to check up on his insurance policies and his will—the fish change their behaviour patterns to suit the wind. When the Spanish tramontana blows the sardines congregate in vast shoals close in to the rocks. They sway in the huge seas that leap out of nowhere, but never allow themselves to be washed into the white foam that surrounds the rocks. And when the tramontana is past the shoals spread out and every fish appears to be on the feed once again.

Yet in the South of France, when the Mistral wind is past, the water is like glass and shockingly cold, and the fish abide by a sort of hush until the water warms again.

Bay after bay in the Mediterranean is carpeted with the green stalks of the posidonia weed. It doesn't grow very high—perhaps two feet at the most—but it provides shelter for the most amazing marine population. Yet the diver can, and often does, swim over it, seeing nothing but its green slim leaves.

It is, I suppose, like blades of grass magnified into the lawn of some land of giants. And the diver who passes over it without some close inspection does himself and his fishwatching a considerable disservice. This weed is so common that the diver has some excuse for treating it as a common part of the underwater landscape. At depth it peters out and the sand and dark rocks of deeper water take its place.

In the posidonia weed there is a fantastic amount of life. It is here that the sea-horses hide. It is here that, if the diver lets himself sink into its grasp—making sure that he is not sinking straight on to the spines of a scorpion fish, for they like to lie up in its tresses too—that blue fish will pop out as though the diver's weight has ejected lesser beings.

These blue fish have a square black mark beneath the main dorsal fin. The black patch is so striking that you can't miss it. These fish belong to the Picarel family and make nests in the weed.

With a little patience and stealth the diver can get so close that the startling blue of these nine-inch long fish is almost dazzling. Though they will freeze in the weed until the diver is almost on top of them they seem to spend most of their life chasing away smaller wrasse with obvious designs on their eggs.

But even though you can get really close to these beautiful fish, little is known about their behaviour. More and more underwater observation is needed.

This is where the diver can help. Your observations, your studies, even just your stray observation of a peculiar pattern of fish behaviour are of use. Note it all down and then you are making some valuable contribution to the study of fish.

The excitement you get from your diving and fish observation are usually equal to the amount of effort you put into it. Certainly that is true of the Mediterranean. If you expect a wonderland when you step off some package-tour hotel balcony into the sea, you will deserve the seabed wasteland of plastic cups and empty bottles. But you may find fish.

If, on the other hand, you struggle down some dried-up river bed with all your equipment because it is the only way to the sea through precipitous cliffs, then you will find an unspoiled seabed. And you will find fish.

There you will find the true Mediterranean. Sars show their black and silver uniform around almost every rock. Yellow-striped saupe wheel in giant schools and turn whole areas into a flicker of tails as they feed head down.

Wrasse colour every cluster of grey stones. Red mullet feed on the sand patches where the sunlight sends shafts down like golden rods through the blue. And a black-backed stingray, disturbed at your approach, beats out towards the open sea like some underwater swan attempting a take-off from the surface of a tranquil lake.

Deeper down, the gorgonia shows yellow tips from encrusted crags, and in some dark cave the moray waits.

And when you find a day like that, then only a fool would say that the Mediterranean is barren. It's different, that's all.

KENDALL MCDONALD

GUIDE TO THE
FISHES OF THE MEDITERRANEAN

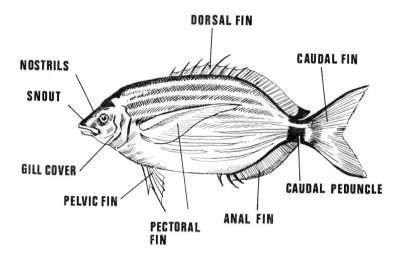

DORSAL FIN

CAUDAL FIN

NOSTRILS

SNOUT

GILL COVER

PELVIC FIN

PECTORAL FIN

ANAL FIN

CAUDAL PEDUNCLE

The Mediterranean differs greatly from the other North European waters, not only in its clarity, but in the species of fish that are found there. Many species, of course, overlap. Red mullet, for example, will be found right up close to the Channel coasts, but are more often seen in the Mediterranean. And the behaviour of the fish in the two seas will not necessarily be the same. But you will find the fish listed in only one of the regional guides, with a note about differing behaviour in other waters.

In previous chapters a reference was made to the sea being a giant highway for fish of all kinds. It is not surprising therefore to find that some Red Sea fish have managed to 'leak' into the Mediterranean.

ROCKS, WEEDS AND WRECKS

Anthias anthias PLATE 34

Fr: Barbier. *G*: Anthias. *It*: Guarracino. *Serb-Cr*: Kiria mala. *Sp*: Borriquete.

There appears to be no well known English name for this Mediterranean species, which seems to take the place of the 'sea flies' (see *Chromis chromis*) at depth. To the diver down at 100 ft they look like grey goldfish with a big forked tail and graceful decorative fins. About 4 in. long at most.

Though this fish looks grey in natural light at depth, due to the lack of red in the light penetrating that far, when lit by a torch or an exploding flash bulb the true colour can be seen—a beautiful pinkish-red shading into yellowish-orange on the fins. Best photographed in small groups though the random movements of this fish, like that of *Chromis chromis*, make a well-composed picture very rare indeed.

Cardinal fish [*Apogon imberbis*] PLATE 42

Fr: Roi des rougets. *G*: Meerbarbenkonig. *It*: Re de triglie. *Sp*: Reyezuelo.

Look just like goldfish from their outline. Can be found at all depths, but are mostly at the back of small caves and clefts in the rocks. Movement slow and purposeful. Are red with a blueish eye, which appears to have an 'eyelid', but which is, in fact, only a darker colouration over the eye.

Not an easy fish to photograph because they rarely venture out from their chosen position in the back of some dark overhang. Can grow up to 10 in. long. The diver will find single specimens in one hole and then up to a dozen in another.

Corb [*Johnius umbra*]

Fr: Corbeau or corb. *G*: Meerrabe. *It*: Corvo. *Serb-Cr*: Vranac. *Sp*: Corvallo or corva.

One of the Mediterranean's most beautiful fish. The great swirling fins make identification easy. At first sight this fish gives the impression of being black, probably because it lives in the shadows under rocks and in small caves formed by rocks overlapping one another.

Once the diver's eyes have become accustomed to the gloom in which he sees the corb, he will realise that his first impression of a black fish is wrong. The corb is the most marvellous mixture of dark colours, golden bronze or olive green with a fantastic violet sheen overall. The leading edges of the lower fins which seem to swirl with every movement have a characteristic white or transparent yellow leading edge.

The corb used to be a common sight in the shallow waters, but that was before the spearfishermen got there. The corb is an easy target as it rarely moves from shelter when first approached.

The fact that its flesh is quite palatable didn't help. Now you will find the corb quite difficult to spot and completely wiped out in shallow tourist areas.

It is difficult to photograph due to the dark places in which it is found. Usually in groups of two to six fish. On the North African coast, groups of these fish all about 18 in. long are quite common still, but even there the fish now favour rocky hiding places with multiple exits. They are usually found in 30 to 40 ft of water.

Salpe [*Boops salpa*]   PLATE 48

Fr: Saupe. *G*: Goldstriemen. *It*: Salpa or Sarpa. *Serb-Cr*: Sopa. *Sp*: Salpa.

Can be seen everywhere in the Mediterranean in schools of over 100 fish. Can be spotted in the clear waters from great distances as their gold–silver markings flash in the sunlight. Adult fish are very pretty in both shape and colouring—silvery-gold with 10–12 yellow stripes along the body. Often swim with their mouths open and this gives the impression of fish notched at both ends—a tiny notch in the head and a nice big V-shape from the tail.

The English name for these fish—'goldline'—is rarely used by divers, who tend to call them by the French 'saupe'. They forage over sandy bottoms or feed on algae on weeds and rocks. The feeding stance—head down—often makes a rock disappear in a waggle of tails and these flashing in the sunlight are a great give-away. Even tiny ones—only 1 in. or so long—have this same feeding attitude, though the youngsters look underwater more of a uniform gold colour. This is a fish whose curiosity can be turned to good account by the diver-photographer.

Feeding schools seem to return to the same area each day, but do not generally spend long in one place. They give the impression of being very busy fish, but they can be lured to the diver.

This is best done by getting as close to the fish as possible—and then taking no notice of them at all. If the diver sits still on the bottom, breathing as gently as possible, and spends his time looking down at the seabed, he will soon become conscious that the whole fleet of fish is wheeling round him. By judging the right moment and bringing up the camera in one swift sweep it is possible to get a good photograph right into the heart of the school. Using this method over 60 fish can be pictured on one 35-mm negative. This is some indication of how close these fish swim to one another.

Shots taken of the fish feeding against a background of shallow grey Mediterranean rocks are always a disappointment. Despite their colouring—or maybe because of it—these fish seem to blend well into the colour of the background. It is not uncommon for other species of fish to join with the saupe. And it is not always easy to spot these extras at first glance. Divers have seen small tuna, bass and mullet moving with the saupe schools.

Grouper, Jewfish, or Dusky Sea Perch [*Epinephelus guaza,*
E. alexandrinus and *Mycteroperca rubra*] PLATE 30

Fr: Merou. G: Zackenbarsch. It: Cernia. Serb-Cr: Kirnia. Sp: Mero.

While the three English names given in the heading are names
that apply to all of these large fish, the Latin names are of three
distinct species. The groupers are all big fish, *Epinephelus guaza*
growing to a length of over 4 ft and being thick round with it.
Colouration varies from yellow brown to almost jet black and
some fish have mottled spots of even lighter colours on the flanks.
The pectoral fins are dark edged. *Epinephelus alexandrinus* is
smaller, not so tubby and young fish have striped flanks against an
overall brown body. *Mycteroperca rubra* has a more pointed head
and is reddish-brown with lighter mottling marks.

The grouper is a rock dweller, living in the same hole for years
—and this has been his downfall in shallow waters. Spearfishermen could spot one and come back day after day and be sure that
the fish would still be there.

But groupers can be found in very shallow water indeed, in
places where the spearfishermen have not turned the sea into a
desert. On some occasions these shallow water groupers have
hardly enough water over them to cover their own immense bulk.
Finding a grouper today in such a situation is rare and not a fact
for broadcasting to all and sundry as the grouper is highly prized
for food as well as for exhibiting as proof of a hunter's prowess.

Now the diver usually has to look much deeper for the
grouper's home, but the fish's behaviour never seems to alter. At
first sight of the diver, the grouper will hang in the water at a
steep angle, tail down, head up, studying the scene. This is
followed by a smart retreat into his home, which is always a hole
in a rock. This hole will have many twists and turns inside and
many entrances—so that even when you have marked the exact
spot, peering into the hole will only give you the impression that
it is empty. The grouper will have sought the cover of one of the
side galleries in the rock or will be making a gliding escape from a
rear exit.

The fish seems to have a well-developed sense of curiosity, and the best method of observing him is not to follow him right up to his hole, but to wait above or to one side.

After a few moments the grouper will poke his head out to see what is going on. This curiosity does, of course, prove fatal if a knowledgeable spearfisherman is about and is another reason for the shortage of groupers in shallow water.

When spearfishermen have mortally wounded a large grouper in his hole they often have great difficulty in getting the fish out even though transfixed by several spears. This is caused by the fish's habit of erecting all his fins in the narrow part of his home and often not relaxing when dead.

The grouper is a majestic fish when viewed underwater at close range. Though giving the impression of laziness when resting or when sliding away from danger, this great bulky fish can go like smoke when disturbed. The main dorsal fin is then folded down and the fish torpedoes through the water and out of sight.

Though now the grouper is usually only met in deep water in the Northern Mediterranean, off the North African coast there are still many groupers of 3 to 4 ft long in reasonable depths of water. They are not afraid of the diver—yet—and Peter Scoones has hand-fed groupers to lure them into suitable positions for underwater photographs. He calls them the most co-operative fish he has ever met and feels that they are intelligent enough to know when harm is meant to them. This sort of thing applies only to unfished areas of course, and there are many stories of groupers which have become accustomed to come to humans in this way and have trustingly swum up to meet a spearfisherman with the obvious fatal result.

Moray eel [*Muraena helena*]   PLATE 31

Fr: Murene. *G*: Murane. *It*: Murena. *Serb-Cr*: Mrina zutosarka.

A brown eel with terrifying display of teeth, body thickening, sometimes dramatically just behind the head—that's the moray. Colouration of the body varies enormously—all shades of brown, even black, are sometimes marbled with yellow, sometimes spotted with the same colour. Some have been seen with giant orange spots.

Despite its legendary reputation for fierceness, the moray is, in fact, a shy fish. But it does possess very powerful jaws and can inflict severe bites. So take care.

But the reason for most of the stories about the ferocious moray is probably due to their habit of opening and shutting their mouths when at rest at the entrance to their holes.

The moray is often difficult to locate in the daytime when it tends to withdraw into a hole which is often inside a cave. The best way to entice the fish into view is to hang at the entrance to the cave until your eyes have become accustomed to the gloom.

The moray will sometimes edge forward to see the intruder. This is probably curiosity and not ferocity. This is the time that most photographs of morays are taken and the fish looks most impressive with just the head and 'shoulders' emerging from the hole.

Morays, however, are not always to be found hiding out of sight. They can sometimes be seen in broad daylight gliding in and out of boulders in very shallow water, sometimes only a matter of inches deep. Nor will you always see the head of a moray first. They appear to have a tendency to leave the tail end hanging out of a hole in the rocks.

At one time the moray was believed to have a poison sac leading to a tooth in the roof of its mouth. This is completely untrue, but from the experience of divers who have been bitten, it does seem that a moray bite will turn septic if not attended to properly and quickly. This is probably due to the decaying pieces of food left in their teeth after a meal and the tearing effect of the teeth themselves. Another theory is that the slime covering the teeth is toxic, but there appears no foundation for this.

Some recent reports from divers indicate that the moray can be hand-fed with pieces of fish so that he becomes tame enough to tickle at the back of the neck. Treat each eel as different. Some might well bite the hand that feeds them!

Parrot fish [*Euscarus cretensis*]

Fr: Poisson-perroquet. *G*: Papageienfisch. *It*: Scaro di Creta. *Serb-Cr*: Papigaca. *Sp*: Vieja colorada.

Found mainly along the North African coast, also Madeira and the Canary Islands. Is red with a large grey saddle at the shoulder, yellow eye and a yellow saddle on the tails talk. Some are grey with a black patch behind the pectoral fin. This is the male. The other markings are the sign of the female. The jaws are modified into a parrot's beak to make feeding on algae on rocks more simple.

These fish are easily identifiable and are easy to approach when browsing on algae, but they will not allow extreme close-ups. They can move very fast indeed when disturbed.

These parrots seem to travel in small groups of three or four. Average size seen by divers is about one foot.

Picarels [Maenidae]

Fr: Mendole. *G*: Sparfisch. *It*: Menola. *Serb-Cr*: Gira oblica. *Sp*: Caramel or Chucla.

Also known as Cackerel or Smares.

Usually to be found in and over underwater prairies of posidonia weed, which is common to many Mediterranean bays, the picarel in summer garb is a striking fish.

There are two main varieties. *Maena maena* grows to about nine inches in length and has a glowing bright blue back and sides shading to yellow near the belly. A square black patch below the dorsal fin is a quick means of identification. *Maena chryselis* is not so brightly coloured with a browny-yellow back and light sides. The square black spot is very much in evidence. And in mating display the male does carry blue 'scribblings' on his flanks.

Earlier reference to picarel's behaviour has been made by Kendall McDonald in his introduction to Mediterranean diving. In this instance he was writing about *Maena maena*, which builds a 'nest' in the weed and defends it against all comers.

Picarels are believed to be hermaphrodites. The 'nests'—shallow pits in the sand in among the posidonia weed—are almost a communal affair with one only a few feet from another. It is for this reason that the diver who penetrates into the posidonia will find that though six or so fish emerge and appear to be a shoal they are in fact the owners of several nests in the neighbourhood.

Sometimes a fish will remain on the nesting site until the diver is literally on top of him or her. But this does not make photography easy. Shooting down from above, though it will show a striking blue back, does not produce a good photograph. The photographer will do better to sink into the weed and photograph the fish that emerge, shooting, if possible, slightly upwards. This will ensure that the posidonia weed background is shown, but without setting the fish against a messy background of green stalks pointing in all directions.

Rabbitfish [*Siganus rivulatus*] PLATE 44

[*Is such a rarely seen fish—until recently—that common names in the various languages do not seem to exist.*]

This fish is a migrant from the Red Sea, and can now be seen in the Mediterranean, particularly off the Libyan coast.

A deep-bodied fish, silvery in colour, it has a similar shape to the John Dory from the point of view of thinness. The body carries indistinct dark spots which may be purple at times. Has a marked gill-plate cover and a rounded V-shaped anal fin.

Peter Scoones's photograph of this fish in Libyan waters is the farthest west that this fish has so far been recorded. He reports that it swims in company with saupe and jacks (horse mackerel) and in the Mediterranean is about eight inches long. Other reports of the fish being sighted come from the Adriatic coast and the Lebanon.

Sars [Sparidae] PLATE 49

Fr: Sargue ordinaire. *G*: Zweibindenbrassen. *It*: Sarago comune. *Serb-Cr*: Spar fratar. *Sp*: Sargo.

The word 'sar' in the Mediterranean area covers a multitude of fins. All the various fish loosely lumped under this heading are bream. You will not look underwater long in the Mediterranean before you meet one of the family. They are the most fish-shaped fish to be seen. Black bands and deep silver bodies added to a twittering of tails and swimming that looks hurried—that's a sar.

To go into the whole family would need almost an entire book so we will take the most common of the sars as an example. *Diplodus vulgaris* is the common or two-banded bream.

The sar have become cautious fish since the advent of spear-fishing and in popular tourist areas you are unlikely to see any really big fish. But small sars will be there. Despite their caution the sars can be attracted by breaking up a sea urchin with a diving knife. They will then rush in to feed on the contents of the prickly shell.

Divers call this method of attracting fish 'chumming', presumably because the diver is making a 'chum' of the fish by feeding it.

Big sars seem to live in ones and twos and not in schools like the youngsters. They tend to shelter under rocks and their large eyes seem to spot trouble a long way off. When injured or attacked by parasites, the sar seems to prefer to live alone in the short time he has left before falling foul of some predator.

Scorpion fishes   [*Scorpaena scrofa* and *S. porcus*] PLATES 38–9, 52

Da: Blakaeft. *Du*: Schorpioen-vissen. *Fr*: Rascasse. *G*: Drachenkopf. *It*: Scorpena. *Norw*: Dvaergulk. *Serb-Cr*: Bodec. *Sp*: Escorpina.

Masters of camouflage and more dangerous because of that. *Scrofa* has tendrils hanging from the chin; *porcus* has plumes over the eyes. The *scrofa* is said to be redder than the *porcus*, but both adapt their colouration to their surroundings so well that the diver is in some identification difficulty. Both are found in shallow water and on deep grounds. Once seen never forgotten. They look evil, and are covered with warts, lumps and protuberances. Eyes look extremely angry. Rather like two empty red jewels than normal fish eyes. Poisonous. Watch out!

Some divers are so worried by these fish that they wear gloves when diving in the warmest waters. Certainly it is true that when diving along a cliff face underwater it is extremely unwise to hold anywhere with a bare hand. The scorpion fishes always seem to be in the exact spot that your unprotected hand is likely to descend.

Only by close examination will you spot the scorpion fish as both varieties melt perfectly into their background. It is the spiny rays in the dorsal fin and the spines on the gill flaps that are poisonous. (For treatment if you are unfortunate enough to be stung, *see* Dangers.)

These fish can be found anywhere from a depth of a few inches to hundreds of feet down. It is interesting to note that some divers describe the scorpions as extremely shy, but others report having shoved close-up lenses within inches of their noses without the fish moving at all. All comment that the eyes look angry and seem to glow with unpleasantness. Both species rely on their camouflage to bring their fish prey within range.

One diver found a particular fish—in the same position each day—reacted in flight at any attempt to approach closely by stealth. But the fish did not mind a really noisy approach. A 'feet first, eyes shut' noisy approach did in fact end with the fish hardly moving even when hit on the nose by the close-up lens on the camera. Even then the fish only shifted a matter of inches. Photographers should try and get the whole fish into the picture for maximum effect.

Scorpion fish do not use their poisonous spines for catching their food. Like the angler fish they are superbly camouflaged and the incautious approach of smaller fish keeps the scorpion's stomach well-filled. The small victims are swallowed whole. The poisonous spines seem to be used only for defence against large predators.

NORTHERN WATERS

Various varieties of scorpion fish are found from the fatherlasher (*Cottus scorpius*), which grows to about 1 ft long, to the more often seen long-spined sea scorpion (*Cottus bubalis*) (Plate 20), which reaches about 6 in. in length.

All sit on the bottom among rocks and stones and are well camouflaged. Will not budge even when a diver approaches really close. Have an air of menace about them. Wounds from the spines often turn septic.

Sea horse [*Hippocampus hippocampus*]

Fr: Cheval marin or hippocampe. *G*: Seepferdchen. *It*: Cavalluccio marino. *Serb-Cr*: Konjic morski. *Sp*: Caballo marino.

There is no fish in the sea which is better named. But, and it is a big 'but', there are few fishes which are more difficult to spot.   It is all very well looking through the glass of a marine aquarium tank boldly labelled 'Sea Horses' and immediately spotting the brown or browny-green bodies of this delightful fish anchored by its tail to the one bush of weed in the tank. It is entirely another matter to spot the sea horse in its natural surroundings.

If you have sharp eyes you will spot the sea horse among the posidonia weed which carpets the bottom of many a Mediterranean bay. They are extremely slow swimmers and when they have to break from cover, swim in a vertical position with the dorsal fins working away like mad. But this open water movement is rare. If you are fortunate enough to come across them in open water then you have all the time in the world to take your pictures, but once the fish has approached a bank of weed you will be driven to distraction attempting to locate the fish.

They feed on tiny marine animals which are sucked up by the tube-like mouth.

The eggs are deposited in the male's brood pouch by the female. Later, when the eggs have hatched, it is the male who seems to suffer 'birth pangs' and hard labour as he ejects the little sea horses one by one from the pouch. (*Note:* This has been observed by study in aquaria, but no divers' reports of this in the open sea are available.)

SAND, MUD, AND SHINGLE

Eagle ray [*Myliobatis aquila*]

> *Fr*: Mourine. *G*: Adlerrochen. *It*: Aquila di mare. *Serb–Cr*: Golub morski.
> *Sp*: Aguila marina.

Another kind of sting ray with much less of an oval shape than the more common variety. Wings are pointed and bent slightly back rather like a very modern jet aircraft. Light brown back, white belly.

These swift mid-water swimmers are usually only seen briefly by the diver, and photographers must be ready for a quick shot before the fish makes a very, very speedy getaway. The best time to approach is if the fish can be found feeding on the bottom on the shellfish that are its main diet. Ideally, photographers should try for an oblique frontal shot from above or below, but as they'll only get one chance this is likely to be a matter of luck.

Red mullet [*Mullus surmuletus*]   PLATE 33

> *Fr*: Rouget. *G*: Streifenbarbe. *It*: Triglia di scoglio. *Serb–Cr*: Trlja
> batoglavka. *Sp*: Salmonete de roca. And just this once we can't help
> adding the *Catalan*: Roger de roca.

The extraordinary thing about the red mullet is that seen underwater there is nothing red about it at all. A silver-grey fish. Square-headed. Looks rather like a swimming door-wedge. Barbels (two) hanging from beneath the lower jaw are very distinctive. Eyes are large and gold-rimmed.

Red mullet are almost always found on a sandy bottom or on sand patches among rocks. They often swim in groups and appear to be fish that don't like to be alone. When not in company with their own kind, they usually have a wrasse or two for company. The attraction between wrasse and red mullet appears to be very strong. It is often the wrasse that take flight first—warning the mullet of the diver's approach. As the mullet feeds, disturbing the sandy bottom with the two barbels, and snapping up the tasty morsels so revealed yet often too small for the diver to see, the wrasse will dart in and take his share.

Red mullet are comparatively easy to approach. But the diver can tell immediately the mullet is about to take fright. They signal their intention by raising the front of the dorsal fin and easing themselves just slightly off the bottom. When they do rush away it is with a peculiar zig-zag darting run. But they do not go far and usually settle down to feed again within a few yards. The larger fish are much shyer than the youngsters—not surprising as the red mullet is a highly prized Mediterranean dish (charcoal grilled after being stuffed with fennel).

NORTHERN WATERS

Red mullet are by no means confined to the Mediterranean and quite recently large specimens were spotted feeding beneath schools of bib just off the Sussex coast. They behaved in exactly the same way as their near relatives in warmer, clearer waters.

OPEN WATER

Anchovy [*Engraulis encrasicolus*]
Sardine [*Sardina pilchardus*]
Sand smelt [*Atherina presbyter*]

ANCHOVY: *Fr*: Anchois. *G*: Sardelle. *It*: Acciuga. *Serb-Cr*: Incun. *Sp*: Boqueron.

SARDINE: *Fr*: Sardine. *G*: Sardine. *It*: Sardina. *Serb-Cr*: Srdjela. *Sp*: Sardina.

SAND SMELT: *Fr*: Cabasson. *G*: Ahrenfisch. *It*: Latterino. *Serb-Cr*: Zelenis batelj. *Sp*: Abichon.

Huge schools of small fish are a common sight in the Mediterranean—probably because of the greater visibility. In Northern waters it is sometimes possible to spot these schools outlined against the surface lightness, but identification is often difficult. Even in the Med when right among the schools of small fish it takes a really expert eye to pick out the anchovies from the sardines and the sand smelts from both the other species.

Basically the anchovy has a pointed nose and is green backed with silvery sides and belly. The sardine has a rounder nose and is darker green on the back, golden on the sides and white on the belly. And the sand smelt has a stumpy nose and a silver line running from head to tail. This line when seen underwater can be an intense light blue.

Probably the most amazing thing about these schools of small fish is their ability to work to one head—that is to move with one accord even when making sudden changes of direction. The result is often like watching a great curtain being swept to and fro. They are usually attracted by light, which accounts, of course, for those romantic offshore lights when the sardine fishermen are out at sea. Photographing these small fish is extremely difficult. Their size calls for the use of close-up lenses, but their usual position in mid-water calls for the finest focusing techniques. Though some fish

30 GROUPER [*Epinephelus guaza*] El Gazela, Libya
  Depth 20 ft Bronica Flash *f*8 Ektacolor S (*Peter Scoones*)

31 MORAY EEL [*Muraena helena*] Giglio, Italy (*Geoff Harwood*)
  Depth 50 ft Flexilette Elec. flash *f*11/125 Kodacolor X

32 DENTEX [*Dentex dentex*] Aiguablava, Spain
Depth 30 ft Nikonos Flash (PF1B) *f*16/60 High Speed
Ektachrome   (*Kendall McDonald*)

33 RED MULLET [*Mullus barbatus*] Malta
Depth 70 ft Rolleimarin Flash Ektachrome (*John Lythgoe*)

34 *Anthias anthias* Giglio, Italy (*Geoff Harwood*)
Depth 100 ft Agfa Flexilette Elec. Flash *f*8/125 Ektachrome-X

35 SPHINX BLENNY [*Blennius sphinx*] Es Cana, Ibiza
Depth 4 ft Bronica *f*5·6/125 Ektachrome-X (*Peter Scoones*)

36 RAINBOW WRASSE [*Coris julis*] Aiguablava, Spain (*Kendall McDonald*)
Depth 20 ft Nikonos *f*11/60 High Speed Ektachrome

37 RAINBOW WRASSE [*Coris julis*] Elba, Italy (*Geoff Harwood*)
Depth 30 ft Exa Elec. flash *f*16/60 Ektachrome-X

38 SCORPION FISH [*Scorpaena porcus*] Punta Escalanya, Spain (*Kendall McDonald*)
Depth 40 ft Nikonos Flash (PF1B) High Speed Ektachrome

39 SCORPION FISH [*Scorpaena scrofa*] Alghero, Sardinia (*Geoff Harwood*)
Depth 60 ft Flexilette Elec. flash *f*16/125 Ektachrome-X

40, 41 *Tripterygion tripteronotus* Porto Fino, Italy
Depth 10 ft Bronica Flash *f*11 Ektachrome-X (*Peter Scoones*)

42 CARDINAL FISH [*Apogon imberbis*] Es Cana, Ibiza
Depth 15 ft Bronica Flash *f*11 Ektachrome-X (*Peter Scoones*)

43 SALPE [*Boops salpa*] Aiguablava, Spain (*Kendall McDonald*)
Depth 20 ft Nikonos *f*11/60 High Speed Ektachrome

44 RABBITFISH [*Siganus* sp.] with SALPE Derna, Libya
   Depth 15 ft Bronica *f*5·6/125 Ektacolor S (*Peter Scoones*)
   Note: This fish is not a native of the Mediterranean but a recent
   migrant from the Red Sea via the Suez Canal

45 SOAPFISH [*Serranus scriba*] Es Cana, Ibiza (*Peter Scoones*)
   Depth 10 ft Bronica Flash *f*5·6/40 Ektachrome-X

46 FLYING GURNARD [*Dactylopterus volitans*] Es Cana, Ibiza
Depth 10 ft Bronica Flash *f*11 Tri-X (*Peter Scoones*)

47 'SEA FLIES' [*Chromis chromis*] Captera, Sardinia
Depth 60 ft Exa *f*8/60 Plus-X (*Geoff Harwood*)

48 SALPE [*Boops salpa*] Aiguablava, Spain
Depth 40 ft Nikonos Flash (PF1B) *f*16/60 High Speed
Ektachrome   (*Kendall McDonald*)

49 SARS [*Diplodus vulgaris*]   Tobruk harbour, Libya
Depth 10 ft   Bronica *f*8/125   Tri-X   (*Peter Scoones*)

50 FIVE-SPOTTED WRASSE [*Crenilabrus quinquemaculatus*] Alghero, Sardinia
Depth 20 ft Flexilette Elec. flash *f*16/125 (*Geoff Harwood*)

51 ANGLER FISH [*Lophias piscatorius*] Giglio, Italy
Depth 120 ft Nikonos *f*2·5/30 Tri-X (*Geoff Harwood*)

52 SCORPION FISH [*Scorpaena porcus*] Es Cana, Ibiza
Depth 15 ft Bronica Flash *f*11 Ektachrome-X (*Peter Scoones*)

53 FRY clustering over tentacles of anemone   Es Cana, Ibiza
Depth 10 ft Bronica Flash *f*11 Ektachrome-X (*Peter Scoones*)

54 ELECTRIC RAY [*Torpedo marmorata*] Malta
Depth 100 ft Rolleimarin *f*5·6/60 Ektachrome (*John Lythgoe*)

in a giant school are bound to come out in correct focus using a standard lens, it is the close-up shot that really shows the beauty of many small fish.

Dentex [*Dentex dentex*]   PLATE 32

Fr: Dente. *G*: Zahnbrassen. *It*: Dentice. *Serb-Cr*: Zubatac. *Sp*: Denton.

A very powerful fish which at first sight can be taken for a bass, but the depth of body and forked tail give it away. Very silver with a humpy head and a stroking swimming motion that drives the fish straight forward.

When seen by the diver is likely to be hunting. The sight of a dentex carving its way through a mass of small fry is a lesson in murderous efficiency. Does not seem particularly put off by the presence of divers when feeding in this way and does not react to flash-bulbs. Best shot from slightly below and to one side to emphasise the depth of the powerful body.

Sea flies [*Chromis chromis*]   PLATE 47

Fr: Castagnole. *G*: Monchsfisch. *It*: Castagnola. *Serb-Cr*: Crnelj. *Sp*: Castanuela or Negrita

The diver who first christened these fish 'sea flies' was inspired. That is just what they are. They are everywhere. Their forked tails make them immediately identifiable as if their habit in moving in shoals of hundreds did not. These shoals—they could not be called schools as they appear to be completely disorganised—hang in the water with their heads pointing in every direction.

Movement is jerky and they will dart a little distance one way and then hang still in the water pointing the other way. The adults are dark black, but the young, up to a length of about one-and-a-half inches are brighter with vivid blue stripes on their flanks. In close up the adult has a purple checked effect on the sides.

But you cannot rely on these fish being in swarms. Sometimes you will find isolated little groups of three or four. In deeper water, you will encounter lonely, but inquisitive single specimens.

Sometimes the smaller fish will retreat into holes at the diver's close approach, but they soon emerge and completely ignore the diver. Photographs of individuals are best taken with flash to offset the fish against its background. In open water photographs of divers in a cloud of these tiny fish can be very effective.

The odd thing about these fish is that they resist 'chumming' (feeding with broken-up sea urchins) and seem to resent other fish getting a free meal. On the island of Giglio where Reg Vallintine (now Director of the British Sub-Aqua Club) ran a diving school, there were chromis which regarded a large rock as their especial territory and would chase rainbow wrasse away from any food offered in this way.

Sharks

BLUE SHARK: *Fr*: Requin bleu. *G*: Blauhai. *It*: Verdesca. *Serb-Cr*: Pas modrulj. *Sp*: Tintorera.

HAMMERHEAD: *Fr*: Requin marteau. *G*: Hammerhai. *It*: Pesce martello. *Serb-Cr*: Mlat. *Sp*: Pez martillo.

Though rarely seen by divers, sharks are present in the Mediterranean. Probably the most common are the blue (*Prionace glauca*), and the hammerheads (*Sphyrnidae*).

Skin divers have reported hammerhead sharks off the coast of Yugoslavia and it is suspected that these and other sharks follow boats up the Adriatic in search of refuse thrown overboard.

The famous Italian underwater photographer Maurizio Sarra was killed when diving off the Italian coast. He was definitely attacked by a shark but was unable to tell, even in a moment of consciousness, exactly what kind of fish it was.

There are fishermen's reports of most varieties of shark in the Mediterranean, but nearly all were seen or hooked in deep waters. This, however, should not be taken as a guarantee that inshore waters are completely safe. (*See* Dangers.)

Sunfish [*Mola mola*]

Fr: Poisson-lune. *G*: Mondfisch. *It*: Pesce luna. *Serb-Cr*: Bucanj veliki. *Sp*: Pez luna or mola.

One of the most extraordinary fish in the sea. At first sight this fish looks like the victim of a shark attack. In fact many people who have seen these fish washed up still believe that what they saw was not a whole fish, but a huge fish that had been bitten off close behind the head. In fact the sunfish is built with more of its body ahead of the dorsal and anal fins than there is behind. In other words, the top and bottom fins give a false centre line, and are really set well back to the tail of the fish. The tail fin extends from the foot of the dorsal right round to the anal fin. Colour: slate-blue or grey. Oddly, most other countries call this a moon-fish.

Can be found in close to the Mediterranean coast in high summer. Sometimes the fish penetrate harbours where they are soon slaughtered and exhibited to wondering groups of landsmen. They are absolutely harmless and underwater look like a dustbin lid with a nose. The fins flap sideways together giving a very odd effect and very slow movement through the water.

The sunfish seems much happier ascending and descending through the water than moving forwards and there is some evidence that they really live very deep down. Perhaps sunfish is the best name for such a fish as they seem to like sunbathing and can often be spotted from inshore boats by the flapping of the dorsal fin on the surface.

They grow very big indeed. The small ones are about two to four feet deep and at times real monsters of 12 feet deep can be spotted close to the surface. The tail fin intrigues divers, and one describes it as 'a bit of perished rubber stuck rather inexpertly to the tail rim of the fish'. Recently it has been suggested that the fish seen on the surface are sick and that this is the reason for their ascent from the depths. But this is one of those cases where little is known and more diver observation will be invaluable.

CHAPTER THREE

Warm Waters and Coral Seas

SYSTEM AND RECORD

It doesn't matter if the coral is poor or the visibility is lousy, the first dive on a coral reef leaves few people quite the same again. The coral is, of course, beautiful in its variety of form and subtle colour; but it is the fishes that leave the greatest impact.

There are fish everywhere, some lurking in holes in the coral, some perched on coral outcrops ready to pounce, some swimming upside down under the roof of a cave, but mostly they seem to wander between the coral heads pecking at the coral, scraping at the weed covered rocks or excavating for food in the sand. But above all the colours are brilliant—far more brilliant it seems than in an aquarium.

My first experience of a true coral reef was in 1960 when I took a holiday from the lower fungi, on which I was working for my Ph.D. thesis. For reasons quite unconnected with diving, I took the direct boat to Seychelles and, like everyone else, went snorkelling on the reefs which are now, sadly, buried beneath the acres of concrete runways of the international airport.

I think I was brainwashed on that first afternoon, although I didn't realise it until later. Slowly the lower fungi seemed to lose their fascination; slowly an interest in fish became more important until now I work full time on the vision and colouration of tropical reef fishes.

Some say that the coral reef is the most productive environment on earth and surely they are right. But, paradoxically, the sheer abundance and variety of life hands the biologist one of his greatest problems—how on earth to sort out, single out and study some behaviour pattern that is simple enough to make sense of, but wide enough to interest life scientists in general?

The Indian Ocean atoll of Aldabra is a dream-come-true for biologists, for its desolate islands have been of little use except to the giant tortoises that live there and the sea turtles that lay their eggs in the sandy beaches. Simply because its commercial potential is so limited, Aldabra has remained to this day almost unharmed by man, whilst neighbouring islands have been stripped for guano or planted totally with coconuts. In the middle of the atoll is a 100-square-mile lagoon opening to the tidal sea by just four deep and treacherous channels.

It is the tidal currents in the channels which make them so interesting. In the largest channel currents of 17 knots have been reported and in the smallest it is just possible to hide behind a coral boulder whilst the current thrums on air tubes and rips at the mask.

Our interest was in the fish which swarm into the channels. The different kinds crowded into great mixed schools of surgeon fish and snapper, unicorn fish and wrasse. Hawksbill turtles clasp onto rocks with their flippers and sharks shelter in the quiet water of caves. There are only a few minutes of slack water in these channels and the question in our minds was how the smaller fish could possibly live and feed through the tremendous four-times-daily current. Did they shelter in caves and crannies or did they somehow keep station snapping up the particles of food that rushed by?

The passe we chose was at the eastern end of the island and is some 50 yd wide and 65 ft deep. It is also nearly two miles long. We had two Zodiacs; one we moored inside the lagoon, whilst the other dropped the three divers well out to sea opposite the passe.

At first there was little movement, just a slight drift, and we had plenty of time to settle down and look around. But gradually it became necessary to grasp a rock or piece of dead coral to look at something more closely; the channel got a little deeper and the walls a little steeper. Hovering in the water were large schools of Jack mackerel and Unicorn fish. On the ground were meadows of garden eels each with its tail anchored in its hole, its body standing upright in the water and its head looking into the current. Drifting over them was a dream-like sensation of never getting where you are going, for, very smoothly and gently, they withdraw into their holes as you approach and simply disappear.

There are never any eels nearby yet always a thick bed of them in the distance.

In the entrance to the passe itself the stinging clumps of *millepora* coral become common. Now the drift gets quite fast and here it is all too easy to get dragged over the coral, picking up a nettle rash on the way. Here, too, the current is about four knots and the sides of the channel are nearly vertical. Occasionally we passed a turtle anchored by its flipper to a rock, and in the caves along the sides there were sharks resting harmlessly on the sand.

During slack water the floor of the channel is flat, coarse sand with small coral nodules; in the flood huge dunes and waves build up, some eight feet high with coral pebbles scampering up the sides with the current and a great boil of sand and debris at the summit. The force of the water must shift hundreds of tons of material back and forth on each tide, but a few feet above the bottom it is strangely quiet like being in an aircraft over clouds. Our cameras and note pads still floated alongside us, yet we must all have been travelling at a good ten knots. Each time we passed a rock outcrop or a narrowness in the passe we were quite gently but briskly nudged from side to side by the turbulence and the occasional 100-lb rock bobbing along like a paper bag gave some idea of the true force of the water.

Finally, after nearly two miles the channel got shallower and the walls less steep, and the gold and blue striped surgeon fish which are only found in the shallow surge zone began to appear, darting back and forth after the morsels of food dislodged in the tide. Slowly the pace slackened and in only a few feet of water we were able to scramble for footholds on the mercifully flat bottom.

As so often happens, we came to rest looking at a distant smudge of land and a universe of water and no boat at all. It is a strange fact that the boats always seem to be exactly behind you perfectly positioned ready for the pick-up. But for a fleeting moment you feel exactly what it's like to be alone and lost in a very wide ocean!

'Well,' said the boat crew when we were all safely picked up, 'did the fishes take shelter?' We felt distinctly sheepish. 'We forgot to look!'

And that underlines one of the real problems of scientific diving. The very human one of forgetfulness that gets much worse underwater. Unless the task is of the simplest, a checklist written on a formica sheet has to be taken down. Nor is it any use expecting to remember some detail of colouration or behaviour. More than likely it will all be forgotten before you are out of the water. So take a camera!

Any diver on air becomes fuddled and forgetful once he reaches a depth of 80 ft or more. If a diver tells you his faculties are all there at 150 ft, he deceives himself; do not let him deceive you! A camera on the other hand is unaffected by depth and the light rays entering the lens will faithfully be recorded on film. If the camera is pointed and focused and exposed correctly, the diver can study the film at his leisure and record details of colour and behaviour lost to him at the time.

Sometimes, however, it is virtually impossible to identify a fish seen in a photograph from a textbook of fishes. Consider, for a moment, *Gnathodentex aurolineatus* (Plate 77). The eye is drawn to the yellow spot behind the dorsal fin and it is that which the eye seeks in the illustrations. But in most illustrations the spot is not there for it fades at death. This is a common fish, yet it is almost never correctly identified in illustrations. Before the advent of underwater photography, its true colouration was quite unknown.

Identifying fish from photographs can be literally impossible—one goby, for instance, looks much like the next and is only distinguished by details of the pelvic fins and scale rows and even more minute features. A common tropical trigger fish is instantly identified by its teeth which are red. Identified in a museum, that is—in life it disobligingly keeps its mouth shut. However, it is possible to make a reasonable shot at identifying most well photographed fish, especially so in the Mediterranean, where the fauna is well known and identification can proceed by a process of elimination. If identification can be difficult from photographs alone, it is enormously better than a sight record. Without a photograph an expert may simply refuse to believe you!

JOHN LYTHGOE

ON THE REEFS

It all started with boats. Wringing the extra knot from a racing yacht involves the regular removal of marine growths from the bottom of the hull. This usually means hauling the boat out on to some slipway for a good scrub. In the tropics, Singapore to be precise, that can be a pretty irksome task. So I decided on the cool way of doing it.

I rigged the crew and myself out with fins, masks and snorkels, issued scrubbing brushes and, thus equipped, we descended over the side. This both amused and upset the crews of the yachts we raced against, for they reckoned it was a downright sneaky caper and ought not to be allowed. They need not have worried, for soon we realised we were not alone. The barnacles and weed we were scraping from the hull attracted a myriad of small fish. Many with impossible shapes and all in 'glorious Technicolor'. The scrubbing was never completed for soon we just hung on to the boat and watched, scraping a small area to keep the show going whenever our small performers began to drift away.

I know now the names of the fish we attracted that day in the Straits of Johore. Sergeant-majors, scat, trunk fish, butterfly fish and many others with unpronounceable Latin names. But then, I had just discovered another world.

A branch of the British Sub-Aqua Club was just being formed, so I promptly signed up, little realising the forms of torture prescribed in the training of a diver. As the waters around Singapore were considered somewhat dangerous, all the laid-down tests were enforced with sadistic zeal. Where a test required a 10-lb weight belt, a few extra backbending pounds would be added. The donning of aqualung and all equipment underwater was carried out with the gear strewn all over the deep end of the pool and a completely flooded demand valve. The test of 500 yds in the open sea was to swim to Malaya and back across a mile of barracuda and shark infested murk stiff with antisocial plankton. By the time I attained second-class status and joined the élite, putting others through the mill, I certainly knew my capabilities and, more important, my limitations.

On branch outings each weekend to the coral reefs around Raffles Light I would watch the beautiful and exotic reef fish and spend many hours sitting among the gorgonian fans observing all that occurred. This type of activity is most economical on air; often rescuers would descend to haul a bored buddy and myself back to the land of the living informing me that my air ran out long ago.

Interest in fish and corals led me to scour the local libraries and museums to identify and put names to my findings. But the more I searched the more frustrated I became. Many fish could not be found in any available books. My thoughts then turned to recording what I saw on film, so that identification could be made later.

My wife Juliet was first persuaded that a cine camera would be a most essential buy (to record the growth of the children), and then assured that the wide angle lens would be the most useful. Next the problem of housing the camera. Being on an RAF base was a great help for several aircraft have perspex windows (an easy material to work that could be welded with trichlorethylene) readily to hand. And aircraft hydraulic couplings were conveniently easy to adapt for control seals.

Now I was ready to go with Kodachrome I in the camera, and a Weston exposure meter in a pickle jar. Fortunately, I was able to charter the Far East Air Force yacht, an ideal craft for a cruise to the fabled islands off the east coast of Malaya. I had been told to expect limitless visibility, giant sharks, manta rays, grouper, barracuda, the lot. These were welcome predictions, but I could find no one who had actually been there. The islands themselves were certainly there. The Admiralty Chart showed excellent coral formations, a warning to mariners about the changing nature of the reefs, and was dated eighteen sixty something.

I will never forget my first dive inside the fringing reef of Pulau Tinggi, the first landfall in the group. It was late in the afternoon as we dropped anchor and we watched it all the way down through the gin-clear water to the white sand 60 ft below. Minutes later, having unearthed our gear, we were in the water finning towards the reef some 40 yds off.

The clarity of the water was phenomenal. From the sandy floor to left and right, pillars of coral strained to within a few feet of the surface, sporting flashy necklaces of dancing gems where the low rays of the sun touched festoons of small demoiselles. Ahead was the reef, a sharply defined dark-blue velvet curtain in the distance, rising to within a few feet of the surface. Close to, the reef face revealed protruding knobs and outcrops of staghorn coral and multitudes of different fish milling around.

The scarlet squirrelfish fidgetted in pairs at small holes, blue and yellow surgeonfish pecked at algae on coral stumps, everywhere butterfly fish were clad Picasso-style. Here and there iridescent blue-striped cleaner fish bounced up and down advertising their trade. A rainbow-hued parrotfish hung askew, cleaners and butterfly fish pecking at invisible parasites, quivering briefly as a sensitive spot was touched.

Atop the reef a panorama of staghorn coral was mirrored in the gently undulating surface sweeping in to meet at the limit of vision. Here and there fine clusters of black urchin needles waved, punctuating the pink tipped ochre coral fingers. Yellow demoiselles flashed golden against the blue-black backdrop.

The tropic sun withdrew its light and warmth swiftly. Life's tempo quickened, tension tangible all around, small fish sheltered beneath protecting arms. The coral heads, now bare with menace, rose dark from out of the ghostly sand. The sea had a sudden chill. The reefs were no more a friendly place. It was night.

Filming around reefs has many problems, not least of which is deciding what to take. Intentions are easily swayed with so many subjects vying for attention. I am sure that many thousands of feet of film are spent on broad vistas seemingly crammed with fish, but these shots seldom recreate the scene as intended. As with surface work, it is often more satisfactory to get in close and concentrate interest on the main subject. This and other lessons from surface filming I try to apply under the sea.

Traps to avoid are: unsteady camera handling, panning too fast, tracking too fast or at an uneven rate. Remember when filming underwater that many of your eventual audience will not be familiar with the undersea scene. Dwell that bit longer on each shot, even longer if the subject is of great interest or difficult to recognise. Tracking shots, pans and the like tend to set their own times, even so I would try to shoot longer than necessary and prune the film at the editing stage. It is not possible to extend what is not there.

My equipment in the Far East was rudimentary to say the least. For a cine, a Bolex in a perspex box had but one control—the shutter release. This forced me to film at pre-determined settings obtained by a quick plunge with the exposure meter. This restriction ensured that my attention was concentrated on selected subjects of a similar type on each dive. This technique, though appearing highly restrictive, does produce a higher proportion of satisfactory work as any other attractions, or distractions, have to be ignored. Though nowadays my equipment is highly sophisticated and capable of tackling all subjects, I still tend to concentrate on certain items per dive, but with the advantage that any alternative subject can be covered in an instant.

My still camera was hardly better, release and wind-on being all the facilities available. I was however able to view my subject in the viewfinder, the camera being an SLR Miranda with a removable prism. This is an important detail for a camera to be used in a housing, even though the position of the ground glass did make me adopt many peculiar attitudes to view it satisfactorily.

While photographing small objects in Telok Tekek, Pulau Tioman, I noticed a fine moray glowering at the entrance to his lair, mouth open, displaying some wicked fangs. What a fine subject for my lens! I settled on the sand, turned the camera on its side for the best composition, a most difficult attitude to view from—with an upside down reversed image—and started edging forward to bring the eel into sharp focus. Nearing the optimum distance the ground glass image dissolved into a blurred pattern of spots. I thought the sea must have swept me back, so I edged forward some more still peering into the ground glass. Then my forehead touched something. Raising my face, I stared cross-eyed at the moray an inch or two from my mask! No more than a half second later, I was spluttering on the surface, the eel back in its hole. A different technique for photography of moray eels would have to be used in future. I nevertheless went back and photographed this eel later and found it a most docile subject.

Another incident which gave me quite a scare occurred in the same bay the following morning. I rose early, just after dawn, the black water mirroring mist-wreathed jungle slopes 300 ft above. Cool air drifted down the cliff and crept out across the water. Dreamily taking in the scene I emptied a bucket of water over the side without realising it contained last night's cutlery. The reef below was strewn with assorted knives, forks and spoons. Damn! I donned my gear and plunged in to collect the hardware.

The water was crystal clear, though the early rays of the sun allowed little light to penetrate and the staghorn reef appeared in sombre tones. The cutlery had come to rest on an area next to a sandy hollow. Easing myself down on to the soft bottom, I started collecting, stuffing handfuls of knives and forks into my swimming trunks. Suddenly there was an alien sound above the crackle of the reef—a rhythmic thump, thump, thump quite unlike anything else I had heard and without the metallic tone of a ship's propeller. Cautiously peering over the coral rim, I stared into the darkness at the limit of visibility. There was nothing seawards, to the right nor left. Then from the direction of the shore, out of the dark curtain, came fast towards me, barely skimming the reef, the largest shark I had ever seen.

The excited tail beats were causing audible shock waves as they cleft the water leaving brief bubbles of cavitation. I was paralysed in position clutching a handful of cutlery to my chest. The shark came straight on stiff and purposeful. Whoosh! Right over my head. A brief glimpse of a blunt snout, a black semicircle and an enormous expanse of grey belly, and I was bowled over by a swirl of turbulence. Whether the shark saw me at the last moment or swept past unseeing I shall never know. I could still hear the thump, thump, thump fading in the distance. I made what must have been the fastest powered ascent in history, clambering aboard fins thrashing porpoise-style. I sat on the cockpit coaming, gasping, cutlery clattering from my trunks. The noise awoke the rest, drowsily enquiring what the hell was all the noise about and please to shut up. Later I noticed there were deep cuts in my hands, where the knives had been clasped.

There were many other encounters with sharks around the islands, but in most cases they seemed more wary, showing little more than passing interest.

The islands in this group stretch seawards from the east coast of Malaya. From Babi Besar a couple of miles off the shore near Mersing, to Aur and Pemanggil, 50 miles out in the South China sea. They provide some of the best undersea scenery in the Far East. From precipitous cliffs strewn with giant boulders plunging to dark depths, to calm and warm coral lagoons, the formations elegant, unstilted like the outer ramparts with their stone-like walls of brain coral and similar types. The visibility can vary from a few feet off the inner islands to over a hundred from Tioman outward. All islands in the group have coconut palms planted around the shores and the mountainous interiors covered with primary rain forest. Typical in fact of the widely held vision of a classic South Sea Island.

Shortly after leaving the island, I returned to England and hung up my fins for eighteen months until I left again for warmer seas, this time to the Middle East. Here, in Aden, I found the ideal fish-watcher's set-up. The working day, from seven to one, left each afternoon free for visits to the reefs, never more than a quarter of an hour away. Water temperature in the eighties, and fish from the Indian ocean and Red Sea sharing the scene.

The only drawback was unpredictable visibility. The in-accessibility of many diving sites, except on foot, and the accompanying heat ruled out the use of heavy aqualungs. Under the surface, terrain varied. There were shallow staghorn patches in the western peninsular bays, and cliffs and a sharp drop-off to seaward, with a shallow sandy area to the east.

Ras Marshag, the southernmost point, provided the most dramatic scenery. A rocky bottom was relieved by craggy submerged ridges jutting out a hundred feet or so to the sharp abyssal slope. The ridges were jagged walls pitted with holes, many housing spiny lobsters, their antennæ bristling and twitching in the currents. Larger holes and caves, some tunnels, provided shelter for large angelfish and groupers. Everywhere the smaller reef fish hovered like clouds of flies.

I spent many afternoons hovering over the end of one of the ridges with the blue-black abyss yawning below. Here all the free swimming oceanic fish paraded past. Great schools of large kingfish took minutes to pass, all purposefully going somewhere fast, and were back again in ten minutes. Pompano schools paused briefly, circling the strange creature hanging on their ceiling. Eagle rays flowed gracefully by in pairs. Often a group of great barracuda would station themselves a few yards off. After several visits these barracuda became a common sight, always the same number and the same distance away. They just hung motionless like myself. Once I swam towards them and they melted away, only to return a few minutes later at the same place. On the few occasions when they weren't there, I felt insecure and nervous as if deserted.

It was near Marshag that others claimed to have seen a giant grouper. Accounts varied, 5 ft, 8 ft, even 12 ft long. By all accounts a large fish, for grouper can be half their length in height. I think that I too saw this fish. I had been engaged by a local firm to assist in the positioning of supports for the outfall end of a large sewer (not yet in operation). The pipe was 4 ft in diameter and had to be supported 4 or more feet from the bottom in order to catch a seaward current. My job was to position cement-filled bags dropped around the pipe where I directed. The operation took several weeks.

One day, when most of the work had been completed, I was

inspecting previously positioned supports, when I noticed in the cement clouded water a large bulk beneath the pipe, where no support should be. I surfaced to remonstrate that bags had been lowered in the wrong place, but I was assured that this could not be so. So I dived again to confirm my report. The cement oozing from lowered bags now reduced visibility to a dirty, dark couple of yards. It was a few minutes before I found the pipe, and then moved along to where the obstruction had been. As I neared the spot, I could see there was still a large bulk dimming what little light there was left. I moved closer and the mass seemed to move up. I noticed clear water beneath the object. I was puzzled and was still moving forward towards it when the entire bulk just disappeared before my eyes.

I am as sure as I can be that what I saw was a giant grouper. Its size could be judged quite accurately, for the depth of the fish was about the same as the pipe it lay below. That would make the length around 8 ft, and by my standards that's a big fish.

All the largest fish were to be found around this area. In the shallow water of Holkat Bay nearby, giant stingray could be found dozing within a few yards of the water's edge. So large were these fish and so sleepy, that I felt sure they could be measured where they lay. I obtained a suitable 8-ft dowel, painted it black and white in foot intervals and with this ruler suitably weighted, I and two others entered the water in search of a suitable ray.

No more than a couple of minutes had elapsed when an excited yell went up and we converged on the spot. At first I could see nothing. Then my friend with the pole pointed down, indicating the outline of a very large stingray, so large in fact that in the seven foot deep water, the whole fish could not be seen without scanning from side to side. I backed off some way to the rear of the fish, and raising my camera indicated the positioning of the measure across the ray's back. As I started the camera, the stick, barely spanning the ray was dropped. All hell was let loose. The ray exploded into action. Sand quickly obscured all vision. Seconds later, still kneeling on the sand, I was crashed into by the fish having taken off in the diametrically opposite direction to that in which he was pointed. I was completely winded, my mask torn away. I lay gasping on the surface, wishing everyone of those grinning apes would go away and let me die in peace.

Along the side of Holkat Bay, a shallow band of small rocks and coral provided shelter for many species. Many cuttle-fish would come here at certain times to perform their egg-laying rites, and thus engaged appeared oblivious of our presence. The cuttles are a weird lot to watch, hovering in the water like miniature blimps with a ridiculous and inadequate skirt rippling along their sides. Cuttles are capable of instant changes of colour, pattern and skin texture, can hover, rotate on the spot, move slowly backwards and forwards, all by means of the undulating skirt. They can move too in any direction. Their instant acceleration is provided by jet propulsion and they often lay a most effective smoke screen when scared.

On the west side, a favourite spot was the short southern side of Elephant Bay, where along the rocky edge there were many overhangs and small caves. One cave in particular was inhabited by a family of chickenfish (lionfish, dragonfish, cobrafish, firefish, stingfish, butterfly cod, are all other names used) of the *Pterois* species. Chickenfish or butterfly cod are most apt names for the look of the fish, indicating its Red Indian feather headdress appearance. The other names lay their stress on the dangerous characteristics of the fish.

It was easy to gather a semi-circle of these fish around you, by merely lying in the knee-deep water outside their cave. They were ideal camera subjects. I would often lie there with close-up lenses attached as the fish inquisitively came up often closer than I could focus. Though exotic in appearance and apparently mild-natured, these fish have a defence mechanism that must be treated with the greatest respect. The long flag-like dorsal spines function like hypodermic syringes. When threatened, the fish tilts its spines in the direction of the danger and the broad pectoral fins are spread out flat on each side of the fish.

When the assailant approaches to within a few inches, the fish beats down the pectorals propelling its body and deadly spines upwards with considerable force. On touching anything the spines compress venom glands at their base injecting the powerful poison. The effect, though seldom fatal, does vary with the size, species, and area. At the very least an extremely painful swelling is caused and often the victim will become delirious.

I induced the defence action a few times by presenting a stick over the fish. They would strike the wood with some force once or twice in quick succession and then could no longer be made to strike even under considerable provocation. However, I never found them the least aggressive except to the small demoiselles who appear to become hypnotised as the chickenfish shimmies forward, flaunting the pectorals again but this time held forward and vertical till the fish is near enough to pounce forward and gulp the small fish whole.

Once, emerging after a dive, I met a bearded character pounding around with Rolleimarin and Calypsophot cameras strung round his neck. He turned out to be Ludwig Sillner, a well-known expert underwater photographer. We got chatting and for a week we took him to our favourite spots. He was at this time searching for a particular fish he wished to catch for identification purposes. I knew that there were many of these fish around Ras Marshag, but during Ludwig's stay the winds blew strong and entry there was impossible. We later captured a specimen. Some weeks later I had a letter from him stating that the fish was a hitherto unrecorded species of *Chaetodontoplus*.

The many species to be observed in the area defy imagination, and of many hundred dives around Aden and the Persian Gulf not one passed without my seeing something new.

This is the heart of underwater adventure and fish photography. Wherever I have dived, the story has been the same—new fish, new creatures, new experiences, new challenges and, best of all, a new, inexhaustible supply of subjects for my cameras.

PETER SCOONES

GUIDE TO THE
FISHES OF WARM WATERS AND
CORAL SEAS

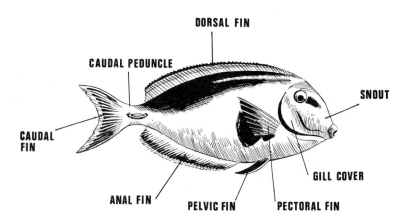

The fish described in this chapter are some of the thousands that a diver will see in tropical and near-tropical waters.

Local names for the fish are not given as they vary so much that one name means nothing only a few miles away down the coast, or on another island. For positive identification of each species, the Latin name is given.

The world of coral fish is one of wonder and beauty. And totally different from that of the fish described in previous chapters.

THE REEF

The Angelfish PLATES 64, 65, 66

The angelfishes include the most colourful and graceful specimens in the sea. All have laterally compressed bodies, which makes them very difficult to see head-on. Oddly enough, this attitude is not used as a method of hiding—the fish is more likely to display itself sideways. This gives any potential enemy a great impression of size. This impression is added to by the long flowing anal and dorsal fins. But the angel fish's defence is not all show—they do have very spiky gill plates and these can be a fearsome weapon if the fish is held by unwary fishermen or if another fish attempts to eat it.

Naming them is not easy, because the young bear no resemblance in colouring to the adult. There is good reason to suspect that there are some fish parading around with long Latin names which are really the young of some other long Latin name!

But names are not everything—the colour and beauty of the angelfish is not in dispute. Certainly they usually swim alone or in pairs, but at times great groups can be seen parading together. The more easily identifiable species are:

Pomacanthus maculosus, a large blue angel fish with a big vertical patch on the side and a yellow tail. At a distance the blue and yellow appear rather dull, but on close approach strengthen in intensity. This is a large fish. Those in the waters around Aden grow to about 18 in. long and are easy to photograph as they swim lazily about.

Pomacanthus imperator, the Emperor Fish, which is probably the most colourful fish of any reef (PLATE 64). A large fish (over 1 ft in length)—the Germans call it the Kaiserfisch—it has some 20 orange-yellow lines running slightly diagonally from head to tail. The tail is bright orange. Towards the lower portions of the flanks, the lines change colour becoming iridescent blue on a crimson ground towards the ventral and anal fin. The head has a large well-defined white area around the mouth, separated from the yellow forehead by a blue-edged black patch over the eye and a further black area around the gill cover.

The young of this magnificent creature are dark blue with white stripes, which become progressively less vertical as they travel away from the head—curving until they become semi-circular near the tail.

Such colourful fish sound like a cinch for the underwater photographer. Unfortunately, the angelfish in this case is shy. It is often seen at the entrance to some coral cave, which has at least two entrances or exits. At the approach of the photographer it will glide into the cave, put its head out and then go back in again. By the time the camera is lined up for its next reappearance, it doesn't! This time it emerges from another entrance. This can go on for some time until the fish just stops coming out of either entrance.

Pygoplites diacanthus (PLATE 66), another brilliantly-coloured angelfish, common in Red Sea and Indo-Pacific areas. Has yellow and white stripes alternating with black ones vertically along the body. The head is yellow with vertical blue stripes, the rear dorsal has a large blue area and the tail is yellow. The ventral fin is blue and pink striped. A most striking fish which when photographed always seems to be tilted at an angle—this is an optical illusion created by the markings.

The Anthias family

In the Mediterranean there is only one member of this family, *Anthias anthias*, but in tropical waters they are very common indeed. A feature of this group is the blue stripe running diagon-ally over the eye. A particular common fellow is *Anthias squami-pinnis*, which can be found at all depths from 30 to 140 ft. They live in great swarms around some handy refuge, usually a branched coral and they dart into the shelter of its arms whenever danger threatens. Average size is 3 in. long.

The Butterfly fishes

Large numbers of these fish are found on all coral reefs for they are coral feeders. Great congregations of them can be seen, tail up, pecking at the spiky coral growths. They are often present in such quantities that one wonders how the coral can survive.

Similar in general shape to the angelfish, they lack the flowing fins and formidable spikes on the gill plates. However, they are still spiky little fish and can erect their sharp dorsal and ventral fins when threatened, much as a cat bristles when threatened by the neighbour's dog.

Colouration is invariably bright with reds and yellows predominant. A large number of butterflies have a dominant dark stripe on the head which passes through the eye. This disguises the direction in which the fish is swimming. Some species take this trick even further with a false 'eye' near the tail. Others have dazzle patterns akin to the old-fashioned warship markings. The mouth of the butterfly has, in some cases, elongated to ridiculous lengths to aid their pecking into coral growths, like *Forcipeger longirostris*. Certain butterflies can also be observed acting as cleaner fish to larger fish.

Chelmon rostratus is the long-nosed butterfly and, as the name suggests, this fish has an elongated snout. It is silvery in colour with four vertical black-edged stripes, the first running vertically through the eye. The caudal fin is transparent and the whole fish appears rather truncated. It is a common fish around Malaya and other Indo-Pacific areas, but is not usually seen in large numbers.

From the photographer's point of view this is the least shy of the butterflies and will hover some 18 in. away from the camera. Most obliging.

Chaetodon auriga (PLATE 71), sometimes called the Herringbone Butterfly, has a shorter snout. Body colour is silver with a dark vertical bar running through the eye. The upper snout has twin yellow-orange stripes and the rear and dorsal areas shade down to orange. A black spot is clear on the upper dorsal fin. The body itself has an overlapped diagonal line pattern. This makes for a dapper little fish. Somewhat shy but not too difficult to photograph.

Another member of the *Chaetodon* family is the Yellow Butterfly. This fish, as the name suggests, is predominantly a bright yellow relieved by one obvious grey diamond-shaped patch over the eye.

There is a slight dark rim to the dorsal and anal fins. This fish is somewhat larger than the majority of the family and can be found in groups of over 20 individuals in the Red Sea and East African waters. Size is about 9 in. long fully grown.

Colour of course plays an important part in the naming of these fish and the Grey Butterfly Fish is grey-blue in colour with a striking and well-defined herringbone pattern along its flanks. The rear of the dorsal and tail fin are black. This dark area is separated from the grey body by a light line and the black areas are rimmed by a bright blue line. This is a dandy fish and gives the impression of being a city gent. This impression is confirmed by the fish's behaviour. It remains aloof, ignoring the diver, and only moves off when inspected closely. Common in the Red Sea and surrounding areas.

The Orange Butterfly Fish is another common Red Sea species and is, of course, bright orange. This colour is ringed with black at the rear and the black area forward of the eye has two yellow stripes vertically arranged.

Sizes vary from 1 in. to 1 ft.

Damselfish [Pomacentridae]   PLATE 56

A large number of different species come under this common name. And they are probably the most numerous fish that the diver sees in tropical and warm seas. A small fish—usually about 3 to 5 in. long, they are readily recognised by the size of the shoals around any rocky area or coral reef. Each coral outcrop however small has its attendant shoal and some species sink right into the coral when threatened. Colouring varies from a drab grey to an unbelievable brilliance. The species most familiar to divers must be the sergeant-major with its vertical stripes. A few of the most common types are listed here:

The sergeant-major (*Abudefduf saxatilis*) is a small black and yellow vertically striped fish, active but heavy-bodied. Grows to a maximum of 6 in. The random movement of each fish in the shoals produces poor still pictures, but in cine these fish are most attractive, particularly if set against a blue water background. Other sergeant-majors commonly seen are *A. septemfasciatus* and *A. sexfasciatus*. In shape they resemble the Mediterranean *Chromis*, but are usually larger.

Abudefduf sordidus is another sergeant-major, but the stripes are less distinct on a silvery base. In older fish the darker areas cover most of the fish and it appears almost a monochrome from a distance.

The damselfish (*Dascyllus reticulatus*) is short and blunt-nosed (PLATE 56). The body is light greenish, almost translucent, when seen underwater at a distance of about 20 ft. The eye has a dark vertical bar, this together with the dark ventral fins and rim of the dorsal, make this a most delightful fish to see in natural light. They drift in small clouds—each fish is about 3 in. long—over their chosen coral clump into which they will dart at the first sign of danger.

Like most of this group the underwater photographer can make them rise and fall by raising and lowering his hand nearby the shoal. Flash, however, will completely kill the delicate translucent colours of the fish and should be used with caution.

Dascyllus aruanus is another damselfish, but this is a white one with three prominent vertical black bars. Not quite so gregarious as the others, this one is found singly or in small groups of 3 or 4. Looks just like a 'humbug' sweet.

Another damsel is the three-spotted variety, *Dascyllus trimaculatus*. This one is black with three white spots—one on the forehead and the other two are placed one on each flank just below the dorsal fin. Grows larger than the others (up to 6 in.). Through the underwater viewfinder this fish looks taller than it is long, but this is particularly due to the dorsal fin being permanently raised like a banner.

These are cleaner fish and can be photographed going about their business of trimming parasites off larger fish. They bounce up and down to attract the customer's attention and even work on large barracuda.

The Groupers   [Seranidae]

There may be only a few groupers left in shallow water in the Mediterranean, but this is not the case around the more rarely spearfished tropical coasts of the world. In these waters there are many different kinds of grouper and despite their size they are extremely difficult to tell apart. This difficulty is due to the incredible variations of colour displayed from age to age. On top of this they show very distinct emotional colours during such social activities as fighting and courtship.

But some groupers are easy to recognise such as *Cephalopholis argus*, which has beautiful blue spots on a dark reddish ground, and when it is excited, dark vertical bands appear on the hind part of the flanks. Another unmistakeable grouper is *Epinephelus flavocoeruleus*, which is boldly patterned with bright blue and yellow and shows up well in the blue water of a tropical reef.

Groupers live on shellfish and octopus and other small fishes. Many like those in the Mediterranean adopt some particular hole, cave or cranny as their home, but they also spend long periods swimming about or just sitting on the bottom and watching.

Divers should be a little careful about visiting these warm water groupers at home. They can get quite aggressive, chasing and bumping the intruder and sometimes biting at his fins. Some huge groupers have mauled a diver quite seriously.

Whimple fish   [*Heniochus acuminatus*]   PLATE 85

Quite well-informed people often refer to this fish as the Moorish Idol. They are wrong. This species is much more common than the real Moorish Idol. They could only be confused with the

Idols on a day of poor visibility—though they both have vertical black-and-white stripes and film-like extension to the dorsal fin.

The *Heniochus* has three black vertical stripes. The first is narrow and extends over the head and stops at the lower edge of the eye. The second broader stripe starts at the first few rays of the dorsal fin and extends down the body to include the ventral fins. The white area next to this stripe continues upwards to the filmy extension of the dorsal fin. This area is bounded by the final broad black stripe, which is slanted and terminates at the anal fin. At this point there is a small white area which extends from the caudal fin to the rear dorsal. Both these fins are yellow. It is a common fish, easy to photograph, which is quite unlike the much shyer Moorish Idol.

Moorish Idol   [*Zanclus cornutus*] PLATE 86

At first glance this beautiful fish resembles the Heniochus, but the dorsal fin of the Moorish Idol is prolonged into a long filament. Often seen in pairs and like the angelfish seems equally at home from the surface water down to at least 140 ft.

Parrotfish   [Scaridae]

These fish are common to all coral reefs and warm seas and take their name from their brilliant colouration and beak-like mouth, which results from the teeth being fused together.

The soft beaches of coral seas owe much to the parrotfish. When they feed they can be heard quite easily underwater as they bite off lumps of coral and crunch it up with rasp-like plates in their throats. The soft parts of the coral are digested and the residue is excreted. This residue will be finally washed ashore to form part of some beach.

Parrotfish vary in size from a few inches in the case of the smaller species to over 5 ft in the largest. And the diver will have difficulty in distinguishing between some parrotfish and wrasse. Both share similar shapes and small specimens are indistinguishable one from another.

Wrasse and parrotfish also have an identical method of propulsion—the pectoral fins are used like the wings of a bird and the body and tail are used for steering.

Parrots are solid and plump fish with rounded heads and broad swallow tails. The large scales are usually prominent and are often outlined in a different hue to the body. Colouration is both brilliant and varied.

Indeed the main identification of many species relies on subtle colour variations and Peter Scoones suspects that there may well be in fact fewer species than those listed at present.

The most prominent colour of the parrots is a bright blue green, but the family includes red, pink, yellow and plain green variations. Some are so multi-coloured that at a distance all the colours merge to give an overall impression of plain grey.

Although they could not be described as fast fish, they are seldom still and provide difficult subjects for the underwater photographer.

The best time for the photographer to approach is when the fish are occupied browsing on coral or foraging among weed. Even then it is seldom possible to approach closer than 5 or 6 ft. The fish do, however, sometimes make close approaches when snap shots can be taken before the fish realise that they are near a diver.

Although difficult for the photographer, they are among the easiest targets for the spearfisherman to shoot at a distance. The killing of these fish is a shame and a waste for the flesh is often toxic and special care has to be taken in their preparation for cooking. As a result many shot fish are left on the shore to rot by the spearfisherman who, though prepared to kill, is not prepared to run the risk of being poisoned.

At night, however, the photographer can approach parrotfish very closely indeed. They will be found lodged in fissures in the reef and are often cocooned in a protective layer of mucus which they secrete and spin around themselves. When they are like this they can be touched without causing instant flight.

As identification of the species is so difficult underwater, only one of the main species is described here. But be warned, so similar are the colour patterns that even this description could fit other species.

Scarus vetula is a parrotfish of 18 in. to 2 ft in length. This round-nosed fish has a stocky body. The dorsal fin extends from above the gill-slit to the caudal peduncle and is striped along its length with pale blue, yellow and pink in that order from the top. The caudal, anal fins and the large pectorals are striped with the same colours.

The tail is broad and swallow-tailed. The head, to the gill-slit, is lighter in tone than the rest of the body and has a few yellow-edged blue stripes extending from the front diagonally upwards to beneath the eyes. The blue scales on the main body are large and rendered more prominent by being edged with pink.

This fish can be seen cruising round the reef, stopping occasionally for another lump of coral, and despite its coat of many colours, the diver will get a first overall impression of a fish of solid blue.

Puffer fish   [Lagocephalidae and Tetraodontidae]   PLATE 61

These fish have two claims to fame. The first is that they can puff themselves up into a ball when provoked and are so almost impossible for a fish to grab. Secondly, their flesh can be deadly poisonous to eat and it is said that chefs in Asian countries have to have a special licence to allow them to prepare these fish for human consumption!

The puffers have a mouth that is really a beak and they use this to crack open crabs and other shellfish to eat. The one that is usually seen inflated and dried swinging from a pub roof is the porcupine variety, but not all possess these sharp spines.

Red Mullet   [Mullidae]

Though there is at the moment only one common red mullet in the Mediterranean and southern North Atlantic, most of the family live in the tropics and are very numerous.

They tend to swim in schools, settling on the bottom to grope

55 LIONFISH [*Pterois volitans*] Malindi, Kenya
Depth 8 ft Bronica Flash *f*8 Ektacolor S (*Peter Scoones*)

56 DAMSELFISH [*Dascyllus reticulatus*] Mida, Kenya
Depth 6 ft Bronica *f*8/125 Ektachrome-X (*Peter Scoones*)

57 SPOTTED SWEETLIP [*Gaterin gaterinus*] Mida, Kenya
Depth 15 ft Bronica Flash *f*8/40 Ektacolor S (*Peter Scoones*)

58 CARDINAL FISH [*Archamia fucata*] East Africa
    Depth 6 ft Bronica $f5\cdot6/125$ Ektachrome-X (*Peter Scoones*)

59 SWEEPERS [*Pempheris oualensis*] East Africa
    Depth 8 ft Calypsophot $f4/60$ Agfacolour CT18 (*Juliet Scoones*)

60 CAESIO [*Caesio pulcherrimus*] Aldabra
    Depth 40 ft Rolleimarin Flash Ektachrome-X (*John Lythgoe*)

61 SHARP-NOSED PUFFER [*Canthigaster valentini*] Mida, Kenya
Depth 6 ft Bronica ƒ8/125 Ektacolor S (*Peter Scoones*)

62 HAWKFISH [*Paracirrhites*] Watamu, Kenya
Depth 40 ft Bronica Flash ƒ11 Ektacolor S (*Peter Scoones*)

63 HAWKFISH [*Paracirrhites sp.*] Red Sea
Depth 15 ft Exa 1A ƒ16 Ektachrome-X (*Geoff Harwood*)

64 EMPEROR FISH [*Pomacanthodes imperator*] Aldabra (*John Lythgoe*)
  Depth 30 ft Calypsophot *f*8/125 High Speed Ektachrome

65 ANGELFISH [*Pomacanthops semicirculatus*] Mida, Kenya
  Depth 7 ft Bronica Flash *f*5·6 Ektachrome-X (*Peter Scoones*)

66 *Pygoplites diacanthus* and small soldier fish Aldabra
  Depth 30 ft Rolleimarin Flash Ektachrome-X (*John Lythgoe*)

67 ANGELFISH [*Pomacanthodes chrysurus*] Mida, Kenya
  Depth 10 ft Bronica Flash *f*5·6/40 Ektachrome-X (*Peter Scoones*)

68 STRIPED SURGEON [*Acanthurus lineatus*] Watamu, Kenya
Depth 15 ft Bronica *f*5·6/250 Ektachrome-X (*Peter Scoones*)

69 POWDER BLUE SURGEON [*Acanthurus leucosternon*] Aldabra
Depth 30 ft Rolleimarin Flash Ektachrome-X (*John Lythgoe*)

70 MAJESTIC SURGEON [*Acanthurus bleekeri*] (*Geoff Harwood*)
Depth 5 ft Nikonos *f*5·6/125 Ektachrome-X

71 BUTTERFLY FISH [*Chaetodon auriga*] Turtle Bay, Kenya
  Depth 15 ft Bronica *f*5·6/250 Ektachrome-X (*Peter Scoones*)

72 BUTTERFLY FISH [*Chaetodon leucopleura*] Mida, Kenya
  Depth 10 ft Bronica *f*5·6/250 Ektachrome-X (*Peter Scoones*)

73 *Plectropomus maculatus* Turtle Bay, Kenya (*Peter Scoones*)
  Depth 40 ft Bronica Flash *f*5·6/40 Ektachrome-X

74 PUFFER FISH Turtle Bay, Kenya
  Depth 4 ft Bronica Flash *f*11/40 Ektachrome-X (*Peter Scoones*)

75 SWEETLIPS [*Gaterin schota*] Turtle Bay, Kenya
Depth 10 ft Bronica *f*8/60 Ektacolor S (*Peter Scoones*)

76 STRIPED SWEETLIP [*Gaterin playfairi*] Turtle Bay, Kenya
Depth 10 ft Bronica Flash *f*11/40 Ektachrome-X (*Peter Scoones*)

77 *Gnathodentex aurolineatus* Malindi Banks, Kenya
Depth 15 ft Bronica Flash $f5.6/40$ Ektacolor S (*Peter Scoones*)

78 TRUMPETFISH [*Aulostomus valentini*] Watamu, Kenya
Depth 25 ft Bronica Flash *f*8/40 Ektachrome-X (*Peter Scoones*)

79 LIZARDFISH [*Synodus* sp.] Turtle Bay, Kenya (*Peter Scoones*)
Depth 30 ft Bronica Flash *f*5·6/40 Ektachrome-X

80 SQUIRRELFISH [*Myripristis* sp.] Turtle Bay, Kenya
   Depth 30 ft (cave) Bronica Flash $f11$ Ektachrome-X (*Peter Scoones*)

81 SOLDIERFISH [*Holocentrus spiniferus*] Aldabra
   Depth 10 ft Rolleimarin Flash Ektachrome-X (*John Lythgoe*)

82 PICASSO TRIGGERFISH [*Rhinecanthus aculeatus*] Aldabra
Depth 10 ft Rolleimarin Ektachrome (*John Lythgoe*)

83 TRIGGERFISH [*Balistoides viridescens*] Aldabra
Depth 15 ft Calypsophot Ektachrome-X (*John Lythgoe*)

84 ORANGE-STRIPED TRIGGERFISH [*Balistes undulatus*] Aden
Depth 15 ft Miranda B Flash *f*11 Ektachrome (*Peter Scoones*)

85 WHIMPLE FISH [*Heniochus acuminatus*] Mida, Kenya
Depth 10 ft Bronica Flash *f*8/40 Ektachrome-X (*Peter Scoones*)

86 MOORISH IDOL [*Zanclus cornutus*] Watamu, Kenya
Depth 15 ft Bronica *f*5·6/125 Ektachrome-X (*Peter Scoones*)

87 YELLOW-STRIPED SNAPPER [*Lutianus kasmira*] Mida, Kenya
Depth 10 ft Bronica *f*5·6/125 Ektachrome-X (*Peter Scoones*)

88 STARRY RABBITFISH [*Siganus stellatus*] Aldabra
Depth 20 ft Rolleimarin Flash Ektachrome-X (*John Lythgoe*)

89 SOLDIERFISH [*Holocentrus sp.*] East Africa
Depth 10 ft Bronica Flash *f*11 Ektacolor S (*Peter Scoones*)

90 CARDINAL FISH [*Ostorhinchus fleurieu*] Turtle Bay, Kenya
Depth 10 ft (cave) Bronica Flash *f*11 Ektacolor S (*Peter Scoones*)

91 SPOTTED JACK [*Caranx melampygus*] Aldabra
Depth 10 ft Rolleimarin Ektachrome (*John Lythgoe*)

92 BARRACUDA [*Sphyraena barracuda*] Aldabra
Depth 30 ft Rolleimarin Ektachrome (*John Lythgoe*)

in sand or mud with their barbels for their food. Some of these mullet such as *Pseudupeneus barberinus*, have 'leaked' into the Eastern Mediterranean and may soon be described as common there.

Scorpion fish [Scorpaenidae and *Pterois*] PLATE 55

Pterois volitans is probably the most commonly noticed fish of this group in tropical waters. It may travel under names like lionfish, turkey fish, fire fish, firework fish, dragon fish, tiger fish. But they all have one thing in common—their sting may kill.

Colouration varies a great deal. The rays of the pectorals and dorsal fins are prolonged into great showy ribbons that are clearly meant to warn of danger, though they can be a beautiful sight in a fan of colours, reds and yellows predominating. The first few spines of the dorsal are sharp, strong and hollow and these contain the poison (*see* Dangers).

Sluggish swimmers, these fish tend to rest on the bottom on sand where there is a slight current running. Sometimes the current gets too strong for them, catches the 'sail' of fins and they are carried for some distance against their will. The diver should be aware at all times of the danger of brushing against one of these fish, particularly when they are both being swept about by wave surge.

Snappers [Lutianidae] PLATE 87

A very fish-shaped fish with an oval body. The large mouth possesses formidable teeth which snap together when the fish is caught and landed. They are important fish on any reef for they are predators and feed on other fish. As they are usually very numerous, their effect on the fish population is considerable.

Except for a few brilliantly coloured forms they are difficult to tell apart underwater. Two small species can, however, be identified at a glance. *Lutianus bohar* has two prominent white spots on the back and *L. kasmira* has blue and gold stripes running lengthways.

Though the snapper takes its name from the snapping together of its teeth, this is in fact a spasmodic contraction of the jaw muscles, due to oxygen starvation which occurs when it is taken from the water.

The various forms vary in size from a few inches up to over 4 ft. The smaller ones go about in big schools. Larger individuals, particularly red snappers, can often be found at the rear of large caves.

Really big fish in this family are very wary and the photographer will be lucky if he gets in close.

Soldierfish   [Holocentridae]   PLATES 81, 89

In almost any dive on a coral reef, provided the depth is below the violent surge zone, the diver will see these bright red fishes lurking in the coral caves or among piled rock. Soldierfish, often called squirrelfish, have very big eyes and are supposed to emerge mainly at night. But at least two species, *Myripristis adustus* and *M. murdjan* seem to spend most of the day hovering in mid-water above their chosen refuge. The soldierfish are very dependent on their coral homes and should the reef be destroyed—through storms or perhaps by the starfish menace of the coral reef, 'The Crown of Thorns', the soldierfish will depart too.

The Crown of Thorns starfish is named after the thicket of poisonous spikes that covers the body and the 16 arms. For hundreds of years this large starfish—it can grow up to 2 ft across —has lived quietly in warm waters.

It feeds by night, extruding its stomach over the surface of the reef and using its gastric juices to dissolve the soft tissue of the young coral buds.

There used to be so few of these starfish about that it was almost a rarity. But about six years ago something seems to have gone wrong with the ecology that kept the Crown of Thorns in check. And a starfish population explosion took place.

Most of the reef around Guam in the Pacific was destroyed. Then came reports of an estimated 200,000 of the creatures chewing away at other reefs. The Great Barrier Reef was next. In the past four years, large parts of the reef have been killed, bringing a risk of flooding to Queensland.

The killing of the living coral weakens the reefs and leaves the way open for wave damage and erosion. Some small Pacific islands could disappear as a result.

In the affected areas, divers have been called in to help and inject formalin into the starfish whenever they find them underwater. The Crown of Thorns is also found in small numbers in the Red Sea, but so far shows no sign there of going on a breeding rampage.

One of the most common soldierfish is *Holocentrus spiniferus* and it is very likely to be this one that you will see with its head poking out of a hole in the coral (PLATE 81). Its downturned mouth gives it a sad and unmistakably mournful air. Another soldierfish, *Holocentrus ruber*, is of particular interest, because this is another of those fishes which have 'leaked' through into the Mediterranean via the Suez Canal. It is now a common sight in the Eastern Mediterranean, particularly around Cyprus.

Stonefish [*Synanceia verrucosa*]

An ugly fish with a great squat head and bloated body, the stonefish is often found in extremely shallow water and this is the reason for wearing good stout shoes when paddling out over the reef. The diver should avoid all contact with the fish, which has a habit of lying among coral rubble and taking on a remarkable camouflage colouration. Its dorsal spines contain poison, are razor sharp and when driven into a limb deliver a venom whose pain is excruciating (*see* Chapter Six).

Surgeonfish [Acanthuridae]   PLATES 68, 69, 70

Tangs, doctorfish, lancetfish—these are all names given to this large family, which is restricted to warm waters. The main feature of all of them is the pair of spines (or scalpel-like knives) set in a groove on each side of the tail stalk. If anyone is foolish enough to handle them—or try to underwater—the knives flick out at right angles to the body and very nasty cuts can result.

As if this wasn't enough, some of the family have poisonous spines in their dorsal or anal fins. The surgeonfish live on algae, but strangely will take baited hooks as local fishermen know well.

A rather plate-like group of fish, there are two easily sorted-out shapes. Both are laterally compressed. One group has a rather tear-shaped profile, the head is round and the dorsal and anal fins are kept in a folded position during normal situations. The tail is extended top and bottom to produce a swallow-tail impression. This type of surgeonfish has usually many horizontal stripes along the body.

The other surgeonfish shape is achieved by the almost permanent erection of the dorsal and anal fins. This gives a quite different profile, which is carried to extremes in the Sailfish Tang.

Acanthurus xanthopterus is the purple surgeonfish, sometimes called the yellow-tailed surgeon. This is a most striking fish with deep purple and blue colouration. It has bright yellow pectoral and caudal fins. The head has reddish spots all over it. A characteristic of all surgeonfish is the way they move through the water. Propulsion is mainly by the pectoral fins which gives the impression of a bird flying and a bouncy movement.

The young purple surgeonfish could easily be confused with butterfly fish as the dorsal and anal fin are large compared with the body. This fish is common to the Southern Red Sea and can be seen in vast groups browsing on the rocky bottoms. Wary and hard to approach. Big fish of this variety will be ten to 15 in. long.

Acanthurus leucosternum is readily recognised (PLATE 69). It has a black head, white throat, blue body, yellow dorsal fin and a black-and-white banded tail. A most quarrelsome fish, it will dart in among a group of parrot fish feeding near its favourite rocks and drive them away.

This fish tends to live in the top 20–30 ft of water and is quite at home moving back and forth with the surge of the waves. Average size: 8–9 in.

Acanthurus trigostegus is another striking fish. It is sometimes called the convict fish or convict tang. Silvery white with thin dark-brown vertical stripes down its body, this fish too is often found in the turbulent areas of the surf line. Always in large shoals. Average size: 8–9 in.

Acanthurus lineatus is the name of the striped surgeonfish (PLATE 68). Has many black-edged blue stripes running horizontally along its yellow body. The lower third of the body is totally white. It is always in water less than a few yards deep.

The orange spot surgeonfish is a streamlined fish common in Red Sea waters. The dorsal, ventral, anal and caudal fins are dark and edged with irridescent blue. The body is grey with horizontal blue stripes. There are bright orange patches on the body. The pectoral fins are also bright orange.

Zebrasoma veliferum is the Latin name for the sailfish tang. High dorsal and deep anal fins with vertical stripes on a dark brown body make this fish very distinctive among the surgeons. Large fish will be 15 in. long, but average 6–9 in.

All tend to be fast-moving fish and, from the photographer's point of view tend to 'jump about a bit' when pecking at coral.

Triggerfish and Filefish   PLATES 82, 83, 84

Though these two groups are not technically the same family they are so similar in appearance that underwater they can easily be mixed up.

The filefish take their name from the fact that they have no scales, but a tough rough hide, which is used, dried, in some areas as sandpaper. This is one place where they differ from the triggerfish; the second is that though both families possess a strong dorsal spine only the triggerfish can lock it in place. And the third difference is that this spine is solitary in the filefish and the triggerfish have two smaller spines joined by a web to the front spine.

Both species are extraordinary too in that they can alter their outline by erecting another spine under the body.

Divers have found that the triggerfish will retreat into a small hole when disturbed and erect the dorsal spine effectively jamming itself into the hole. No amount of tugging will dislodge the fish until the first ray of the soft dorsal is depressed like a trigger. The spine lock is then released and the fish can be removed. It then appears to be indignant and grunts audibly.

This trigger arrangement may well have another use. Peter Scoones has observed a dozen small grey triggerfish in a horizontal crack in an undersea cliff. All the fish had both lower and upper spines raised and in contact with top and bottom of the crack. In this position they pivoted like weathercocks in the surge of waves above. Scoones believes that this may be the normal procedure for sleep.

The orange-tailed filefish (*Monocanthus tomentosus*). Colour change is quick and variable. Body colours can range from a dull grey overall to mauve or dull orange. The tail of all, however, is bright orange—not so obvious when folded but quite clear when fully open. The fish appears to have a habit of opening and closing the tail fin while feeding and this often draws attention to what can be a rather insignificant small fish. Not a fast mover, the fish can be persuaded to pose for the camera without trouble and will readily take titbits from the fingers.

The blue-spotted filefish is a large shy fellow with bright blue spots and stripes on a greenish base. It has a habit of hiding behind rocks and surveying the scene with just an eye poked gingerly from its hiding place.

Not easy to photograph as at the slightest disturbance it will hurry away to the next rock for a repeat performance.

The Orange-striped Triggerfish (*Balistoides undulatus*) is a pugnacious looking fish with a temper to fit (PLATE 84). The head is enormous and is accentuated by the small mouth and eyes set very high. Has bright orange diagonal stripes on a green body. The tail is orange and so are the spots on the upper snout. Moves through the water by an undulating motion of the rear dorsal and anal fins rather than flapping along like other species of triggerfish.

The Green Triggerfish (*Balistoides viridescens*) is one of the largest triggerfish—up to at least 30 in.! It has a rounded tail and large olive scales each outlined in darker green. They nest in the sheltered part of the reef around January. The eggs are laid straight onto the exposed bottom, a delectable plate of caviar, each little egg just a handy mouthful size for the swarm of little fishes that gather round.

The poor parent triggerfish gets quite demented. First it has to blow a current of water through the egg mass to oxygenate it and then it has to chase off all the little fishes intent on stealing the eggs. But there is no peace! A hungry rock cod comes prowling up and the only way to shift the intruder is to swim straight at it, bumping it out of the way—by which time a quarter of the eggs are in peril from the small fishes again, most of which have grabbed a mouthful.

The eggs have then to be oxygenated again, by which time the rock cod has worked his courage up again. A diver with his camera is not welcome. Indeed, if you want to know what it's like to be an unwanted grouper, try photographing a harassed triggerfish! It spots you from 30 ft away, turns and charges straight at you and it doesn't stop. Thump!

Unicornfish [*Naso brevirostris*]

A fish with an outrageous shape—and because of that absolutely unmistakeable for anything else. A big horn juts from the forehead, even beyond the snout. They spend most of their time swimming in mid-water and are not usually easy to photograph in close-up. But whereas an individual specimen may be extremely shy and avoid all attempts to move in close, the photographer may sometimes find himself surrounded by a shoal of these dark fish— they come in all shades from black through dark brown to grey— and have no difficulty in getting his camera right up to the fish.

Wrasse [Labridae]

In warm waters there are even more wrasse around than there are in the Mediterranean—and even greater difficulty for the diver in picking out the various members of the family. But there is one exception. And that is the giant humphead wrasse (*Cheilinus undulatus*). One of the largest bony fish in the sea, it may exceed 6 ft in length. There is no doubt about the identification—a great hump behind the eye. The green scales are huge and well-defined. Unfortunately this fish's flesh is excellent eating—most unusual for a wrasse—and its sheer bulk makes it a prime target for any spearfishermen in the area.

Another interesting warm water wrasse is the cleaner fish (*Labroides dimidiatus*). Near any outstanding feature on the seabed there will be two or three of these little blue and black striped fishes waiting for a customer to come along nicely infested with fish lice and fungus.

The client invites cleaning by spreading out its fins, gaping mouth and gill covers and hanging in the water in an unnatural head-up or head-down position. The little cleaner fish at once start work picking the parasites off its sides, even entering its mouth and leaving through the gills.

It is worth noting here that if a diver has some tropical ulcer on his leg—and this is common after a week or two of reef diving—then these little fish may come and clean him up too! All that is felt is a little tweak or two and all the pus and dead skin is cleaned out and the healthy flesh left untouched.

A word of caution . . . there is a little goby (*Aspidontus trigloides*) whose shape and colour is nearly identical to the true cleaner fish, but this little brute comes darting out and punches a hole out of fish or diver's leg. Not recommended, so beware of imitations!

OPEN WATER

Barracuda [Sphyraenidae] PLATE 92

Impossible to mistake. Looks like a pike with the same power-driver of a tail. The mouth is large and overteethed for the diver's comfort. Silver body, dark fins. They look nasty and they are. Their habit of circling round and round a diver gazing at him with large cold eyes is disconcerting to say the least, but they do not *usually* attack, though there are records of unprovoked attacks. They are much feared in the Caribbean. Are usually not a big fish—about 2 ft long, but the Great Barracuda is known to grow to 8 ft and weight over 100 lb. All the varieties appear to be curious about the diver, but will usually retreat if faced with a determined advance. Photographers find this habit infuriating and usually try ignoring the fish and letting him approach as closely as possible before taking a snapshot.

Horse Mackerel [Carangidae]

Perhaps it is because these fish hunt by day that to the diver they seem to be the most important predator of the reef.

The schools of small reef fish know when the horse mackerel are coming long before the diver can see them. The little fish show their concern by bunching tighter or by moving down into the shelter of the jagged heads of coral. After a pause the diver can spot the horse mackerel. They come in groups of three or four, balanced on their pectoral fins, poised like a boxer waiting for the right moment to strike. They will swim round and round a diver just as barracuda do—so fast that it is difficult to hold them in the camera-viewfinder. After a while, they tire of this and resume their patrolling up and down the reef.

When they strike a fish, they swim incredibly fast in short bursts, right down among the coral heads. So fast is this strike that it is difficult to know how they manage to avoid the jagged corals among which they find their prey.

Very difficult to tell one of the species from another. It doesn't help that they are very good eating and little time is available if one is caught before the cook claims it!

Underwater only one very common member of the group, the Spotted Jack (*Caranx melampygus*), is easy to recognise. This is because of its blue sheen and dark speckled body.

Sharks

All divers in warm waters will be conscious of sharks, whether seen or not. And though, fortunately, unprovoked attacks by sharks on divers are relatively few when compared with the attacks on bathers, a diver in waters which sharks are known to frequent would be lying if he said that sharks do not frighten him.

Even putting the attacks on divers into perspective—most have occurred because of the presence of blood in the water from speared fish—will not cure a diver of this fear. The plain fact is that sharks of all species can be dangerous; they are unpredictable and should be treated with great respect.

Though the great majority of shark species are not regarded as aggressive, a diver should proceed with great caution when in the same water as a shark of any kind.

The sight of a shark underwater immediately gives the impression of a creature supremely adapted to and at ease in its natural environment—a sleek grey shape undulating, apparently idly, along a reef in some ceaseless search—probably for food.

However, the shark keeps on the move for another reason almost as important as the search for food. Unlike most fishes, the shark does not possess a swim bladder, and the lack of this makes it impossible for him to maintain position without swimming. Sharks can rest on the bottom and many do, but in open water if the shark stops swimming he will sink down and down until he reaches the ocean floor no matter how deep down that is.

But even if a diver finds a shark, *apparently* asleep (for we don't know if they really can sleep as we do) on the seabed or in some cave, there will be no doubt in the diver's mind that what he is seeing really is a shark. A shark, yes, but what kind? Accurate identification presents a great problem.

Experience has shown that the identification of a shark by divers underwater is haphazard in the extreme. This may well be due to fear with its consequent loss of clear thought. On the other hand it may well be the fact that the slotting of sharks into quick categories is not easy. In some cases, even when the shark is landed by shark fishermen safe and sound in a nice dry boat, the wrong identification is made.

Seven of the basic sharks are listed below. Treat all with care and ignore anything said about the harmlessness of any of them. (*See also* Dangers.)

GREAT WHITE SHARK   [*Carcharodon carcharias*]

This one is sometimes known as the white pointer. It has a reputation of being a man-eater and as a result is probably the most feared of them all. It frequently reaches lengths of over 20 ft and some have been recorded well over 35 ft in length. The colour of mature specimens is a dull grey, giving it a ghost-like appearance underwater. The body is somewhat more thickset than other sharks and it has a large dorsal fin. The caudal fin is nearly symmetrical and the snout is pointed, though not as much as the Mako.

Young specimens do not necessarily have the same 'white' colour of their parents, but range from light grey, through brown to black. However, the change of colour from the back to the white belly is abrupt and this serves as a useful quick guide to instant identification.

TIGER SHARK   [*Galeocerdo cuvier*]

This one is easier to identify. Has a short blunt rounded snout, which looks somewhat flattened. The younger ones—up to about 10 ft—have a distinctive striped or blotchy pattern on their upper body, which gives the shark its name. There is some doubt about the appetite of this shark for live divers as it is basically a scavenger. But it would be as well to give it the benefit of the doubt and stay clear.

NURSE SHARK [*Ginglymostoma cirratum*]

An indolent bottom-dwelling shark rather like a large dogfish, but with a stockier body. This one will be familiar to Hollywood film devotees. Whenever the man-eating shark sweeps in to the attack, it is, sad to say, our old friend the nurse. It looks sufficiently shark-like to impress cinema audiences.

But it is in fact the most docile of all the sharks. The mouth is small and situated almost at the tip of the blunt snout. The give-away is the barbels on either side of the snout just in front of the mouth. The dorsal fin and the second dorsal fin, which is large in comparison with other sharks, are set well to the rear. Colour varies from brown to greyish. Is often found in caves and under overhangs of the reef. When disturbed it will move smartly to the next sheltered spot for another snooze. *Note:* Should not be con-fused with the grey nurse which is not so docile.

HAMMERHEAD SHARK [*Sphyrna zygaena*]

The hammerheads are readily identified by the head which is greatly extended laterally, like a double-bladed axe, with the eyes at the outside ends of these extensions. The dorsal fin is very tall and curved and so is the tail. Viewed from the side the head extensions may not be noticed at once. The hammerhead has long pointed teeth and a reputation for aggression—and as 14 ft is the length of a mature specimen, it pays not to take chances.

WHITE TIP SHARK [*Carcharhinus albimarginatus*]

This is the most common shark seen by divers on the reef. It is a 'shark-shaped' shark easily identified by the white tips on the dorsal, pectoral and caudal fins. Its length is usually around the 7 or 8 ft mark and it can often be seen in considerable numbers on one dive. It is an active shark—with teeth—and should not be ignored however much familiarity tends to breed contempt.

PORBEAGLE or MACKEREL SHARK   [*Lamna nasus*]   PLATE 14

This one is hard to tell from the Mako. Both are typical shark outlines—pointed snouts, slender bodies, and crescent-shaped caudal fins. Dark-blue grey bodies set off the usual white bellies. The main difference seems to be in size—the Porbeagle goes from 6 to 8 ft and the Mako from 10 to 12 ft. Detailed examination of the teeth structure is the only foolproof way of telling them apart, but only a fool would try underwater. The porbeagle is not a real tropical species, but when encountered in any water should be treated with great respect. Little is known of its attitude to divers and it must be regarded as potentially dangerous.

WHALE SHARK   [*Rhincodon typus*]

This is the largest of the shark family and whatever effect its size may have on the diver, it is a plankton eater. It has been reported to reach a length of over 60 ft and has light spots on a brownish body. Lateral ridges are present on both back and sides. The whale shark moves slowly through the water at about 2 to 3 knots and will allow divers to clamber all over it. Arab legends tell of a small boy who having fallen into the water rode the dorsal fin of one of these sharks for four days before being rescued!

CHAPTER FOUR

Associated Marine Creatures

You are never alone in the sea. And fish, of course, are never seen in isolation. There is always a background of other marine creatures.

In fact the underwater photographer would be less than human if, at times, he did not stray from his photography of fish to concentrate on some other aspect of life under the sea.

This book is concerned with fish. It would take another book to deal with each of the various sections of marine life that the diver sees as he fins over the seabed. It is no exaggeration to say that the diver will come into range of enough marine life on one dive to fill several books—if he were able to discuss and explore all the ramifications and life cycles of this background material.

The underwater photographer finds distractions enough on any dive. Anemones make beautiful pictures (PLATES 99, 110), especially the plumose variety, when fully extended to take advantage of the goodies that the tides bring to them.

Starfish are another distraction (PLATES 107, 118). They are often purple in Northern waters, but are brought to glowing yellow or orange life by the explosion of a flash-bulb.

In Mediterranean waters of course the starfish is more often the conventional red of travel posters.

Sea urchins (PLATE 117), purple and pink, cling to the underside of rock shelves in Northern waters like those off Cornwall's rugged coast. And black urchins with longer spines dot the rocks under the softer grandeur of the cliffs of the Costa Brava, French Riviera or Italian coast. All these will make pictures for the diver.

The sea cucumber, again in the Mediterranean, will stand up and sway in the current when the South-West wind blows. It

148

would take a completely insensitive photographer to ignore this phenomenon. Why do they do it? Why only in these circumstances? Obviously another book is needed.

There is, it is said, enough material on one growth-encrusted rock to keep a marine biologist busy for his entire life, so all that the fish photographer can really do is to photograph this extraordinary world in microcosm in the way that he thinks will make a good picture and then move on in search of his speciality, fish.

But there are, of course, bigger marine creatures than the sponges on a rock. Lobsters and crabs tend to be very much easier to photograph underwater than free-swimming and fast-moving fish. But if the fish photographer is distracted into this field, all is not simple.

Lobster photography (PLATES 93, 101, 116) tends to have the same problems as those which come when photographing a conger—poor illumination in dark and inaccessible holes. This can sometimes be overcome, if you care to cheat, by moving the lobster into a lighter place.

But you have to be careful because this kind of photograph can look artificial. Lobsters just don't sit out in the middle of a sun-dappled patch of sand in the middle of the day, although it is hard to make any general rule and they can be found out in the open when travelling.

Philip Smith, who has taken a great number of classic lobster photographs, insists that a photographer should try to take a lobster in his chosen home—and if the lobster will not co-operate, then you should save your pictures for a more photogenically-sited creature.

Crabs, he says, especially edible and spider crabs, are more helpful and will either remain stationary where they are or will creep off at a sea snail's pace.

Spider crabs do make ideal subjects for the beginner to try out his underwater photography (PLATE 115). They are easily visible to start off with and can be found clinging to the sides of rocks or laminaria fronds. They are harmless and slow-moving, but at the same time they do possess a cheery bright orange shell colour.

And they do have a habit of planting live pieces of growing weed on the top of their shell in what seems to be a poor attempt at camouflage. This makes them look like a mobile cabbage.

The handsome edible crab (PLATE 111) with his beautiful rosy-mauve shell and smart black tips to his claws makes an attractive subject for colour. The crab is usually a patient sitter and rarely makes any attempt to move unless caught in the open away from the rocks—and then he will high-tail it sideways in search of cover.

Should there be insufficient natural light for close-up shots of a crab, then once again flash will have to be used. But Phil Smith has found that the concentrated harsh light from even a small bulb is enough to cast rather unsightly shadows behind the crab's angular legs.

To overcome this he uses an opal Perspex screen placed over the whole reflector, which is sufficient to spread and diffuse the light. The subsequent softening of the shadows gives a much more natural look to the finished picture. Of course, sea water itself is a great diffuser of light and at distances of more than 3 or 4 ft the screen becomes unnecessary.

The problem facing underwater photographers is not usually what to photograph, but what to photograph first. And some find great difficulty in concentrating on the fish.

For example, one of my last dives of the season before completing work on this book was into the Mixon Hole, off Selsey Bill, Sussex.

It is fair to say that the Mixon Hole is one of the most amazing underwater features of the British coastline. I can still remember my first dive there.

John Messent, a diver from Bromley branch of the British Sub-Aqua Club, took us in his fast boat out to the Mixon Beacon.

As we anchored in what can only be described as a tide rip over a shallow bottom and the boat bounced in the choppy water, the gulls that cluster round the top of the Beacon uttered mournful squawks. I was inclined to agree with their verdict on the sort of diving we were likely to find there.

93 LOBSTER [*Homarus vulgaris*] Kimmeridge, Dorset (*Philip Smith*)
Depth 20 ft Rolleimarin Flash *f*16/125 Ektacolor S

94 JELLYFISH [*Aequorea forskalea*] St Abbs, Berwickshire (*Colin Doeg*)
Depth 3 ft Rolleimarin + supp. lens *f*8/50 High Speed Ektachrome

95 GLASS PRAWN [*Leander squilla*] Swanage Pier, Dorset
Depth 5 ft Bronica Flash *f*16 Ektacolor S (*Peter Scoones*)

96 CUTTLEFISH [*Sepia* sp.] Holkat Bay, Aden (*Peter Scoones*)
Depth 4 ft Miranda B $f5·6/150$ High Speed Ektachrome

97 OCTOPUS [*Octopus vulgaris*] Sa Tuna, Spain (*Kendall McDonald*)
Depth 35 ft Nikonos $f11/60$ High Speed Ektachrome

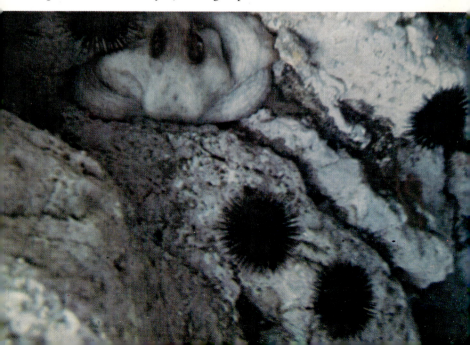

98 LION'S MANE JELLYFISH [*Cyanea capillata*] and young fish
Bradda Head, Isle of Man (*Ron Hook*)
Depth 20 ft Calypsophot Elec. flash *f*4/30 Kodachrome II

99 ANEMONES [*Parazoanthus axinella*] Porto Fino, Italy
Depth 15 ft Bronica Flash *f*11 Ektachrome-X (*Peter Scoones*)

100 SEA SQUIRT [*Halocynthia papillosa*] Porto Fino, Italy
Depth 6 ft Bronica Flash *f*11 Ektachrome-X (*Peter Scoones*)

101 SPINY LOBSTER [*Palinurus vulgaris*] Punta Escalanya, Spain
Depth 40 ft Nikonos+20 cm close-up Flash (PF1B) *f*22/60
High Speed Ektachrome   (*Kendall McDonald*)

102 CLAM [*Tridacna*] Telok Tekek, Tioman, S. China Sea
Depth 10 ft Miranda B *f*4/60 Ektachrome (*Peter Scoones*)

103 PRAWNS Mida, Kenya
Depth 12 ft Bronica Flash *f*11 Ektachrome-X (*Peter Scoones*)

104 DEADMEN'S FINGERS [*Alcyonium digitatum*] Bognor, Sussex
  Depth 30 ft Nikonos + close-up Flash (PF1B) *f*16/60 High
  Speed Ektachrome   (*Kendall McDonald*)

105 SOFT CORAL Mida, Kenya
  Depth 6 ft Bronica *f*5·6/125 Ektacolor S (*Peter Scoones*)

106 SEA SLUG on sea rose Mida, Kenya
  Depth 7 ft Bronica *f*5·6/125 Ektacolor S (*Peter Scoones*)

107 CRINOID STARFISH Pulau Tioman, S. China Sea
  Depth 10 ft Bronica *f*4/60 Ektachrome (*Peter Scoones*)

108 CLAM and Gorgonian East Africa
Depth 20 ft Bronica Flash *f*8 Ektacolor S (*Peter Scoones*)

109 CUTTLEFISH [*Sepia officinalis*] Swanage, Dorset
Depth 10 ft Nikonos Flash (PF1B) *f*16/60 Tri-X (*Colin Doeg*)

110 DAHLIA ANEMONE [*Tealia felina*] Durdle Door, Dorset
Depth 6 ft Bronica Flash *f*11 Ektachrome-X (*Peter Scoones*)

111 EDIBLE CRAB [*Cancer pagurus*] Chapman's Pool, Dorset
Depth 12 ft Nikonos *f*5·5/125 Tri-X (*Leo Zanelli*)

112 COMMON HERMIT CRAB [*Eupagurus bernhardus*] Swanage, Dorset
Depth 5 ft Bronica Flash *f*16 Tri-X (*Peter Scoones*)

113 COMMON WHELK [*Buccinum undatum*] Swanage, Dorset (*Colin Doeg*)
Depth 6 ft Calypsophot + 20 cm close-up *f*5·6/125 Tri-X

114 SEA HARE [*Aplysia*] Swanage Pier, Dorset
Depth 10 ft Exa *f*8/60 Plus-X (*Geoff Harwood*)

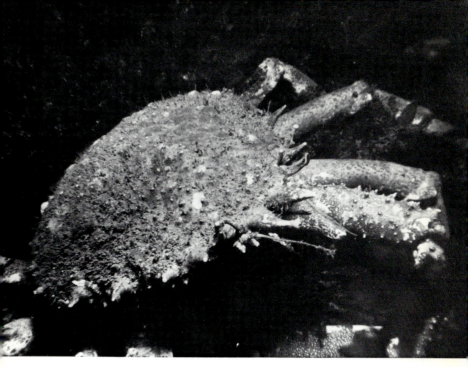

15 SPIDER CRAB [*Maia squinado*] Swanage, Dorset (*Geoff Harwood*)
Depth 10 ft Exa Flash *f*11 Ektachrome-X

16 BABY LOBSTER [*Homarus vulgaris*] Newhaven, Sussex (*Tony Baverstock*)
Depth 30 ft Calypsophot + close-up Flash *f*22/125 Tri-X

117 SEA URCHIN [*Echinus esculentus*] Land's End
Depth 40 ft Exa Flash *f*16/60 Plus-X (*Geoff Harwood*)

118 SPINY STARFISH [*Marthasterias glacialis*] Harlyn Bay, Cornwall
Depth 6 ft Bronica Flash *f*16 Tri-X (*Peter Scoones*)

119 DIVER [*Homo aquaticus!*] and
Turtle [*Chelonia mydas*] Malta
Depth 25 ft Calypsophot
*f*11/125 Plus-X (*Philip Smith*)

120 FEMALE DIVER [*Femina
aquatica!*] Giglio, Italy
Depth 20 ft Agfa Flexilette
*f*5·6/125 Plus-X
(*Geoff Harwood*)

At first, when the water cleared of the bubbles from our backward-roll entries, it seemed that the gulls were right. Twenty feet below was a flat weed-covered uninteresting seabed. Sand patches here and there looked hopeful places for flat-fish, but that was hardly the object of the exercise.

Penny and I finned after John and his brother, Robin. And then it happened. One minute you were over weed, the next the weed stopped and you were dropping over the lip of a sheer wall and down to a ledge some 15 ft below.

Looking back up you could see the flat fronds of laminaria marking the edge of the Hole. The fronds hung down only a few feet and underneath this, a wall of grey clay had been undercut by the tide.

But the ledge on which we hesitated was only the beginning of the Hole. From here down into the limit of misty vision was a steepening slope. It runs down, in fact, to nearly 80 ft before meeting the floor of the sea.

Every hole in the slope—and it seemed as though a monstrous home handy-man had been trying out his gigantic drill all over the surface—contained a crab. This cratered moonscape allows no weed to grow.

In one of the holes though, as I drifted down, was a brown mass as though some monster fist had stuffed it full of weed. I hesitated. It seemed so out of keeping with the rest. But then the answer to the puzzle swam into view. A female cuckoo wrasse with weed in her mouth brought fresh supplies for her nest. She poked and prodded the new material into place. And thrust at me aggressively as I looked closer.

What chance would she have when the eggs were laid of raising her brood? I would guess at practically none—from every crack, cranny and crevice stared the black eyes of edible crabs and the red eyes of the swimming kind.

I took some pictures but the light was very poor (when developed they were hardly worth keeping) and so I slid on . . .

We have dived the Hole many times since. In the spring, when the tides are right and you can dodge the Mixon race, lobster and crab are well up on the steep walls of the Hole, a crumbling moonscape of clay.

Go there again as summer fades into autumn on a day when the wind carries a touch of winter's approaching bite and you'll have to drop deep down into the depths of the Hole to find the slightest sign of lobsters or crab.

With the coming of winter the shellfish obviously move into deeper water. Yet any diver making his first visit to the Hole in autumn would say that you have to go jolly deep before there is anything of the slightest interest.

Obviously it is no good the diver making a report—and drawing any conclusions from it—unless he has dived the area at all seasons.

Incidentally, it was a series of dives on the Mixon that convinced us that lobsters—and possibly crabs—feed on seaweed if nothing else is available. The stomachs of some of these shellfish were completely full of green material. And the words of Bernard Rogers, a diving friend in Cornwall, came immediately to mind. He said: 'If you think about it, how often is it likely that a lobster finds a dead fish? How often do you see a dead fish on the bottom? To feed all the lobsters that fishermen catch in their pots the seabed would have to be carpeted with dead fish at least once a month!'

He believed that lobster, crayfish and crabs ate seaweed. His idea was ridiculed by professional lobster-pot fishermen. Yet it is quite clear that he is right.

Not only were the stomachs of shellfish found on the Mixon completely crammed with green material, but it was also clear that unless they fed on each other all the time—and possibly at times they do—there was not enough fishy food in that crumbling grey clay ravine to feed one, let alone all the shellfish which made their home there in the spring.

Yet there is no seaweed on those grey slopes even though it grows in profusion on the seabed above the sheer lip that marks the hole. Was that what the shellfish were doing high up in the spring? Do they stock up on green vegetables early in the year before sinking down to a more lethargic life in the depths later on?

It is this sort of question that the diver alone will be able to answer as the years go on. No surface-bound marine biologist will find the answer to that sort of question in the contents of a net tipped on to the deck of his boat. Nor will he ever find out the true colours of any living undersea creature unless a diver has been down to photograph it in its real surroundings.

This loses none of its importance because British waters do not contain many highly-coloured creatures—though the cuckoo wrasse in courtship is beautiful and the cuttlefish can go one better.

When the cuttles are mating, then they throw all their normal caution to the waves. Usually when seen underwater they blend in perfectly with their background and, if alarmed, jet off very rapidly showing instantaneous changes of colour as they pass over different colourations in the seabed. But at mating time both adopt a striking zebra pattern.

Cuttlefish (PLATE 96) are not normally extremely difficult to approach and photograph, but the photographer must be prepared for them to shoot away suddenly. However, when they are mating they seem completely oblivious to the diver and give the underwater cameraman the distinct impression of being a Peeping Tom.

It is difficult to say exactly what other marine creatures any diver will associate with the background to his own dives. Certainly in British waters, the background will be one of swaying weed, starfish, deadmen's fingers (PLATE 104), mussels, crab, lobsters, anemones, whelk shells, and sometimes the beautifully marked blue-rayed limpets clinging to the upper fronds of laminaria forests.

Closer examination will make the diver believe that the encrusting yellow of the breadcrumb sponge covers nearly everything.

He will see that here and there in season the spawn of the sea lemon makes yellow ringlets on the rocks, that sometimes the winkles and limpets are a solid surface on the walls of some underwater ravine. That sometimes the sea hares (PLATE 114) or big-eared sea slugs mate on the bottom before their brief life is over.

In the Mediterranean the background changes once again. Here the diver will be conscious of the many-spined black sea urchins everywhere. On the seabed below him are the obscene shapes of sea cucumbers.

The underside of rocks are covered with blood-red sponge-like growths. And sea-squirts (PLATE 100), sea-fans and the flower-like white pavonia are almost everywhere.

And though some surface swimmers might like to think that the octopus is an unusual sight—one extraordinary article recently said that the octopus was rarely seen except at night—the truth is of course that the octopus is a common part of the daytime Mediterranean background (PLATE 97). And Med divers regard him or her with something approaching affection.

The octopus rarely measures more than 1 ft across with tentacles reaching out from the 'soup-plate' of the body to 3 ft. Yet Bernard Heuvelmans in his book *In the Wake of the Sea Serpents* says 'Even the largest octopuses in the Mediterranean have never been more than 25 ft across or weighed more than 130 lbs.'

This sort of size might account for stories that divers tell of certain areas in the Mediterranean—the reef off Tamariu in Spain is an example—where the divers say whole sections of the seabed move and great eyes frighten the underwater photographer out of his wits.

This, thank goodness, is not part of the normal background!

The octopus is a highly intelligent creature and as interested in the diver as he is in it.

John Lythgoe notes that very often octopi select their 'nesting sites' on a rising piece of seabed so that—in the words of the human house-agent—they 'command extensive views over the surrounding countryside'.

The octopus generally builds a little wall of shells and pebbles round his home and from this looks out on the underwater world. Unfortunately, these walls betray them to the experienced eye.

This is not to say that you will not find an octopus out in the open. They do seem to travel at certain times, but when approached will jet their way to the nearest rock shelter.

Make no mistake about it, octopi are inquisitive creatures, and the only time that they can be watched in a state of nature, interested in nothing but themselves, is when they are copulating. This process can go on for several hours with the pair perched side by side.

It is a particular feature of the octopus that the choice of nuptial couch is the depth where the water changes sharply from surface warmth to the colder temperature of the deeper water.

This boundary is often abrupt and it is possible to put your hand through from warm water into the cold water with your fingers in 'ice' and your wrist in the warmth.

It seems an extraordinary sexual arrangement. One octopus stations itself in the warm water; its mate in the colder water below. With such eight-armed creatures one can only suspect that the octopus Kama Sutra undoubtedly extends into several volumes!

In warmer waters, there is no doubt about the real background to it all—the coral (PLATE 105), twisted into a myriad shapes, dominates everything.

It is, however, one of the thrills of diving that the unexpected happens all the time. The trouble usually is that the underwater photographer is often caught by the unexpected.

However ready he may have been for strange encounters at the beginning of his dive, it seems to be a rule that when his camera jams or he is out of film, then into sight comes the shot of a lifetime.

Phil Smith says about this: 'Nine times out of ten the unexpected catches you unprepared. To increase the chances of this happening try leaving your camera behind. Then you will see that school of dolphin, that inquisitive seal, that giant unknown fish.

'Yet it doesn't always work this way. On one of my diving

holidays in the Mediterranean off the coast of Malta, I was fortunate enough to encounter a sea turtle—and I had my loaded camera with me (PLATE 119).

'It is amazing the power that even a small turtle can produce in his own element. We found that if you clutched him firmly on both sides of his shell you could be taken for an underwater ride of at least one turtle power. After thirty minutes of photographing the turtle sculling about the sea towing various divers behind him, we felt that he had earned his freedom. Our last sight of him was as he moved into deep waters, relieved at last of his unwanted riders.'

And so it goes on. The list of marine creatures that a diver will associate with his dives is almost endless. And each dive may lead him to something completely new.

Man is said to have come from the sea. Now he returns to it. Which must make the latest associated marine creature—from the fish's point of view—MAN (PLATE 120).

KENDALL McDONALD

CHAPTER FIVE

Freshwater diving

Though this book is mainly about the sea and fish, it would not be complete without some recognition of another field of fish-watching and photography. This takes place in fresh water—in lakes, rivers, ponds, even streams.

Many of Britain's divers live far enough from the sea to make regular visits there something of a safari. But they live close to sizeable amounts of fresh water and spend considerable periods of time beneath these surfaces.

This diving is, like the greater amount of diving in the sea, bringing to light a great deal of new knowledge—in this case about freshwater fish and life of all kinds. And our knowledge up to now of the way freshwater creatures behave has been even more skimpy than that of marine life.

Take that much fished-for 'monster' which is reputed to haunt every puddle in the British countryside, the pike (END PAPER). Like the conger in the sea, the stories of the pike's ferocity are part of the line-fisherman's life. Divers preparing to enter waters that are known to hold pike have often been solemnly warned by onlookers to 'be careful of the monster pike'. And there is no doubt that the warning was truly meant.

For has not the pike been observed to take ducklings, pulling them beneath the surface with little more than a widening circle of ripples to mark their end? Has not the pike even been credited with pulling adult moorhens to destruction the same way?

This sort of pike behaviour is not in doubt. These acts were observed by naturalists and carefully documented. Though the story of a pike swallowing the head of a swan and drowning it is open to considerable doubt, the pike would seem to be a considerable menace to the wild-life of any stretch of water that he inhabits.

Would he then attack man? Well, a pike of 47 lb 11 oz, the British record fish taken from Loch Lomond, is several feet long and a thick powerful fish. Perhaps he might—if he was as ferocious as legend has it.

But the truth is that there is only one report of a diver being attacked by a pike—in the Norfolk Broads—but the diver concerned stated at the time that he believed the fish was only striking at the flashes of sunlight from the underwater watch that he wore on his wrist.

Divers have now completed many hours' underwater in pike-bearing lakes and ponds. No other instance of aggressive behaviour has been reported—aggressive behaviour, that is, that involves an actual attack. The divers' experience of pike cover all seasons.

For example, John Lythgoe was once trying to measure the light that penetrates through water and had decided to carry out his experiments in a very clear freshwater lake (or rather large pond) in Norfolk. He describes what happened like this:

'It was a freezing December day with a fine cold drizzle coming out of the usual North-east wind. Plunging in with an unwieldy device, I was at once surrounded by an impenetrable cloud of fine silt and little floating pieces of sedge. I also got tickled most intimately with the released marsh gases—possibly an interesting situation had it not been so cold.

'Obviously delicate measurements were out so I left my apparatus on the bank and paddled off round the lake to have a look. I had made three-quarters of a circuit and there seemed to be nothing much about except a snail or two and some weed. Then the knife which was strapped to my leg snagged on a reed; turning to release it, I came face to face with two huge pike each hovering and watching me with their pale yellow eyes.

'As I turned, they turned too, until realising that this new and noisy fish was even bigger than themselves, they sidled off and eventually swam out of sight. I visited the pond several times after that and each time saw pike. Once they were chasing small roach back and forth amongst the weeds, snapping their jaws. Even now I am not sure if I heard their teeth or just imagined it.'

My own first experience of pike came when, thanks to Allan Chambers and the other members of Coventry Branch of the British Sub-Aqua Club, Colin Doeg and I were allowed into a huge lake for which they hold the diving rights.

It was a hot day in early June when the dive took place and I really didn't expect to see any big fish despite the stories of huge pike and giant carp with which we were regaled on our sweaty climb down to the water. Full wet suits and aqualungs are not the perfect gear for this sort of land exercise.

The water was cold at over 50 ft, but quite warm near the surface. And it was near the surface, coming up from the green 'aquarium' weed that carpeted the lower slopes of the lake, that I saw my first living pike.

I was looking up to the same silver screen of surface that you see on a similar ascent from a sea dive. And the pike was a still dark shape against the silver surface. Closer, you could see his fins paddling slowly against his deep body. He was just outside the place where the roots of the reeds that ringed the edges of this part of the lake sank into the soft ooze of the lake bed.

Once having spotted one, I began to see others. They were all in shallow water and the best way to find them was to look hard at the point where the dead weed and other debris floated up to the edge of the reed bed. They always seemed to be hanging about a foot below the surface. And the first few all seemed to have the same markings—a mottled brown with darker speckling and barring. Then I noticed that the larger ones seemed a paler colour with markings that were almost white.

Now I had not the slightest idea about how a pike would react to a diver. Of course, the other divers who had told us about the pike did not seem to be afraid of them, but no one had actually asked outright if they would attack.

Well, the pike did not attack me, but I must say I was impressed by the way that they didn't seem the slightest bit afraid of me.

They would hang very still, just those fins paddling slowly away to hold them in position as you came closer and closer. They seemed curious about you, but the eyes were cold like congers'.

When you got within touching distance they would glide slowly away. Some fish don't like turning their back on you in a situation like this, but not the pike. He would present his tail to you, contemptuously it seemed, though you were still being watched in a sort of over-the-shoulder way.

This turn-tail attitude was infuriating. I was trying to take pictures and each time you got really close all you saw in your viewfinder was a tail. I began to evolve a technique for dealing with this. I found that if you swam outside the fish—between him and the open water—he would turn into the reeds and when about a foot inside this cover, again hang motionless in the water.

The barring on a pike's sides provides very good camouflage in this position. So good that if you take your eyes off one for a second you won't spot him again. And they seem to be able to slide through the close-packed reed stems without disturbing them in the slightest.

Once the pike was in this position in the reeds, it was often possible to part them and manoeuvre the camera gently into position. Slowly and gently was the key to the whole thing. Any swift movement would send the fish shooting away through the reed bed and then there wasn't the slightest hope of finding it again.

While parting the weeds to do this on one occasion I gave myself a real fright. As I pushed the reed stems out of the way of a clear view of one pike, I came face to face with another, which had chosen almost the same hiding place as the one I was trying to photograph. My fingers must have brushed his nose. For a moment we stared at each other eyeball to eyeball—so close that I found difficulty in focusing my eyes on that lethal-looking nose —and then he slid away.

Only twice have I seen a pike take aggressive action—if it can be interpreted as that. Once was when I was photographing a 'baby' of a foot long. This one was letting me pull weed out of the way all around him and even lift a small branch of a dead tree under which he was hiding. As I did so, something made me look over my shoulder at the open water behind me. And there was a real 'monster' almost white in colour and fully three feet long speeding towards me.

Of course he may not have been bent on aggression, but was merely interested in what was going on. However, my violent reaction—I must have jumped about a foot—sent him away very fast.

John Lythgoe has a good idea of the reason for that big pike's interest. He says: 'One way I found to photograph pike came as the result of my clumsy changing of a flash bulb. This usually seems to involve wallowing all over the bottom, fishing out the new bulb from some recess, burning your finger on the old one and digging out bits of glass from the socket. The result is, naturally enough, an opaque cloud of silt and detritus.

'In fact the cloud is quite small and there is a crisp edge between the cloudy and the clear water. Coming back on one of these clouds on one occasion I found there were three pike hovering in the clear water and staring into the cloudy. I suppose they thought that some Drama of Nature was being played out inside and there was likely to be food. These clouds of disturbed mud frequently attract pike and after a while I deliberately turned up the bottom to bring them in.'

Well, when the big pike came at me I was certainly stirring up the bottom by moving that tree branch, so perhaps that is the explanation.

The second occasion on which a pike made a threatening move came as I manoeuvred the head of the flash-gun to within a few inches of a large pike's nose.

Suddenly put his head down and bucked at it. 'Bucked' is the only word for it, for he looked for all the world like a stallion pawing the ground before charging. He bucked not once, but twice. And then fled when I moved the flash gun in even closer. If the flash gun had carried a polished reflector, I should have said that he was challenging his own reflection, but the cup of the Nikonos flash is satin-finished.

Incidentally, pike do not seem to be worried by the flash-bulb going off even if it is right in their face. They still hang there, mouth closed, but with pectoral fins fanning all the time. They behave rather like sea wrasse in their long unhurried swings in and out of weed.

The long nose is very prominent underwater as is the thickening of the fish towards the tail fin. Incidentally, this tail fin looks just the power supply it obviously is.

The acceleration of a frightened pike is amazing—from motionless to disappearance among weeds is literally impossible to follow.

John Lythgoe, too, has found photographing pike difficult. 'Pike,' he says, 'are one of those fish that always seem to present a three-quarter profile to the camera with the head pointing away. One technique that sometimes works is to spot a pike on the bottom, then swim round in a wide circle so that you come up to him head-on after making the approach run from as far off as possible. Then the pike takes a little time to paddle his body round clear of the bottom and, if he doesn't dart off in a panic, he works his way round Zeppelin-like and you can get a good head and side view.'

We have still a lot to learn about pike underwater. They justify the 'devil in the lake' type of stories because they look sinister. They look sinister underwater. Perhaps more so there because though quick movements will frighten them off, other sights and sounds that must be unusual to them do not.

Aqualung bubbles do not seem to worry them, nor does panting through a snorkel tube—nor the bright orange of a lifejacket. They give the impression that they know that little will hurt them (fishermen's hooks excepted)—that they are the kings and queens of the lakes. And they undoubtedly are.

Pike are, of course, only one of the species that divers see and study on their freshwater dives. I have chosen to describe meetings with pike because they typify the sort of excitement that divers can find in inland waters. And they are a species about whose behaviour underwater, despite all the fishing books, little is known.

Here, as in the sea, more and more diving is needed. More and more observation is required. More and more needs to be written about the way fish behave when they are at home underwater.

In this book we have made a start. We have, however, if you will forgive the expression, only just scratched the surface.

KENDALL McDONALD

CHAPTER SIX

Dangers

There are dangers in the underwater world. But they are not always the dangers that will leap immediately to the non-diver's mind.

Ask a non-diver what he would think would be the greatest danger in going underwater to watch or photograph fish and he would almost certainly reply—Sharks.

Well, sharks do certainly count as one of the dangers, but they do not usually present as great a hazard to the underwater photographer as other much more commonplace things. For example, though it sounds like gross carelessness, one of the main dangers to the underwater photographer is that he will run out of air at depth.

Air

This can happen when he becomes so engrossed in taking pictures of some photogenic subject that he forgets that he is dependent on the supply of air from the cylinders on his back. It is only when breathing becomes tight and difficult telling him that his air is almost exhausted that the diver-photographer is forced to become aware once again that he is in an alien environment.

It shouldn't happen, but it does. Fortunately as the diver rises back to the surface he will, as the pressure lessens, be able to get one or two more breaths from his near-empty cylinder.

But the length of time that a diver can stay underwater depends not only on the size of the cylinders of air he has on his back or on the depth at which he is working. If he is working hard, he will use up more air at whatever depth he is.

And if he has been some time at depth he may well need to decompress below the surface for a given time on his ascent. For this reason the diver-photographer cannot afford to take the risk of running out of air at depth. If he does, though he may well be able to reach the surface, he will not have enough air for decompression and then runs the risk of the crippling (or in severe cases, fatal) diver's disease called 'the bends'.

What can an underwater photographer do to avoid running out of air?

The answer really is that he should resist the temptation to hang on for just one more picture. It is easier said than done. The best solution is to train himself to use a contents gauge with his aqualung—and to look at it regularly as a check on the amount of air he has left.

Danger: Running out of air. Action: Check your air supply at all times.

★   ★   ★

Cuts

Another underwater hazard that will hardly have entered the landsman's head is the danger of cuts.

Because of his interest in fish the photographer will be bound at some time or another to work in and around wrecks or rocks.

Wrecks are a particular menace to the hands of a diver. Though underwater it seems the most natural thing in the world to reach out and grasp a piece of wreckage to steady yourself before taking a picture, the result can be disastrous.

Wreckage is honed to a razor's edge by the action of rust and decay. So sharp are these edges that you can cut yourself seriously —to the bone—without even noticing that the damage has been done. Rocks, too, carry sharp marine growths which can cut in the same painless fashion.

Many a diver at depth has only become aware that he has cut himself badly by noticing a strange green stream coming from, say, his hand. Blood then looks green due to the lack of red light penetrating to the depths.

The diving-photographer is particularly prone to this sort of injury because of his dislike of gloves, which, he feels, will hamper his use of the camera's controls. (It is probably not necessary to stress that a release of blood of this kind into the water will attract sharks.)

But the diver-photographer who refuses to wear gloves on these grounds is either using a camera with controls that are too small or is unaware of the fine pliable five-fingered neoprene gloves that E. T. Skinner now market.

Danger: Cuts. Action: Wear gloves.

Treatment: Cleaning the wound should not be necessary as the sea should have cleansed it. But obviously if it is dirty or contains pieces of rust, clean it up. A big cut that is going to need stitches should be wrapped in a clean cloth. But any cloth within reason will do provided it is thoroughly rinsed in sea-water. Tie the cloth tightly round the wound to stop bleeding. If it is not possible to get to a doctor quickly—or if the wound is small—use an antibiotic cream on it. As a precaution, carry a tube of aureomycin cream in your first-aid kit.

★　　　★　　　★

Wrecks

As we have already mentioned wrecks, do note that there is a danger in going inside any wreck. If you have to go in, use a lifeline so that you will be able to find your way back through the silt that is bound to be stirred up.

And bear in mind that there is always a danger of collapse of any structure that has been in the sea for any length of time.

Danger: Trapped in a wreck. Action: Use a lifeline. Better still don't go in.

★　　　★　　　★

Overweighting

Another danger which may arise from the photographer's obsession with getting good pictures is that of overweighting.

The underwater photographer does this so that he can maintain a reasonably stable position on the seabed while taking pictures. The ordinary diver, if he is sensible, arranges his weights so that he is neutrally buoyant—that is so that he can rise or fall dependent on the amount he breathes into his lungs—at the depth that he intends to spend most of his time underwater.

Overweighting brings obvious problems. It is all right to be overweight in shallow water, but if the dive leads into deeper water, then the diver who is overweight will find, at least, that he is bumping all over the bottom and stirring up unwanted sediment with each contact with the seabed. He will also find that he has to swim that bit harder to reach the surface on the termination of the dive.

There is only one way in which the diver-photographer can ensure that he is sufficiently weighted to stay on the bottom and take pictures without running the risk of being so foolishly overweight that the return to the surface is a ghastly struggle. And this is to use a compressed-air lifejacket.

With such a lifejacket the diver can bleed off air from the small compressed air cylinder that these lifejackets use until his buoyancy is adjusted to the depth.

Danger: Overweight. Action: Buy a lifejacket of the Fenzy type and take a course in how to use it. These jackets do need training in their use. Incorrect use could lead to a high-speed ascent which might kill the diver.

★   ★   ★

Lifejackets

All these dangers do exist. But it is important to realise that emergencies of the kind envisaged here should not catch the diver unawares if he has been fully trained on a British Sub-Aqua Club course. Such dangers and their avoidance are stressed during training.

But emergencies do happen. I can remember a dive for red coral in Spanish waters that started out as a happy care-free expedition, but which could have ended in tragedy.

The entry in my logbook is short. It reads: 'Formigas Islands. Maximum depth: 100 ft, duration 35 mins. Visibility 50–70 ft. Rock bottom. Strong current South-west. Coral hunt. Large wreck.'

And as I look across the room to a large spray of precious red coral, I remember why that entry was so short. I remember the fear that came into me during that dive. And the things that went wrong. . . .

We set off early. At least, early by Spanish standards, from the little port of San Feliu de Guixols. Eight a.m. was the meeting time, but we finally got away by nine. The boat was old, but big—at least 22 ft if my memory serves me right. And the engine was one of those thump-thump Spanish jobs that goes on for ever. This, mind you, was in the days before coral diving was forbidden without special permission from the Spanish authorities.

We lolled in the early morning sunshine as the boat headed up the coast. I say 'we'—one Belgian, four English, and one Spanish diver of great experience—but I don't then include the two-man Spanish crew. I suppose you could call the journey to the Formigas uneventful—if you forget a momentary panic when the engine cover caught alight due to the exhaust stack becoming red-hot. However a good bucketful of Mediterranean blue soon put a stop to that.

The dive started strangely—the Spanish captain refused to stop his engine and we all had to jump into the sea as he circled the islands.

I remember being a bit perturbed about this, but thought no more about it in the excitement of the chance of finding coral down below. We soon had a casualty though. The Belgian had to be shoved aboard on the next circuit of the boat because his demand valve refused to supply him air below the surface. And then the boat, still with engine working, steamed off and left us.

We all found our coral, but I got separated from the rest; my ears wouldn't clear quickly enough to keep up. Imagine a vast bowl of sight—like swimming in a vast aquarium. That was the visibility in the Formigas. I was alone and I let the current carry me through the vast underwater complexes of the islands. I felt lonely, but happy. I cruised along some 20 ft down, confident that the boat would soon be round to pick me up.

It was then that I saw my first barracuda. The first one I have seen in the Mediterranean and I hope my last. A big, long silver fish, he had what I can only describe as a great evil grin on his face as he cruised happily—for him—just a few feet below me. (If anyone is doubtful about the presence of this fish in the Mediterranean, they should see the pictures taken by Captain Ted Falcon-Barker of barracuda schools near Ibiza.)

I have never felt so alone as I did then. But finally, to my great relief, he went away. I found a rock that enabled me to stand with my head just above the water and waited for the boat to pick me up. And waited and waited. By twisting round I could see the yellow shapes of lifejackets all over the sea behind me. The other divers had finished their dive and, like me, were waiting for the boat.

But the boat didn't come. And the lifejackets and divers drifted farther and farther away. Anyone who thinks of the Mediterranean as a sea without currents and tides should have been with me then. When the farthest diver was just a yellow speck on the horizon the boat appeared. But to my horror, instead of the steady thump-thump of the engine, it was moving silently and as slowly as it is possible for a boat to be driven by the vast sweeps that passed for oars on a boat of that size.

Finally it got close enough for me to swim to it. I was in a right panic now—not for myself, but for those who floated in life-jackets almost out of sight. When I finally got aboard and demanded in my bastard Spanish for explanations, I was told that to start the engine we needed a blow-lamp—to heat the top of the cylinder and explode the engine into life. The blow-lamp they had, but the paraffin for it, not a drop.

Was there no paraffin at all? The whole expedition got stranger and stranger. There was no paraffin on board, but, just by chance, a man in a small fishing dinghy nearby had got some. 'But he's a robber,' they said, 'he wants ten pesetas for a small bottle!' Rather than pay this exorbitant sum our crew, it seemed, were prepared to row all the way back to San Feliu (about ten miles).

If I had known the words I would have said them. The only coin I had was a 25-peseta piece and the fisherman in the small boat got this for his paraffin.

Then, with the engine started, we picked up all the divers. And never have men been so glad of obeying the rules and wearing lifejackets. All the way back the crew grumbled among themselves about the way I had inflated the price of paraffin around the Formigas Islands. But all I cared about was that we were going back with the same number of divers as we had when we set out.

Danger: Not being picked up quickly by the diving boat. Action: Wear a lifejacket on every dive.

★   ★   ★

Diving alone

The classic rule of safe diving says thou shalt not dive alone. This is sense and all divers believe it. It should be observed at all times. Having said that, there are few things more infuriating than a partner of dirty habits.

He will rush around stirring up the bottom. He will point out the fish that you have been carefully stalking and frighten it away. He insists on being included in every photograph. The temptation is to turn off his air supply, but the moderate diver-photographer will change partners to a diving photographer who appreciates what's going on and keeps clear, but near.

The truth is that to be an underwater photographer you must

be an experienced diver. A person to whom existence underwater has become an almost automatic technique.

You must be able to cope with all the demands of ordinary diving and still have enough in hand to cope safely with all the added camera equipment. For however compact that equipment is, it will still hinder movement to some extent and diving with cameras must be planned properly.

To cope with all this in his local waters, Tony Baverstock has evolved a special shallow water technique. It breaks the rule, but only just. The photographer goes in with a safety line tied to the boat. He has up to 300 ft of line on a compact reel which is carried by a loop around his wrist. As he swims away—into depths not over 40 ft—the reel unwinds with the line passing through his fingers. In this way he can feel a signal or series of tugs from the boat.

The limit of the dive is the extent of the line. The return to the boat is made by either winding oneself back or leaving the reel and swimming back along the line.

'This is just permissible,' says Baverstock, 'in shallow water. In deeper water, I never dive without a partner. In all cases there is a standby diver on the boat ready for emergencies. And of course the condition of the sea affects the method we use.

'Only in conditions of calm when the expired air bubbles can be seen from the boat do we use the reel method. And we have used this method safely and reasonably successfully for ten years. Lifejackets are always worn and the Fenzy with its separate bottle of compressed air for inflation is the one we choose to wear.

'But there is really no substitute for the safety afforded by a diving partner. I remember a time when I came badly unstuck. It was on a dive to 90 ft. A wreck was located by shore marks and echo sounder. The anchor was dropped and, because I was diving officer, I dived to check that we were indeed on the wreck. We were, near enough. I surfaced and then with my diving partner and camera went down again. This time we took with us a lead line which we attached to the anchor chain before swimming over to the wreck paying out the line as we went.

'I became engrossed in photography. First a lobster and then a conger. So much so that I didn't notice I was getting low on air until my breathing started to get hard. I signalled to my partner who was on the line four feet behind me and we turned round to follow the line back to the boat's anchor. We stirred up the silt and by the time we reached the anchor the visibility was nil and I was so low on air that breathing was really difficult.

'And then it happened. I couldn't move—and I couldn't see what was holding me. In fact the lead line had snagged on the wreck and around the flash arm of the camera. I couldn't see. I could hardly breathe. And there was 90 ft of water over me.

'However with the assistance of my diving partner, I managed to jettison camera, aqualung and weight-belt and did a very swift and very free ascent to the surface.

'I regained the boat in a grey, ashen and considerably shaken state, but was rapidly cheered by a large gin and water and the recovery of all my equipment by the other divers on board. My last activity on that trip was to dive and free the anchor—and to recover my nerve. Having done this, I thought how nice it would be to have another gin, and also to wonder how gin got on the diving boat.

'No one would confess to having gin aboard. The mystery was solved, however, when a kind lady member of the Club told me that she had administered the well-known treatment for shock—sal volatile in water!'

Danger: Snagged up. Action: Never dive alone.

Treatment: Always carry a knife. If snagged by fishing net or line, don't panic, keep still and cut yourself free.

★   ★   ★

Jellyfish

Jellyfish are usually not so much a danger to the diver as the bather. For one thing the diver can often see the jellyfish before coming into contact with the tentacles—though some of the more venomous forms have an incredible spread of fine 'stingers' in the water around them. And the diver is usually wearing at least the top of a wet suit in all but the warmest waters and this protects a great deal of his body from the stings.

But even so, the sting of a jellyfish should not be underrated. It can be severe enough to raise great welts on the skin and cause unconsciousness possibly leading to death.

Danger: Jellyfish sting. Action: Avoid being stung.

To do this, don't forget to keep an eye open in mid-water or on the bottom for jellyfish. It is a popular belief that all jellyfish float along the surface and it is wrong. At certain times jellyfish seem to want to keep out of the full sunlight and will home onto a diver as a source of shadow.

Treatment: Remove all tentacles in any way possible. Sand and seaweed will do as wiping agents if nothing else is to hand. Avoid rubbing broken tentacles on to fresh portions of skin or fresh stings will result. Swabbing with alcohol or baking soda in water may help. An old sailors' remedy may help too.

This is simply to soak a cigarette in a little seawater and to rub the resultant mess on to the affected part. It will take out the sting from some jellyfish 'bites'. Cortisone cream may help. In severe cases get a doctor quickly.

★   ★   ★

Sea urchins

Sea urchin spines are a danger that most divers take as an occupational hazard. Sooner or later the diver who is intent on getting close to some fish will accidentally brush against the spines of an urchin and get some imbedded in his flesh. They are incredibly sharp and will penetrate wet suit or fin heels with diabolical efficiency. Can cause a nasty wound if struck with force.

Danger: Sea urchin spines. Action: Almost impossible to avoid at some time or another, but try.

Treatment: Pull out as many as possible with eyebrow tweezers or pliers without breaking them off in the flesh. Clean with antiseptic. Will usually work themselves out in time, even after months. If infection starts, see a doctor.

Note: There seem to be some sea urchin spines which produce much more violent symptoms—swelling, aching, burning pain, irregular pulse. If any such symptoms appear, seek medical attention at once.

★   ★   ★

Sea anemones

At the risk of making divers nervous of everything underwater, it is only right to say that there is a slight danger in the colourful sea anemone. While skin is normally tough enough to provide the perfect defence against the minor stings of the sea anemones' tiny tentacles, there are tender areas of the body where such a sting can have an effect. Examples of these tender areas are the edges of the lips, the lips themselves and the inside of the mouth.

Surely no diver is going to go around kissing sea anemones no matter how beautiful they are?! Of course not, but it is interesting to note that my daughter, Joanna, did get a badly swollen and sore lip as a result of being touched there by an anemone's tentacles.

We were playing a game while snorkelling in the Mediterranean. She had just started to enjoy snorkelling and would dive down and place a small pebble into the 'mouth' of one particular anemone. As soon as she had popped it in, I would dive down, take it out and give it back to her . . . and so the game went on. It seemed an innocent way of improving her skin-diving.

But on one occasion when I dived down and pulled out the stone I must have pulled away a few tentacles too. These floated in the water and drifted against her mouth. She felt the sting, but took little notice. Two days later she had a large septic sore on her mouth. And it took several more days to go down.

Danger: Stung by a sea anemone. Action: Keep tentacles away from tender skin.

Treatment: Ask a doctor for a suitable cream to apply.

Note. In many instances in this chapter for further treatment (or immediate treatment in urgent cases), it is suggested that you consult a doctor. It would be a wise precaution for those planning to dive in strange areas to make sure that they know where the nearest doctor is.

In most cases a small first-aid kit will be sufficient to cope—indeed many expeditions spend days at sea or travelling without having a resident doctor with them—but it is better to be safe than sorry.

In a strange or foreign town it is sometimes difficult to follow directions given quickly especially by locals to those under stress or in pain. So make sure you know where to find a doctor before you start diving.

★　　　★　　　★

Octopus

Octopi have a story-book reputation of holding divers down until they drown. This is extremely unlikely as octopus rarely grow to a size that would make this sort of incident even faintly possible. But some danger does attach to a bite from the beak of even the common octopus. It can produce bleeding and swelling.

Danger: Bitten by octopus. Action: When touching even small specimens avoid beak area.

Treatment: Control bleeding if heavy. Get to a doctor.

★　　　★　　　★

Stings

Stinging fish do present a danger. Weevers, scorpion fish, stone-fish, lionfish and sting-rays all can cause intense pain and such a

175

wound must never be treated as anything but a serious emergency. This is because nobody reacts to the venom in an absolutely identical way. The onset of pain may be immediate—it may be delayed as much as ten minutes.

Danger: Stung by a fish. Action: Know your fish and keep well clear of these stingers.

Treatment: Clean the wound and apply heat. This should be done by getting the injured part into water as hot as can be borne. Be careful not to scald. Get medical aid quickly. Vomiting, fainting and sweating are likely to occur very soon after the diver is wounded.

★ ★ ★

Sunburn

Sunburn is not the sort of danger you would expect the average diver to be exposed to. But divers do spend long periods wearing a wet suit and then strip off for a 'few moments' in the sun. As they are not accustomed as is the average holidaymaker to tanning gradually, broken by intervals lolling under an umbrella on some tourist beach, the diver does frequently get a touch of sunburn as a result of a short period of pure thoughtlessness spent on some rocky point or boat deck.

Danger: Careless sunbathing after a dive. Action: Sunbathe sensibly.

Treatment: Apply Calamine lotion thickly or some preparation like 'Aftersun' over the affected area. In severe cases see a doctor.

★ ★ ★

Oxygen

There is one danger which comes from the use of the wrong equipment. Some people who want to approach fish very closely feel that the aqualung with its noisy exhaust bubbles has often spoiled their chances of getting really in among the fish. When they feel like this they cast glances at the oxygen rebreather system that was used by the wartime naval frogmen. This apparatus, it is true, does not have any noisy exhaust, as the air is recirculated with the deadly carbon dioxide being taken out of the system by chemicals.

But the trouble is that the pure oxygen used can itself become toxic only a few feet down, leading to convulsions and death. Some famous pioneer divers have been lost through using this equipment.

Danger: Oxygen apparatus. Action: Don't use it.

★   ★   ★

Sharks

And finally the danger from sharks. And let us be quite clear about it at the beginning—no shark is safe. They are completely unpredictable and action that will scare one away may well cause another to attack.

Despite all the research that has been done recently on shark attacks, there is no sure method of frightening them away.

Screaming at a shark underwater will, it is said, frighten some away, but not all. Shark repellents do not work. The only safe shark is a dead one—and then take care that it is really dead, not stunned.

In tropical waters—there seems *some* evidence that a shark is more inclined to attack in warm water—divers would be well advised to carry a shark billy with them whenever they are in the water. (A shark billy is a wooden pole with a metal tip or an all metal rod and photographers could make this double as a measuring stick.)

Attacks on skin divers are not numerous, but such attacks generally seem to be associated with spearfishing. It has been known for ages that blood in the water will attract sharks and so will the struggling noises transmitted by a speared fish. So the diving-photographer would do well to stay away from areas that are being spearfished.

And this advice does not just hold good for tropical waters. As you will have read elsewhere in this book, shark attacks are recorded in the Mediterranean. But they are not frequent enough to warrant the diver there carrying the ultimate weapon against sharks, which is now often employed in tropical waters.

I refer to the 'bang-stick', which is really a twelve-bore shotgun cartridge mounted on the end of a rod. This is pushed against the shark's head and the action of pushing forces the firing pin against the cartridge cap. The resulting explosion will kill a shark outright in most cases, but only a head hit is sure to be fatal.

It is easy to say, but the worst possible thing you can do if you appear to be in danger of becoming the object of a shark's attentions, is to panic. Try to keep your back to rocks or form a back-to-back link with your diving partner. This will at least give you a chance to beat off any attack with stick or camera. A good bang on the nose with a camera housing has been known to frighten off a shark. Move smoothly and quietly away if the shark does not come in close and get out of the water as soon as possible.

Danger: Sharks. Action: Get out of the water as soon as possible. Never take chances with any shark.

Treatment: Any shark bite victim will suffer from shock and probably from great loss of blood. Apply tourniquet. And get to a doctor fast. The chances of recovery of the victim of a severe attack will depend on the speed that medical aid is obtained.

KENDALL MCDONALD

PART TWO

Photography

YOU HAVE TO START SOMEWHERE

The very name 'conger' has a fearsome ring to it and I well recall the first time I saw and speared a conger eel underwater. I had gone to Dancing Ledge on the Dorset coast with a few spear-fishing friends from the Bournemouth Branch in the early summer of 1955 and we entered the water expecting to shoot a few mullet or bass.

After snorkelling for a short while, I was suddenly startled to see a blue-grey shape sinuously twisting its way through a large clump of thick brown kelp. For a few moments I watched fascina-ted at the elegant ease with which this eel swam through the apparently impenetrable weed stalks, disappearing one moment and reappearing in a different spot a yard or two further on.

I mustered up a little courage and, drawing a deep breath through the snorkel, dived down towards the unsuspecting creature, harpoon gun outstretched in front of me. I then com-mitted the basic error of shooting the conger halfway down his body; the spear went well and truly home, but then the trouble started! There is really only one way to shoot a conger and that is just behind the head either from above or from the side. If anyone does, as I did that first time some fifteen years ago, shoot a conger in the side of his body, the fish will writhe and twist with tre-mendous muscular power. It can easily bend the shaft of a steel harpoon, possibly breaking free in the process.

With mild panic setting in, I swam for the rocky shore towing the enraged conger at the fully extended length of my harpoon line. My diving buddy, swimming nearby and seeing some com-motion in the water, joined me on a rock. We hauled the still fighting fish out of the water and attempted to administer the coup-de-grâce with a knife. To this day, I can still see that conger's head turning and twisting, his eyes apparently following every move of the knife blade poised above.

That bungled beginning to my acquaintance with congers tended to enhance for me the evil reputation this much maligned eel has. Over the years, however, having seen many hundreds of congers underwater, I have found that far from being the fearsome creatures they are made out to be in angling books, they are shy retiring fish and quite harmless unless actually speared, when they can do considerable damage to an unwary hand.

However, despite this familiarity, my heart still misses a beat at the sight of a gold-rimmed eye the size of a penny sunken into a head like a terrier dog, staring out from the darkness of a weed-shrouded wreck. A pair of rubbery white lips and a slate blue thigh-thick body complete my mental picture of a 30-lb conger eel. Perhaps it was the very nature of the beast and his hostile appearance that challenged me to bring back some good under-water portraits. And so I bought my first camera, which was the highly versatile amphibious Calypsophot.

My first results were, to say the least, disappointing. Either every frame was completely blank or there were only some faint ghost-like images located at the bottom of the negatives. It was obvious that flash illumination was going to be the only way to penetrate the Stygian blackness of the conger's lair. So I progressed to a Rolleimarin, and with it more sophisticated lenses and flash equipment.

This still left problems, for it was difficult to see into the gloom on the Rollei's ground glass focusing screen and so ensure a sharp subject. After much trial and error I found one successful method was to locate a conger and attempt to lure him out of his home with a freshly speared fish such as a pout whiting which are usually available in profusion near most conger holes.

Once I had gained the fish's confidence, and I must confess first overcome my own uneasiness, the camera would be lined up and the flash arm removed and placed either to one side or resting on the sea bed at the entrance of the conger's cave. Often the big shiny reflector would prove too much for Mr Conger's curiosity and he would stealthily glide out to investigate. My best results were obtained by setting the camera lens to its closest focusing distance and, keeping as still as possible, wait for the subject to move into sharp focus, all the time viewing the image on the camera screen. Pop! The brilliant flash of a bulb momentarily penetrated the blackness causing the fish to recoil violently. This was the usual reaction of most congers, but there have been some I have photographed that totally ignore the brief flash and continue to stare out with bland unconcern.

The techniques I learnt from photographing conger eels I then applied to other slow moving or stationary marine creatures, and as my method of off-camera flash improved, I began to look for other ways of adding a little impact to underwater photography. I decided to experiment with the use of coloured filters over the flash reflectors.

I approached a local plastics manufacturer and asked him to cut a series of coloured Perspex discs which slotted into three lugs welded on to the aluminium reflector to hold the filters in place. The Perspex had to be as thin as possible, but the colour had to be strong and I chose a vibrant red to start with, as the seas around our coasts tend to be lacking in red.

Whilst the idea was all right in theory it was a little difficult to implement in practice. The amount of light absorbed by the filter necessitated the use of a more powerful bulb, and it was difficult to place the second flash head with the coloured disc in the correct position for maximum effect whilst at the same time judging the correct exposure for the main unfiltered light source on the camera. What invariably happened is that one or other of the bulbs would fail to fire and I would be left with either a faint red glow from one side or a bright white flash from the other.

I can well remember spending over forty minutes wedged underneath a rock ledge in the middle of Kimmeridge Bay trying to get a close-up shot of a pout whiting using the two flash system. I am convinced that if fish possessed a sense of humour, this particular pouting would have had a good belly laugh at my expense. It was ludicrous. I was lying prone on the sea-bed, some ten or more pounds of extra lead ensuring that I didn't float up out of position, my head firmly lodged under this overhang of rock and equipment in the form of light meters, reflectors, spare bulbs etc., strewn all around me. Every time the poor little fish poked his nose out there would be a flash and then an ensuing struggle on my part to remove the filters, replace the bulbs and re-position the reflectors.

While all this was going on the cheeky little chap would swim sublimely up and down in front of my mask expressing an acute interest in all this frenzied activity. The moment I was ready to shoot again, all I would see would be a tail disappearing into some inaccessible crevice. Understandably, I rather treasure the one and only respectable photograph which resulted from this rather fraught session of underwater photography!

PHILIP SMITH

OBJECT LESSONS

Ideally an underwater photographer should live within sight of the sea, have a nice flexible job that allows him to work in his stuffy office while the gales lash and the rain comes down, and nip off for a dive any time the weather looks good.

He should have a fully equipped workshop and darkroom for use on those blowy-rainy days when he isn't required to work for a living, and he should have limitless knowledge of optics, engineering, photography, diving, seamanship and marine biology.

Unfortunately my own circumstances fall a little short of this. My nearest salt water is the River Thames. I work weekdays, have to book holidays weeks ahead and always pick the worst weather. My fully equipped workshop is still a lovingly marked-out area in the garden awaiting the blessing of the Borough Surveyor. The darkroom is only dark when it's dark outside. As to knowledge, I read what I can.

So I have to make the best of it. I really do enjoy making gadgets. And designing underwater cameras provides a wonderful source of problems just asking to be solved by such gadgets. If a psychoanalyst was to try and find out why I spend so much of my time diving he would probably deduce that I dive to experiment with the gadgets and perhaps to find any little fault with the whole system which will give me the excuse to go home and make some more gadgets to get around the trouble.

Eventually perhaps, I shall have a system which can tackle any possible subject underwater and guarantee a perfect result every time. I've got a long way to go and many more square yards of half-inch Perspex will be consumed before I get anywhere near that.

So now you know my driving force; trial and error is my modus operandi. When I started in underwater photography, there wasn't much in the way of literature on the subject and trial and error was the only way. Luckily a scientific education had taught me to keep records of my experiments, including the unsuccessful ones, so progress in the early stages was rapid. After a couple of years and my fourth camera (an Agfa Flexilette 35-mm Twin Lens Reflex) I was getting some fairly decent results. Then I started really looking at subjects underwater and working out modifications to the camera and technique, and came up with some rules to help ensure better and more consistent results.

Perhaps a few anecdotes will help to illustrate the problems and the lessons learned from them.

★   ★   ★

Setting: Anchored near the Eddystone lighthouse on a beautiful calm day. Beneath the boat, a gigantic shoal of large grey fish.
Action: The fish were all so large and closely packed that my first thought was to obtain a few for supper before the dive. Without bothering to don a wet suit I borrowed a speargun and slithered into the water. It was an unbelievable sight. I was literally surrounded by 2-ft long bass milling around like knights in shining armour within a few feet of me. I took careful aim at a large specimen who was particularly close. Schpoomph! The spear sped through the imperceptible gaps between the fish in the shoal. This was repeated a few dozen times before it occurred to me that I stood a better chance with the camera. The shoal seemed amused by my antics and made no attempt to move away. But by the time I had gone back to the boat, loaded up the camera, kitted up and gone in again there wasn't a fish to be seen.
Lesson: Photographs first, dinner afterwards. I still haven't managed to get a recognisable picture of a bass.

★   ★   ★

Setting: The remains of a Mulberry harbour sitting on the bottom in about 15 ft of water off Pagham, Sussex.

Action: A conger eel eyes me from his home under a pile of pieces of broken concrete. He is too far back in the hole for a reasonable picture because my flash head is on an arm above the camera. I want him much further out, preferably showing his teeth in a threatening manner. I signal to my buddy to find the other end of his hole (underwater photographers soon develop an uncanny system of conveying instructions underwater!) This results in both ends of the conger withdrawing into the hole, presumably by some sort of folding in his invisible middle region. Further efforts to attract him out by offering him tasty flippers etc. have no effect whatever, and by this time the silt is stirred up and so we leave him to it.

Lesson: Take an insurance shot first before you try persuading any fish to do something he doesn't want to. At least you'll have some sort of picture.

Tailpiece: A spearfishing type went down after we finished and nailed our conger. When he got home late Sunday night he put it in the fridge. The following morning his mother nearly had a heart attack when she opened the fridge door and 6 ft of slimy conger slithered out and lay twitching at her feet!

★   ★   ★

Setting: The tiny island of Ras Garib off the Egyptian Coast in the Red Sea. The chart shows sundry soundings around 100 ft enclosed by a vague dotted line. Just outside the dotted line the nearest sounding is 6,000 ft.

Action: The felucca crew tossed the anchor (a piece of bent scaffolding pole tied to a length of thick but very woolly looking rope) overboard, and the boat pulled up to a stiff tide. Bearing this in mind, I decided to leave the cine camera behind and just take the Flexilette and Nikonos, the former with Kodacolor X for flash shots in the deeps and the latter with Tri-X for available light.

We went in and made a brave attempt to go down the anchor line, but eventually let go and got down to the friendly bottom where we scrambled hand over hand into the tide towards the cliff edge which we could just see over a hill. Occasionally a hand hold would turn out to be the soft squashy breed of coral instead of the hard stuff and we would go sailing backwards and demolish a swathe through the fine porcelain type until a firm hold came to hand.

When we eventually arrived at the cliff and looked over the edge we felt like fledgling seagulls contemplating their first leap off Beachy Head. The chart was dead right! The cliff was absolutely vertical and was patrolled by fish which defy description. There were shoals of 'jacks' each about 6 ft long (PLATE 91). Groupers as big as horses and unicorn fish with bizarre horns sticking out of their heads swam by in shoals.

I was so awestruck that I was frozen to the spot and it never occurred to me to take any photographs until my air was beginning to tighten and I was suddenly jerked to my senses. I had to take some pictures if only to prove to myself that it had really happened. If only I'd taken the cine camera. If . . . If . . . .

Lesson: Try to develop an imperturbable nature. Remember that a memorable dive is only a memory without photographs!

★   ★   ★

Setting: The wreck of the freighter *Heliopes* sunk in 140 ft of water in Mounts Bay during the First World War.

Action: I was trying out my very latest camera and another diver had borrowed my previous effort, the Agfa Flexilette in fact. Well, as every diver knows, 9 minutes is all the time you get at 140 ft. unless you're working from a shot line and can do decompression stops. As inevitably happens on this type of dive an interesting souvenir was spotted after about 7 minutes' browsing among the boilers and engine room machinery. The villain of this piece parked my old camera on a convenient hook and set to work to dig out his find. At $8\frac{1}{2}$ minutes I remind him that it's time to go back to the sunshine. He looks around him and a panic-stricken expression streams into his mask which conveyed to me that the camera and hook were no longer where he'd left them. Below the place was a big black hole leading into a big black boiler.

The next day we went back and spent 8½ minutes finding the boiler again. On subsequent trips we haven't even found the wreck.

Although by now the housing can't be expected to be still supporting 70 odd p.s.i. it would be jolly interesting to find out what has happened to it since August 1965. It is in the starboard boiler and I suggest you take with you a 10-ft pole with a hook and a torch on one end.

Lessons: One, don't park your camera on the bottom, carry it with you on your arm by a short loop if you want to keep both hands free. (A neck strap always gets in the way and keeps the camera in exactly the wrong place, between you and what you're trying to do.) Two, don't trust the strength of anything on a wreck, especially an old wreck. Three, don't cancel the insurance on your retired camera even if you don't think you'll be using it any more. Someone is bound to want to borrow it to see if they like it enough to buy it from you.

★   ★   ★

Setting: Swanage Piers on numerous occasions over the past few years.

Action: There are two piers at Swanage, one is an old wooden structure more or less in ruins and the other is a 'new' one made mostly of concrete. They both offer some of the best fish-watching territory in Britain and they could hardly be more convenient for divers. Bob and Dennis Wright have a fully equipped diving centre within feet of the water, with compressor and equipment hire facilities and it is possible to park cars on the actual root of the pier.

Underwater, although the visibility is not usually as good as it is further out to sea, it is normally quite good enough to see what's going on and to get some really good photographs. Apart from occasional plaice, pollack, weeverfish, scorpionfish, pipefish, sticklebacks and what-have-you, probably the most entertaining fish are the spotted dragonets. They are incredibly common and there is one place at the foot of the old pier on a sandy bottom where dozens of dragonets congregate. They are a photographer's delight because they sit still most of the time eating the sand, picking out the tasty bits and ejecting the unwanted bits out through 'holes' in the backs of their heads. It's true—I've a photograph to prove it!

On one occasion I decided that it might be an idea to try feeding dragonets with those lovely juicy ragworms they sell on the pier for anglers' bait. This idea led to a highly entertaining dive. I put the worms in a plastic bag and leaped into the water. The dragonet patch was full of dragonets as usual, so I unpacked a worm and the fun started. Ragworms seem to be such docile creatures when they are wrapped in newspaper in a handful of sand. Get them underwater in their natural environment and they go beserk. They wriggle at unbelievable speed and unless you are a bit nimble in catching them they take a flying dive into the nearest patch of sand and are gone. This vital experience gained, I went and found a patch where the sand was a bit more compacted, and difficult to wriggle into. The next worm merely squirmed about on this in frustration, and a dragonet spotted it. Focusing on the worm, I watched it carefully through the viewfinder, ready for a series of studies of the ensuing meal. Suddenly there was a brown blur and the dragonet, with the worm as long as itself in its mouth, was a couple of yards away.

I tried again, this time with the worm pinned down with a stone. The result was the same except that the dragonet only got half the worm. Next time I kept one eye on the nearest dragonet and the other on the worm in the viewfinder. I pressed the shutter when I first saw a movement in the dragonet. The result was a picture, frozen by the electronic flash, of the dragonet at the moment of snaffling the worm. It wasn't in the middle of the picture, but we were getting somewhere.

Another fairly common fish under the piers at Swanage is the pipefish (PLATE 19). An odd character who seems as if he hasn't really worked out how to swim. He appears a little bit heavy and has just enough power in his dorsal and pectoral fins to haul himself along if he considers it really essential. Another photographer's fish because he can't get away. If you find him in an unsuitable place, you can always pick him up gently and move him to a more suitable setting. His little beady eyes and long inquisitive-looking nose are always good for an amusing picture. *Lesson:* You don't have to go on 'hairy' dives all the time to find interesting fish; some of the best hunting-grounds are the easiest places of all to dive in. Also, in shallow water you have enough light for photography and time to get to know the inhabitants.

★   ★   ★

Setting: St Abbs, Berwickshire, amongst the rocks within a hundred yards or so of the harbour entrance.

Action: We had heard reports of a lonely or maladjusted porpoise who teamed up with divers in the area of St Abbs, a spot much frequented by divers from Scotland and the North of England. We decided that although the chances of meeting the porpoise would be pretty slim, the diving should be pretty good in any case, otherwise the area wouldn't be so popular. While we were chugging out to our first dive in our inflatable boat, what should appear but the famous porpoise, following us out. When we got into the water the porpoise joined us, and I felt a little of the awe that had struck me in the Red Sea.

He was so big. He looked big enough on the surface, but underwater he looked enormous due to the magnification of the water. It was a little difficult to be quite convinced by all the tales we had heard of his harmlessness, as he was obviously quite capable of eating any one of us in a couple of mouthfuls. His grace of movement and acrobatics made me wish I had his shape and power. He rolled over on to his side and offered us his belly. I thought about scratching it, for that is what he seemed to want. I decided against it just in case that wasn't what he wanted at all.

I took a few pictures in the gloom as he swam overhead, and

when he next came in close I plugged in the flash for a portrait. When the flash went off there was instant turmoil, and we found ourselves 20 ft from where we were previously and a great tail was beating into the distance. We never saw him again on that dive.

Lesson: Although some fish are absolutely undisturbed by flash, it seems on the basis of this one experience that the porpoise, being a mammal and not a fish, was very much affected by the sudden light. The next time I meet a porpoise (or seal for that matter) I shall get as many shots as I can by available light before trying a last one with flash, just to see whether the St Abbs porpoise was an isolated case—nervous, as well as kinky enough to prefer divers to its own kind!

★   ★   ★

Setting: A tiny cove between the Yealm Estuary and Stoke Bay, South Devon, after a mighty struggle down the cliffs with all our gear on a hot day.

Action: This is a real picture-book cove. About 20 yds wide and 50 yds long with 20–30 ft of water near the sides and a sharp spine of rock running up the centre reaching to within 10 ft of the surface. The water was quite clear and we were having a pleasant ordinary dive when I spotted a cuttlefish, apparently asleep on the bottom. I really went to town on him, taking pictures as fast as the electronic flash would charge up. At first he lay there, gently changing colour. When I found him he was an exact replica of the little patch of sand, but as I watched and photographed, bands of stripes appeared and slowly spread over his body. Then he gradually lifted up off the bottom and glided slowly along the gully by a beautiful sinuous movement of the frill around the bottom of his body. We followed him, and I took pictures with every conceivable background. By the time I was down to my last few exposures he had had enough, and raising two of his tentacles in a defiant gesture, he sped off under jet propulsion.

I emerged from the water secure in the knowledge that in that little cassette were 30-odd shots which had been taken with as much care as it is possible to give—if I didn't have a winner, it wasn't my fault! I continued to think that until I developed the film. It had some beautiful negatives on it, but also had a series of dark patches. The reason slowly dawned. I had spooled the film from a tin of bulk film which I had found in a cupboard at work and which was no longer needed. As I developed my pictures I realised with horror that the film had been exposed before. A technician had exposed a whole roll, torn off a small length for a test process, found it was underexposed and repeated the test. Someone must have rescued the tin from the waste box.

Lesson: The cost of a good fresh roll of film in the maker's original packing is very small when you compare it with all the other costs of diving. Luckily this was no further away than Devon, and some of the shots were relatively unaffected. But I can imagine how I would have felt if it had been the film I took on my once-in-a-lifetime trip to the Red Sea. Don't take risks with film.

★   ★   ★

I could carry on with anecdotes like this ad infinitum. In fact one learns something new on every dive—but it all boils down to the same thing: *learn from your mistakes.* Talk to all the underwater photographers you can and learn from their mistakes as well. It's cheaper, and as by now most of the mistakes have already been made by someone somewhere, there is no point in repeating them. It is amazing that even now, people seem to start from square one, in spite of all the pioneering that was done years ago. So if you're just starting out in underwater photography, meet as many experienced underwater photographers as you can, buy them all a pint (it's worth it!) and let the anecdotes sink in.

A word of warning though—be wary of any advice given or tales told in the few weeks that come before the closing date for any major underwater film competition. Then all the underwater photographers are trying to do is to throw a smokescreen over the secrets of their proposed entries!

GEOFF HARWOOD

CHAPTER SEVEN

Basic Equipment and Technique

Although underwater photography could hardly be described as an ancient art, there is already so much photographic equipment on the market which is suitable for use underwater, that the beginner must take advice before buying.

Mistakes in buying camera equipment are usually costly ones. With land photography, even if you buy a camera or accessories that are not exactly suited to the circumstances, you can still get acceptable results. With underwater photography, however, the wrong equipment is useless.

Most people do not realise the vast differences there are between taking pictures on land and underwater. Obviously, underwater you cannot see as far as you can on land. On land, for example, when visibility is reduced to 50 yds because of fog or mist, warnings are put out on the radio and the hazard lights begin to flash on the motorways—and any photographic club faced with these conditions would cancel their planned outing.

Yet when you plunge down into the underwater world, you will hardly ever find visibility as good as 50 yds. It is just possible that you will be able to see that far in some particularly warm sea's waters, but you will be lucky if you can see more than 30 ft in any direction on an average day in British waters. On land this is the sort of visibility that would have you driving at a snail's pace and probably thinking of abandoning your car. But it is the sort of sight bowl in which underwater photographers regularly —and happily—work.

However, there is no need to be discouraged by such conditions. In fact, in that sort of visibility the underwater photographer succeeds in taking excellent pictures of fish and marine life.

And it is worth stressing right away that you are unlikely to spend a great deal of time photographing the 'monsters of the deep'. Of course, big fish will come your way and let's hope that you capture them on film, but a great deal of your photography will be concerned with fish of quite ordinary size.

This is no drawback at all. Small common fish are perfect subjects for your camera. Indeed, fish, regardless of size, make some of the most superb natural history photographs that anyone could wish to see. And some underwater photographers spend almost all their time on a dive trying to capture in close-up the delicate colours and movements of very small fish.

Vast areas of the sea, even the shallows close inshore are virtu-ally unexplored. And only the camera can bring back an accurate and useful record of the marine creatures, large or small, at home there. In order to do this, the underwater photographer's equip-ment has to be suited to the conditions and the land photographer has to adapt his surface techniques to meet the difficulties of taking pictures down below.

The problems are both physical and optical. Cameras don't like water—so it has to be kept out. The sea exerts pressure on both the diver and the camera—at 100 ft the weight of water is equivalent to having a small car balanced on the camera housing. Optically, the general lighting conditions are poor compared with land. Furthermore, suspended particles in the sea reduce definition and quality.

So to get the best results you have to get your camera really close to your subject. The idea is to get as little sea as possible between camera and target. A wide-angle lens helps here because basically it enables you to take the same picture that you would with a standard lens . . . but from a much closer distance.

Refraction adds to your problems. This is the name given to the way light bends when it passes from one substance to another if their 'refractive indices' are different—and those of water and air definitely are. You can see this for yourself if you thrust a straight stick into water. The stick appears to bend at the air/water interface although you know that it is straight.

This happens underwater when you look through the air gap in your face mask into the sea. Everything appears to be either a third larger or a third nearer. This is no problem as amphibious cameras and cameras in underwater housings normally look out through portholes which have a similar air gap. And there is no problem about focusing and composition—the camera with a flat porthole sees exactly the same thing as your eye does. But the fact that the object is actually further away than it appears to be does make it even more important to get as close as possible and so reduce the amount of water between lens and subject.

These differences between land and underwater photography are the reason that your choice of equipment must be absolutely right. This is particularly true when photographing fish.

Fish are a real challenge to the photographer. You have got to get down into their natural environment. You have got to get your camera close to them. There is no substitute for getting close—and it's the same whether you are photographing a basking shark as big as a lorry or a dragonet about the size of a teaspoon.

On land, of course, it is easier. If you don't want to go right up to an elephant or you can't get close to a mouse, you merely fit a telephoto lens to your camera. Underwater you can't do that. The telephoto lens is not usually suitable because you get too much water—and suspended matter—between the lens and the fish and so the quality is spoilt.

But before you choose your equipment for working underwater, you have got to decide about the kind of pictures you plan to take—do you want to work in still or cine?

It is best to begin with a still camera unless it is vitally important that you get results that show actual movements of fish—behaviour studies or research into fin action would, of course, require cine film.

For the ordinary person, the still camera is best. This is because to start with you do not need elaborate equipment. And you can select only your most successful pictures to show people.

If you start with cine you may well find that a whole sequence is ruined because a portion of it was incorrectly exposed or composed. Still film often can be given special processing to 'save' it when some of these mistakes occur. Similar treatment of cine stock is not so easy. And there are more high-speed films available for still camera work than there are for cine use.

Now to the right kind of still camera for photographing fish. The right one need not be expensive—it might cost as little as £5. Or it might be short-sighted to spend less than £500.

Your choice is determined by two main factors. First—where are you going to take most of your pictures? Will you be spending most of your time in the fine conditions of the Mediterranean, Red Sea, or tropical waters—or in the poorer visibility of more Northern waters?

Secondly—what standard of results do you want? Will it be sufficient to produce a selection of Enprints—or do you want superb marine biological illustrations?

The answer to those questions is either a modestly priced simple camera or an expensive sophisticated piece of equipment. A modest camera will produce acceptable results if used in good conditions.

A sophisticated outfit will be more versatile—it will focus closer and have a better quality lens—and so will produce good results in poorer conditions. The difference between the cameras becomes more dramatic when you bear in mind that one of the general rules of underwater photography is not to take pictures from farther away than a quarter of the distance of visibility.

For example, if you are working in visibility of 120 ft you will get good results at up to 30 ft and superb quality with subjects much nearer. But if the visibility drops to 10 ft, you won't get much of a result with a camera that can only focus down to 5 ft. In that sort of visibility you need to get to within at least 2 to $2\frac{1}{2}$ ft.

Still cameras

If you intend to begin modestly the best advice is to buy a *Kodak Instamatic* or something similar. They cost about £5 to £10 (later on we'll tell you how to make a housing for one for less than another £5).

These cameras will produce good results in good conditions and acceptable pictures in British waters provided you realise their limitations.

They do not focus particularly close so, except in the best conditions, it is advisable to fit a close-up lens. At present only the slower speed films are available in rapid-load cartridges for these cameras, so you must seek well-lit areas either by going abroad or remaining in shallow water.

A different start to your underwater photography could be made by buying an amphibious camera such as the Siluro, or for the more ambitious, the Nikonos, or Rolleimarin.

The *Siluro* is a box camera which has been fully waterproofed. It was obviously designed with Mediterranean conditions in mind because it will only focus down to 5 ft. In fact the focus is not adjustable, nor is the speed setting. It is really more of a fun camera than an instrument for the use of the serious underwater photographer, though some excellent pictures have come from the Siluro even in British waters by using the flash gun which is part of the outfit. Complete with flash it costs nearly £30.

The *Nikonos* is a better buy if you can afford it. This is regarded by many divers as the ideal, all-round underwater camera. It was developed from a camera designed by the pioneer of modern aqualung diving Captain Jacques-Yves Cousteau and one of his colleagues.

The Nikonos is a normal-size 35-mm camera with all the conventional controls. It is waterproof down to about 160 ft. It is extremely easy to use, both on land and underwater and is so small that it can be taken on every dive whether you intend to use it or not.

The price of the Nikonos (later models are called *Calypso-*

Nikkor or *Nikonos II*) is about £135. There are various accessories available, including a reliable flashgun for bulbs, and different close-up and wide-angle lenses. If you can't afford a new Nikonos, then go for a second-hand one at about £70–£80.

A cheaper second-hand alternative is the Nikonos's predecessor, the *Calypsophot* at about £30–40, but remember that this camera is no longer in production and that, at some point in time, spares will become a problem.

The *Rolleimarin* is for the photographer who wants the improved quality that comes from the larger negative ($2\frac{1}{4} \times 2\frac{1}{4}$ in.) Rolleimarin is the name given to an outfit made up of the Rolleiflex camera and a housing developed by Hans Hass, another pioneer of modern diving, whose specialist field was underwater photography.

The complete outfit costs about £500, but second-hand models can be obtained for as little as £100/£200. This is because the unit has now been on the market for twenty years.

There are four versions of the housing, each designed for a different series of the camera. So it is important, if you buy one second-hand, to get the housing first and then a camera to fit it. Buy a second-hand camera first and you may find it impossible to track down a suitable housing.

The Rolleimarin is widely used. Nikonos addicts say that swimming with it is like having a small dustbin hanging round your neck, but the fact is that more award winning pictures have been taken with this combination than by any other underwater outfit.

As the years have gone by, various modifications have been made to the housings and the latest, the Mark IV, has an arrangement to enable close-up lenses to be moved in front of both the taking and viewing lenses while underwater.

Without doubt, despite its age the Rolleimarin is still the best-designed of all the underwater housings. It will be just as widely used as it is now for many years to come.

However, the Rolleiflex camera itself has two disadvantages for underwater use. The wide-angle lens model will not fit into the housings and there is always the possibility that in use you might not notice that the taking lens is obscured by weed because the viewing lens is a short distance above the lens taking the picture. You do, of course, run the same risk with the Nikonos when looking through its 'gunsight' viewfinder.

Single Lens Reflex Cameras

Now the single lens reflex (SLR) cameras. They have a number of features which particularly suit them for underwater work. You can fit a variety of lenses, including wide-angle ones which will focus extremely closely. And, most important, with these cameras when you look through the viewfinder you are in fact looking through the lens so you see exactly what it will take. This is a great advantage when taking close-ups.

Provided you can afford to support these sophisticated cameras in the manner in which the manufacturers intended, there are several available.

The most widely known is the *Hasselblad* outfit, which costs upwards of £500 for case and camera—depending on the lens and type of body. Other accessories add even more to the bill.

The 'Hassel' has the advantage that the camera has been available for a considerable time and, therefore, the camera and its accessories are widely stocked and items can be hired if required for only a short period. The housing itself is produced by Hugy-Phot to the exacting standards that one would expect from equipment for the Hasselblad, but its design could be improved.

Setting up the camera to go into the housing is a laborious business and the outfit is not easy to use underwater. The control knobs do not come readily to hand and the viewing screen is dim. We understand a new housing is being developed, and no doubt attention will be given to these points.

New lenses have been added to the Hasselblad range, but none focus as closely as one would like for underwater photography, particularly in Northern waters, without the addition of a supplementary lens. This is limiting. They have to be fitted before the camera is inserted into the housing and you cannot switch to them underwater. But despite this criticism the Hasselblad does of course take magnificent pictures.

A 'best buy' in this price range of cameras is the *Bronica*. It is well-suited for 'boxing up' and it has the important advantage that its wide-angle lenses will focus from infinity to a few inches by a single twirl of the control ring. This makes the camera extremely versatile, though the shutter is inclined to be noisy.

A metal housing is available in Britain from Tony Dixon (*see* Appendix 3) and there is also an American one on the market. You could, of course, make your own.

There are a number of other $2\frac{1}{4}$-in. square single lens reflex (SLR) cameras available that are worth considering for putting into housings.

The most versatile of all is the *Rollei SL 66*. At £650 it is also the most expensive. But it will focus down to 1:1. There is no regular housing available. Those in use are custom made.

More modestly priced $2\frac{1}{4}$-in. SLR cameras are being introduced.

The *Kowa 6* looks particularly promising. Its shape would fit the Rolleimarin style of housing and it might even be possible to modify such a case to take one.

If you wish to have the advantages of the SLR camera at a quarter of the big format price, then there is a range of 35-mm models available. For these, there are many wide-angle lenses—some of which will focus very close indeed. However, with the smaller negative you cannot expect to produce pictures that will 'live' alongside those from the bigger cameras unless you are an exceptionally meticulous worker.

But before you decide to put any camera into a housing—having one specially made or making your own—you should realise that there are only two justifications for doing so.

One is if the total cost of camera-and-case is less than the price of a Nikonos or a Rolleimarin. The other is if your completed outfit will produce facilities for picture taking that are not available from a Nikonos or a Rolleimarin. Box up a camera for any other reason and you are wasting your money.

Cine cameras

An exception to this rule comes when you are dealing with a cine camera—there just are not any amphibious models manufactured, so all have to go into housings.

For home viewing and showing to small audiences, the Super 8 cameras produce excellent results and beginners should start their underwater filming with one of these models.

You will have little trouble finding a housing for these cine cameras. There are ranges of Perspex cases and metal housings including one from Aquasnap for the Kodak Instamatic and other simple cameras.

The combination of Eumig Vienette and Hugy-Phot housing is a good one, well designed, easy and pleasant to use.

The 8-mm cameras are in fact ideal for putting into housings. If you choose one with a fixed focus lens, automatic iris and electric drive, it means that only one control is needed, the shutter release.

There are no 16-mm or 35-mm cine cameras with similar features in commercially available housings although a 16-mm outfit is being developed. The housings for these wider gauge cameras are heavy and bulky, although, of course, they do become easier to handle in the water due to their buoyancy. Long-run magazines and special lighting systems have been developed for these cameras.

Probably the best-known 16-mm cine camera is that manufactured by Bolex—and with its Bolex housing it is the standard underwater outfit used by professionals. The camera will take a particularly wide-angle and close-focusing lens. It sells for about £200, but second-hand ones can be bought for about £100. To this, of course, you have got to add the cost of the housing (about £300).

Film shot for professional purposes is 16-mm or 35-mm. This is not to decry Super 8 as long as most of the underwater scenes are shot in close-up. But the professionals demand a quality of which Super 8 is just not capable.

The drawback to using the wider gauge is, of course, the fact that the cost of the equipment and the film soars upwards as the negative increases in size. One compensation for this extra cost is that both 16-mm and 35-mm film can be 'pushed' to compensate for under exposure or poor contrast, whereas the same facilities for Super 8 are difficult to find.

Film

The basics of underwater photography have been described in a number of excellent books (*see* Bibliography). However both fish photography and the techniques of working in poor visibility require a more expert approach.

Most books recommend that you begin by using the slowest film that conditions will allow. This is all right as far as it goes, but the slowest suitable film for Northern waters usually happens to be one of the fastest available—Tri-X (400 ASA) in black and white and High Speed Ektachrome (160 ASA) in colour positive! You cannot blame the authors of these earlier books for this—it is the tremendous improvements in film emulsions in recent years that have made their books out of date.

In their books too they were not usually talking about photographing fast-moving creatures like fish, but usually some pastoral underwater scene composed of a few starfish and anemones.

Another reason for using these fast films is that you are unlikely to be photographing a fish that has not already noticed your presence. The fish will be alert and suspicious. Its movements are likely to be quicker than normal. And the light may well be poor.

In order to stop rapid movement you need a fast shutter speed. Rarely less than 1/125 and often you need to shoot at 1/500. In order to work in poor light you need to give adequate exposure. And, in order to show something of the fish's environment, you need to use an aperture of at least $f/5 \cdot 6$ in natural light. So you must go for a fast film.

If you have the facilities to develop your own, begin with

Tri-X. It has tremendous latitude and if needed its speed can be boosted by extended development.

It is fast enough, for example, to get quite reasonable results in 140 ft of water off the coast of Britain. And just as a matter of interest for those non-divers who ask so often: 'But isn't it cold and dark down there?'—light has been observed from one of America's deep-diving submersibles at over 1,000 ft below the surface of the Mediterranean.

If the thought of having to process your own film fills you with horror, then don't add to your problems—work in colour. Colour film has many advantages over black and white, but it also has limitations that must be understood if you are to have even reasonable success.

Firstly, as a general rule, colour transparency film can only be given one exposure—the correct one—to give a good result. And only one kind of processing to produce a good result—the right one.

Thus there are fewer margins for either error or experiment. Either your transparency will be good or it will be poor. There isn't likely to be any half-way stage. So you have to be more accurate. But the rewards of correct exposure and correct processing are, as far as portrayal of the underwater scene is concerned, far greater than the same scene in black and white.

Exposures

Accuracy of exposure also becomes a matter of prime importance if you use those slower films that older books write about—unless the lighting is so good that you do not have to sacrifice shutter speed and aperture for the added quality that you can get out of a slow speed emulsion. The alternative, of course, is to take your own artificial light with you in the form of bulb or electronic flash. This is a technique that we will deal with at length later on.

At this stage we will deal with natural light techniques only. Stating the obvious—the most important thing is to expose the film correctly. But underwater this is often easier said than done.

Some people find it easier to talk underwater than they do to hold an exposure meter!

Underwater we must use the reflected light method with our meter. Readings by incident light are just not satisfactory. But all picture taking does not have to stop because you haven't got an exposure meter with you.

The correct exposure can be estimated by working from the following table, which is for clear British waters (visibility over 30 ft; 10 metres) and for both colour and black and white films rated at 64 ASA using a shutter speed of 1/60 or 1/50 second. The table assumes that the time is the middle of the day and that the sun is shining.

Depth	Over light sand	Average and in open water	Over dark rock or weed
Down to 2 ft (0·6 m)	$f/16$	$f/11$	$f/8$
5 ft (1·5 m)	$f/11$	$f/8$	$f/5·6$
10 ft (3 m)	$f/8$	$f/5·6$	$f/4$
20 ft (6 m)	$f/5·6$	$f/4$	$f/2·8$
40 ft (12 m)	$f/4$	$f/2·8$	$f/2$
80 ft (24 m)	$f/2·8$	$f/2$	$f/1·4$

In conditions such as the Red Sea of course, less compensation is needed with depth because of vertical sun and light seabed.

But there really is no effective substitute for an exposure meter, especially in murky waters. For the proper way to use an exposure meter and the right kind to buy, see Chapter Ten.

In any case, if you are a beginner, it is best to straddle your exposures—take alternative shots at one and two stops either side of the indicated setting in order to 'fail safe'.

As your experience grows you will find it unnecessary to take so many pictures on alternative settings. But the professional is not too proud to do the same thing when he wants to be really sure that he has an exciting scene or important picture locked safely into his camera.

In other words, when in doubt, take lots of pictures and play safe. The sea changes every day and that fantastic scene may never come your way again—even if you live to dive forever! It is amazing how many photographers, especially when they are learning, fail to follow this elementary rule. It may be adequate on land to take only one exposure of the North wall of that interesting church. It will never be sufficient to take just one picture of a fast-moving wild creature and then expect to have captured the most immortal natural history picture of all time.

If you are taking up underwater photography there are other reasons to indulge yourself a little with film. You are recording a new and exciting world. You cannot know how many of the subjects you see have been recorded on film before. Think about it. Is it likely that there are hundreds of shots of that fish in that position in that situation?

The truth is, of course, that though at times magazines are full of underwater pictures—or seem to be—the quantity of under-water pictures in existence compared with land subjects is very small indeed. So use up a bit of film—you may well be able to sell your pictures; at least you will be contributing to man's know-ledge of an unexplored wilderness.

Another reason for using more film than a land photographer is that the effects possible with underwater photography are still largely unknown. Not unnaturally, many people shy away from this technique on the grounds of cost. And shooting a lot of film is, of course, more expensive.

No one can afford to blaze his way through miles of film unless he is fortunate enough to be a millionaire. But you do have to decide which you would rather do—use this technique to ensure that when you have a good subject you produce an excellent result? Or be mean with film and hardly ever have a picture worth the paper it's printed on? Put that way, it is obvious what your answer should be.

Composition

But what is a good fish picture? It is certainly simpler to obtain a straight-forward record shot than a picture of a fish with some special effect. Each expert that you ask about this will disagree with the others. But, despite their strong views, they are agreed on certain things that do help to make a good picture of fish.

They all think it should be a well-lit photograph of the fish doing something natural in its normal environment. They all agree that it is important that you should see at least one of the fish's eyes—otherwise the picture will be lifeless. All the experts agree about this, but when you ask them the way that they set out to achieve that ideal, then they will start to differ.

For example, Geoff Harwood and Peter Scoones endeavour to obtain a result that is technically correct in the marine biological sense, but Colin Doeg is more interested in trying to capture the mood and atmosphere of the situation in which he finds the fish.

To achieve either effect you will have to return to the basics of fish photography. The style of picture you take is obviously determined by the moment you press the shutter and the composition before the camera at that instant. At first, the best moment to release the shutter must be determined by trial and error.

Take a shot every time you like what you see through the viewfinder. Then look at your results when processed. On your next dive concentrate on getting more of the style of photographs that most appealed to you on the previous occasion.

There are a number of principles that will help you to do this. The first is still to show the fish's eye. Whether you are showing the fish head-on, sideways, or going away from you at an angle, it is essential to show that eye. It can be much more difficult than it sounds.

Some fish (dragonets are a good example), have eyes that work independently of each other. It's ten to one on that you'll end up with a picture of a boss-eyed fish unless you are very careful.

Once again in these circumstances you must be prepared to expend a great deal of film to make sure that you have got it right. Bass—to take another example—present a different problem, because they so often speed away leaving only a fast-disappearing view of their powerful tail. Result: No eye. And poor picture.

Method

But not all fish are so difficult. Mullet and wrasse will look at you —all you've got to do is to persuade them to let you come close enough for that prize-winning shot.

One obvious technique to allow you to get close to fish is to feed them. Often this is a waste of time. It brings the fish close all right, but you can end up attracting so many fish of all types that you can't get a decent photograph of any of them. They dart about in great excitement, stirring up sediment and generally having a fine time while the poor photographer just isn't.

Next try to show the fish in a natural position. For example, pollack can frequently be seen hanging at an angle in the water. They can be head down or head up. So when photographing this characteristic pose do make sure that there is some vertical object also in the viewfinder—part of a wreck, rock or pier which makes it immediately obvious that the fish is at an angle.

There are many other examples of 'natural positions'. Basking sharks strain their food out of the sea by swimming near the surface with their mouths open like a gigantic sieve. The ideal picture should show all of this. Fast-moving fish like bass or mullet can be shown to be swift and agile if they can be caught at the right moment—in the middle of a turn for example.

Other fish are elaborately camouflaged. Take the whole family of flat-fishes. They blend so well into the background that they will sometimes not show up at all on your pictures unless you take your shot at the moment they raise themselves up on their 'skirts' before shooting off out of range.

The angler fish has to be taken from the right angle. A particularly good head-on view was taken by Tony Baverstock and is in this book. It shows the camouflage 'netting' well.

Every fish has its own required technique. The thing to do is to practise on the slow-moving species and then move on to the faster fellows. Bottom-living fish do tend to be slower, so watch out for these on your first few photographic dives. The easiest way to photograph most bottom-dwellers is to pre-focus the camera and then put it down on the seabed at the spot you judge to be the correct distance from the fish.

But don't then start trying to get down behind the camera and squint through the viewfinder. You'll only stir up so much sediment that all photography will be impossible. Look at your camera and the fish from the side and judge the moment to fire.

This method is advisable with most bottom-living fish. You'll find they tend to move around a bit when the camera is plonked in front of their noses, but it is much easier to follow them by this method than peering through the viewfinder. It's all a matter of judgement—of angle and moment—but you'll be surprised how quickly it becomes a matter of course.

The Nikonos is well-suited for this technique. With larger cameras—if the fish will stand it—it may become necessary to dig a small hole in the seabed to get the lens down to fish-eye level.

For most other photographs of fish it is usually better to take the pictures looking slightly upward. This reduces the amount of bottom distractions, such as weed, and, if the fish is well camouflaged, it will make it stand out from the background. Pictures taken looking down are usually failures.

It is, of course, important that the camera is held steady. At times you must make yourself into a living tripod, either by lying or kneeling on the seabed, leaning against a rock, wedging yourself into a crevice (don't do this when there are sea-urchins about!) or gripping a rock or pier column with a leg scissors.

But if you do employ these methods, remember that you are bound to stir up a bit of sediment and be prepared to wait until the tide has carried it away. If you get it wrong, the whole subject will be blotted out by a cloud of debris and the fish will be gone when it has cleared.

If you are using a camera with a viewing screen, it is best to obtain your final focus by rocking gently back and forward rather than by twiddling the control knobs.

Remember everything underwater is on the move even if very gently. It all moves—the background scenery of weed, the fish you are trying to photograph, you and, of course, the water.

Consequently, shutter speeds of 1/125 or faster should be used if conditions permit. Sacrifice aperture rather than speed if it comes to the crunch. For fast-moving fish try to use 1/500 or 1/250.

A ground-glass viewing screen may often be a disadvantage when compared with the frame-sight. It is often impossible to see clearly underwater on a viewing screen. The easiest way to get your focus right in these conditions is to line up the camera on a nearby piece of weed or anything else with a clear shape and then compose the picture by means of the external frame finder.

When you use a frame finder it is, however, easy to be misled about lighting conditions. The human eye has the finest system of automatic light (and colour) compensating equipment you could wish for. Consequently the eye adjusts very well to gloomy conditions and you will begin to think that things are better than they really are.

For a land example of this, you have only got to wait for a few minutes to be able to read a newspaper by moonlight. As far as colour is concerned, you will not realise how green things were on that dive until you look at the colour pictures you have taken.

As steadiness is an essential of good photography, it is always more satisfactory to be negatively buoyant for underwater photography. Use an extra 4 to 8 lb of lead and push the weights to the front of your belt to obtain a 'keel' effect. But overweighting can be dangerous (*see* Dangers).

Cine

Now to cine photography underwater. It is easier to produce results with a cine camera than a still camera. And cine is also much easier to operate. For a start you can get cameras that do it all for you—fixed focus, automatic exposure and electric film wind. All you have to do is point and press. The average 8-mm cine camera has such a large depth of field that there is no need for focusing control, especially when using a wide-angle lens. And whatever your experience of automatic still cameras may be, the cine variety work well and produce correctly exposed results.

The visual opportunities are enormous—you can run four minutes of film without stopping to rewind. This means that you could show a diver entering the water, follow him down to 100 ft and then leisurely come in to a close-up shot of the piece of coral he has gone down to collect—and you can do all of this without rewinding.

Putting a cine camera into a housing is much simpler than 'boxing' a still camera. You will probably need only a single control going through the wall of the case to release the shutter.

However, it is much more expensive to start from scratch with cine. You need a camera, a projector, a screen and an editor. And you can't make do with less if you are going to produce worthwhile results. Film-making is not just a matter of exposing reels of film and then joining them up for running through a projector. This is the perfect short cut to losing friends and boring people.

Regardless of whether you are making a film of fish life in order to show your friends the creatures that fascinate you in the undersea world, or whether you are producing footage to enable the fin movements of cod or whiting to be studied, the results of your filming must be edited before they become interesting.

Editing is a highly skilled and important part of film making. It is at this stage that the pace, mood, drama and vitality are injected into the film. And this is the stage where you must be ruthless. You will have to throw away a lot of material you have shot simply because it does not contribute enough to the final result.

So when you begin filming underwater, you should start in shallow well-lit water. Find a quiet bay and go in on a sunny day. And as these are ideal conditions you won't have to worry about taking special lights down with you.

As you go deeper you will find that your film sequences become greener and greener. Ocean waters are blue, but all water eventually is seen as greyish-green by colour film.

You have to be careful of this effect when you become more ambitious with your filming. Otherwise you will flit from a greenish picture of a fish to a greyish shot of a diver and back to a shallower bluer sequence of a spearfisherman.

There are three ways to avoid this colour contrast. You can use artificial light—taking lights down with you—for everything. You can use coloured filters to correct the effect so that the general appearance of all your film will be the same wherever they are taken. Or you can group together the shallow water shots, then those taken at moderate depth and then the really deep ones and show them in that order as though you were progressing downwards on a dive. In this final method, the differences are not so obvious and can be an important part of building up atmosphere.

The cameraman underwater has greater freedom than anywhere else, including the moon. He can swoop and glide taking endless tracking shots or plunge down rapidly to the seabed. He can stand on his head, lie on his side, or hover weightless in midwater.

But when you are filming underwater you must be careful not to abuse this freedom. If you fin too vigorously your superb tracking sequence will end up as a weaving, wavering unsteady picture, which will send your audience rushing for their seasickness pills. You must learn to move gently and slowly capturing the tranquillity and beauty that you know exists beneath the waves.

Another point to bear in mind is that an underwater sequence should be held longer than you would do with a similar sequence on land. Most audiences are unfamiliar with the underwater scene and so they have to be given longer to become accustomed to it.

You will find that considerable charm can be added to your film if you shoot the sequences at a faster speed than you project them. Many cameras have this facility and by showing the final result in slow-motion the film will have a dreamy, slightly unreal quality that suits the underwater world very well.

If you aspire to making really good underwater films, it is important that you work to some sort of basic idea or theme. You must get order and planning into what you are doing despite the difficulties of doing so underwater.

It is unlikely that you can write a precise script for shooting underwater—and then go out and take it. You will be unlikely, too, to have that much control over the principal characters—fish or divers. But it is feasible to decide on your basic theme and then go out and take pictures that will fit into the film's pattern. All you will need then are some linking shots to join everything together.

With fish, of course, it is impossible to script sequences in precise detail. You must take that sort of sequence as it happens. But you will do it more effectively if you can decide when taking it roughly where it fits into your final plan. This sort of thinking may well alter the way you film the fish.

Let's face it, underwater photography has an element of luck about it. But more often than not, luck can be given a helping shove.

An octopus will look better if it is red rather than grey. You know it goes red when annoyed—so annoy it.

A basking shark feeds on a cloud of plankton—which ruin visibility—so drive it into clearer water if you can (they seem to dislike the sound of an outboard motor and this can be used to good effect).

But remember that some fish are very shy so try not to have streams of exhaust bubbles pouring from your demand valve when actually filming.

If you really can't get close to the fish try shortening the distance by holding the camera out at arm's length. Precise composition is not easy with this method, but it does give you the chance of better close-up than with the camera, still or cine, held close to your eye.

Of course, lots of your still pictures, lots of the cine sequences will not turn out as you had hoped. But you must continue to be adventurous. If you want to take pictures that have that some-thing extra—try shooting straight into the sun. Dive when its raining. Dive in the winter. Dive in clear water. Dive in muddy. Then study the results.

There is always the chance that you could produce special pictures of fish in a way that no one has ever seen before.

COLIN DOEG
GEOFF HARWOOD
PETER SCOONES

CHAPTER EIGHT

Making your own housing

Should such-and-such a camera be put into an underwater housing? Simple answer—no.

This blunt advice should be given more often to the person who is asking about taking up underwater photography. For the truth is that the camera is often quite unsuitable for housing and it would be a waste of time to attempt it.

It would be better to sell the camera and buy a Nikonos or Rolleimarin instead.

There are only two reasons for putting a camera into an underwater case—and neither of them is concerned with the fact that you have already got the camera in your possession. The reasons for casing a camera are: (1) it is cheaper, or (2) the result will be better than anything commercially available.

For example, if you have a camera which you use a great deal on land and from which you regularly get superb results, then it is obviously worth considering making an underwater housing for it. But if you rush out and spend £100 on a camera and then wonder how you can waterproof it, you are obviously going the wrong way about taking up underwater photography.

So let's begin at the beginning. Is the camera you own or which you are contemplating buying suitable for putting into an underwater case? It only takes 60 seconds to find out. Try the Harwood Test. The only equipment required is a pair of thick gloves—gloves not mitts—and the camera. Put the gloves on. Now see if you can operate the camera easily.

Can you wind on the film? Can you fire the shutter? Can you alter the aperture and shutter speeds? If it's easy with the gloves on, then the odds are that it will be a simple matter to fit underwater controls to it.

However, if the controls are difficult to work with gloved hands then you need to give serious thought to its suitability for housing. It probably isn't.

The controls that cause a lot of trouble when you come to 'box' a camera are things like particularly long film wind-on levers, speed and aperture settings operated by rings which have to be pulled apart before they can be moved—or which can only be adjusted by minute levers which need your thumbnail.

It is also a good idea to avoid a camera which has lots of separate controls to do things. For instance, some cameras have one control to wind-on the film and another to set the shutter. All this is done by one stroke of the lever-wind on other types of cameras.

Extreme suitability for putting into an underwater case is typified by the Super 8 cine camera which requires only one control—the shutter release—and which is so compact that it will slip into a particularly small housing.

So avoid fussy controls of all types. Go for a focus knob that has to be moved only through 90° because this can be worked easily underwater by a lever arrangement. If it has to be turned more than this you might end up having to use an expensive series of gear wheels, which have to be positioned in the housing with great accuracy.

Avoid cameras with speed control knobs which spin round when the shutter is released or those on which the whole lens rotates when you alter focus—taking the aperture lever or ring with it.

If you are selecting a camera especially for putting in a housing, you don't need an elaborate one. For instance, shutter speeds from 1/30 to 1/125 might well be adequate—and such a camera body would only cost about £10 or £15. Then you can invest the remainder of your money in a top quality lens. If you do that you are putting your money where it really matters.

This is exactly what Geoff Harwood did with his specially

designed 35-mm outfit. He bought an Exa 1 body which cost him £10—and a Flektagon wide-angle lens which was £50. The body has only four shutter speeds, but they are the ones which are most used underwater. (You are hardly ever likely to find bright enough light to use 1/1000 and even 1/500 is not essential.)

At the other end of the price scale Colin Doeg uses a Bronica, which is well suited for a case. The camera cost £180 second-hand and the case, specially made, about the same.

Although the Bronica is a sophisticated camera it has a simple square shape. Focusing is by means of a large ring at the front. Film wind-on is by a lever or knob on one side and the speeds are set by rotating another knob on the other side. This means that the controls are well spaced out on the exterior of the housing, but in positions where they come easily to hand.

And do note that it is worthwhile buying a camera of this kind with a removable pentaprism. This is preferable to removing the top with a hacksaw! If your camera hasn't got this feature, it is difficult to see how you will arrange a viewing system which lets you see all of the screen.

One final piece of general advice: Before you rush out into your workshop and box up your camera, do spend some time looking at and handling other housings and studying how the controls are fitted in them. This will save you a lot of disappointment later. And you can learn from other people's mistakes.

Practically every home-made housing—and several of the commercially made ones—have some shortcomings. The main troubles are usually control knobs that do not come easily to hand and which are too stiff to operate easily. Other housings have such complicated sealing arrangements that it takes forever to reload with more film.

After you have studied other housings, and not before, you can come round to planning your own case. Most existing books on underwater photography mention stuffing boxes for sealing control rods. Stuffing boxes went out of diving with the steam engine.

How then should you go about making your case and fitting

controls? This, of course, depends on the sort of case you have in mind. It is true that a cheap, but effective, shallow water case can be made from a long-sleeved industrial glove and the front glass of a facemask. It is probably not what you have in mind, but it might suit the man or woman who just wants to take a few under-water snaps on an annual Continental holiday.

All you have to do is to turn the glove partly inside out, pulling the cuff back over the hand. Put your camera inside the cuff and then insert the face plate, clamping the end of the glove over the glass with the rim band from the mask.

If you cradle the camera in one hand and insert the other into the finger part of the glove, you will find that you can hold the camera against the glass plate and work all the simple controls without difficulty.

But remember this type of cheap housing is only suitable for very shallow water. Try it out first of all without the camera inside and check for leaks. Only if it doesn't put the camera in. That sounds obvious, but you would be surprised how many divers rush into the water with their camera already set up in a brand-new housing and then get upset when water leaks in on their precious camera. Surely it doesn't take much patience to test the case out empty to the sort of depths you plan to use it!

The industrial glove and face plate is a crude case. More substantial ones are made from both Perspex and metal. The former is by far the easiest to work and any home handyman can make a Perspex case.

Whichever material you decide to use, the first step of all is to put your camera down on a sheet of paper and make several accurate drawings of it—front, side and top. When you do so make sure that the lens is fully extended and also draw in the area covered by the lever-wind when it is operated.

Now draw the smallest rectangle you can round each outline of the camera, allowing an extra $\frac{1}{4}$ in. in front of the lens to make provision for a filter, and about 1 in. above the top of a 35-mm camera to leave enough room for the fitting of controls (or $\frac{1}{2}$ to

1 in. all round a 2¼-in. square SLR.) These rectangles will represent the inside dimensions of your housing.

All you have to do now is to draw the outside of the case round those rectangles—most case-makers prefer ½-in. thick Perspex —and you can work out the actual dimensions of the box you require. When doing this make sure that the smaller sides support the larger ones. If you make it the other way round it is possible that water pressure will push the sides into the case.

When you know the exact sizes of the pieces of Perspex you require order them from a stockist who will cut the sheet with a circular saw. This ensures that you have clean, accurately cut edges. The only other item that you need at the moment is the Perspex cement, Tensol No. 7.

Lay one of the large sides down on a flat, clean surface and pour a ribbon of glue along at each end. Then carefully lower the two sides down on to the glue. You don't have to rush, the glue won't set for about 20 minutes. Make sure when you lower the sides that all the glue does not squeeze out. Let the weight of the Perspex sink it into the glue.

If there is any surplus glue about try to ooze it out to the inside of the case. Don't clamp the parts together. It is a popular fallacy that clamping is best, but all it does is to squeeze all the glue out of the joint.

When the sides are reasonably rigid pour ribbons of glue along the other edges of the large piece of Perspex and lower down the other sides.

While they are drying, you must keep checking that they are all square. If the large side is not lying on a level surface you will find that the other sides will slide off.

A word of warning: If you haven't worked with Perspex before get some off-cuts and play around with them before you start making the actual case. In other words, get the feel of using both Perspex and glue before you start major operations.

Once you have made your basic box, you will have to fit the controls. The easiest way is to buy special assemblies from Aqua-snap (see Appendix 3). These assemblies consist of a control knob and shaft set in a bush, which is sealed with sufficiently large washers to enable it to be floated around to some extent in an oversize hole through the case. This means that you do not have to be particularly accurate in positioning the hole in the first place.

To make the holes use sharp drills. Once again experiment first with your scraps of Perspex. Use a handbrace to work the drills or if you are using an electric drill take small bites at the Perspex so that the plastic does not get hot and melt.

It is often a good idea to fix the camera to the 'lid' of the box by a bolt going through the Perspex into the tripod bush of the camera. The bolt can be sealed by an O-ring, as are the control rods you bought from Aquasnap. The 'lid' then becomes the bottom of the case and the camera fixed to it is pushed on to the various controls as you close the case.

Making the controls work is a matter for individual ingenuity. A lot can be done with Meccano wheels with rubber tyres on them. Rubber bands are another useful method if stretched over the lens and to a pulley wheel fixed on the control shaft.

Control knobs can be bought from Aquasnap or from a local radio shop. If you use radio control knobs, don't forget to replace the grub screws with ones made from stainless steel or brass or you'll never get those knobs off after the first dive. Sea water can corrode amazingly fast.

One of the most important features of the housing is the main seal. The simplest system is to use a flat gasket, which should be cut from $\frac{1}{8}$ in. flat fairly soft rubber—you can buy a sheet of material specially for this purpose.

Strange things can happen to gaskets underwater. They can be squeezed out of position by pressure on the 'lid' or pushed right inside the housing by the pressure of the water at depth.

The solution is to hold the lid in place by bolts through every 3 inches so that it cannot distort and free the gasket. You should also make a thin rim round the inside of the lid to prevent the rubber being forced in.

An even simpler way of making a Perspex case—if you have the necessary skill and facilities—is from large diameter tube.

All you need to do then to make a watertight case is to turn a couple of end caps on a lathe and machine grooves for O-rings in each one. But you do need skill and great care is needed when drilling through the circular sides to fit the control rods. In fact when doing this it is best to provide a supporting shoulder of Perspex rod both inside and outside the wall of the tube.

If you are going all out for superb results, it might be worth while fitting a dome porthole or one of optically flat glass into the case for the camera to look out of. Glass is easier to clean without scratching than Perspex.

However, glass has to be fitted very carefully. It has either to be screwed against a seal by means of a large diameter locking ring as with the Rolleimarin, or it has to be secured by means of a large number of screws or bolts to make sure that the pressure exerted on it is absolutely even. Stresses may be created if this is not done which can break the glass.

Of course, one advantage of Perspex is that if it gets knocked accidentally against a rock, it may scratch, but it will not shatter. And it is easier and cheaper to replace. For example the Perspex porthole in Colin Doeg's alloy housing for his Bronica is circular and fitted with an O-ring seal. It is a push-fit into the case and so takes only seconds to replace if damaged.

Don't rush the manufacture of your case. Remember it has got to stand up to the equivalent of having a small car sitting on it when you get it down to 100 ft.

One photographer found that the pressure at depth was sufficient to push in the front of his case about $\frac{1}{16}$ in.—enough to prevent him being able to extend his lens fully for close-ups. Another had a similar experience. This time the side of the housing was pushed in enough to prevent his cine camera working.

No matter when or where you are using your camera in its housing, it is vitally important that you check that the seals are clean before you close the case. Even a hair can make an O-ring leak and grains of sand or a tiny fleck of weed can let the whole ocean come flooding in.

These examples might seem to be extreme, but they have happened to really expert underwater photographers at depth. Even in shallow water particles of sand will let water through the strongest seal.

When you open the housing to reload always keep uppermost the edges which seal together. Don't put the sealing parts in direct contact with the ground—or even with the thwart of a boat—sand gets everywhere. Double check each time if you dive from sandy beaches.

You will be an extremely fortunate underwater photographer if disaster never strikes and seawater does not penetrate your housing. If water gets in, don't panic. This is the moment for strong nerves, and positive action will come more easily if you have thought out in advance what you should do.

If it is only a small quantity of water, you may well find that you can tip it into the corner of your housing and finish both the dive and your roll of film. This has been done on several occasions; some divers have ignored successfully as much as half a cup of sea.

But if the situation is worse than that, you must do a quick sum and decide which part of the camera is the most expensive. For example both Colin Doeg and Peter Scoones use cameras with lenses which cost about £230 new. The bodies of the cameras are about £100 and the filmbacks cost £76 each. Obviously if the worst comes to the worst, it is best for them to save the lens.

Geoff Harwood's camera has a lens costing five times the price of the body. So once again it is best to keep the water away from the lens. With most 35-mm cameras it is advisable to keep the lens, shutter and top of the camera out of the water and let it gather at the back of the camera, particularly the corner where the film cassette fits since this usually has nothing more expensive in it than your exposed film.

After keeping the water away from the vital part of your camera you have to decide what to do when you surface. Air can be as harmful as sea-water because it causes corrosion to set in. So the first thing to do is to keep the air out of the camera by leaving the camera and the sea inside the housing until you are ready to begin the rather drastic life-saving operation that is now necessary to get your camera working again. Although to be honest, it is doubtful if your camera will ever work as sweetly again as it did before it was drowned.

Peter Scoones is the expert on reviving drowned cameras. He has managed to soak both still and cine cameras in various parts of the world from Swanage to Singapore—and restore them sufficiently to be able to use them—and be still using them six years later.

This is his advice: If only part of the camera has got wet then only treat that. But let's assume that the worst has happened and the whole lot has been flooded.

Don't run about bemoaning your fate and showing everyone what has happened. Put the sodden thing down in the water-filled case while you get out of your wet suit and then beg, borrow or steal a bucket and a supply of fresh water, from a tap if possible.

Now take a firm grip of yourself, fill the bucket with water, open the housing, take out the camera and put it in the bucket. Keep working the controls while the camera is literally underwater and let fresh water flow through the bucket.

If possible feed a supply of fresh water by hose to the bottom of the bucket so that you get as little aeration as possible. Do this for at least 15 to 20 minutes. Change the water several times, letting the excess spill out over the edges of the bucket.

The camera is now ready to travel home with you provided you can keep it completely immersed in water all the time. The housing is a good container—provided the leak is not too big.

The camera can stay in fresh water for about a week without any more harm coming to it. But once you get home, if you can put the camera into water that has been boiled, and allowed to cool, it will be better still.

Work the controls at intervals and change the water as often as you can. Then switch the routine to distilled water. After that we are ready to start getting rid of the water.

Take the camera out of the bucket and dunk it in methylated spirit. It is fierce stuff, but if you want to save your camera, it is a good idea to be prepared for such emergencies and have a pint or so in the garage. Water mixes with meths and then evaporates away as the spirit vaporises. So immerse the camera in the meths, work the controls a few times and then bring it out and shake any surplus moisture off.

At this point in Operation Rescue you will need one or two watchmakers' screwdrivers and some brake fluid. Strip the camera down and put all the bits in the brake fluid. To do this, first of all you should remove the 'leathers'—the fabric or plastic pieces stuck on to the case. They just pull off and are easily replaced.

When you have done this you will see various small screw-heads exposed. If not you may have to dig around to find them amid the remains of the rubber-based adhesive which held the 'leathers' in position.

Undo these screws and you will be able to remove the sides of the camera. Now you will be able to see all the delicate parts that hate seawater.

Keep on unscrewing everything and put it in the brake fluid (*but see Note at end of Chapter*). If you are able to do so it helps either to photograph each side of the camera before you strip it down, or to make sketches of where the various parts go. This is advisable if you intend to reassemble it yourself later on.

It is also a good idea to try to keep the parts in their various assemblies. Put them into separate containers—jars or saucers are fine provided the parts are completely immersed.

Several items will be ruined by the meths—particularly such parts as freznel screens, plastic windows and so on. Meths also removes grease and oil so parts will have to be properly lubricated before re-assembly.

Anyway, you've done it now. Your treasured camera is just a few piles of gears and other pieces swimming around in brake fluid. But, don't worry, something can be done with them because you have taken the correct—and prompt—action.

If you had delayed even half-an-hour your camera would have been white inside with dried salt and solid with corrosion when you opened it. This is why it is important to do these drastic things yourself.

It's no good taking your flooded camera to a photographic shop. You'll find out later that some clot merely took it out of the water, gave it a shake, and then posted it to the importer or a camera repairer for attention.

Well, there you are with your jars and saucers and bits in brake fluid. If you don't feel competent to reassemble the camera take it direct to a camera repairer or to the importer's workshop.

Camera repairers are listed in the Yellow Pages of your local telephone directories. It might be a good idea to telephone first and then go to the one who has the most experience with your type of camera. Tell them what happened. What action you took —and why. And then let them get on with it.

It is not an easy job to reassemble a camera and it will not be cheap. But it is better to pay £20 or £30 to an expert to have this done than have to find £150 for a new camera. Of course, you should have insured a valuable camera for diving anyway.

The parts most likely to be affected by all this will be the blades of Compur shutters, which are never the same again, the blades of the automatic diaphragms, the slow escapements and the roller blinds of focal plane shutters. The blinds, for example, go brittle after going through the water-meths-brake-fluid routine. And it's not surprising.

Note: If you have an expensive lens then it is important to try to prevent it getting wet because the cement holding the various elements together can deteriorate.

It is then extremely costly to get the elements cemented together again satisfactorily. If your lens has got wet, you stop at the meths bath and do not put it in the brake fluid. The lens diaphragm should, however, be removed and put in brake fluid.

May your camera never get wet. But at least if it does, now you will know what to do.

Here is a quick check on the seven rules for dealing with a drowned camera:

1. Don't panic.
2. Immerse camera in fresh water. Keep in housing if housing will hold water.
3. Work controls and change water as often as you can.
4. Switch to distilled water.
5. Dunk camera in methylated spirits. Shake off surplus water.
6. Strip down and place parts (except compound lenses) in brake fluid. Make notes of where everything goes.
7. Take to expert repairer.

CHAPTER NINE

Sophisticated hardware

The most sophisticated underwater camera in the world is undoubtedly the Rebikoff torpedo *Pegasus*. This is a chariot that is piloted by the photographer. Cameras and lighting equipment are housed in the nose and the cameraman 'flies' over the seabed as he carries out photographic surveys and other tasks. For more modest applications, there are smaller-sized torpedoes without propulsion units which contain cameras and lights mounted in the front in the same manner.

However, even the most experienced underwater photographers wouldn't expect to be able to commute to their pictorial work on a miniature submarine. They would probably choose a camera which they could carry and which was versatile without being too bulky and unwieldy—and they would fin their way to the photographic site. But what is the experts' ideal camera?

Colin Doeg, Geoff Harwood and Peter Scoones spent an entertaining time dreaming up their ideal underwater cameras, and one feature they each wanted was the ability to focus from infinity down into the macro range.

Another feature they all chose was electric drive so that they could take pictures in quick succession—ideal for sequences showing fish movement. Wanted as well was the capability of taking longer lengths of film than standard magazines allow.

Each wanted a single lens reflex but were divided on format. Peter Scoones went for $2\frac{1}{4} \times 2\frac{1}{4}$ in. Geoff Harwood preferred to continue with 35-mm because he thinks that, at the rate film emulsions are improving nowadays, big-negative quality will eventually result from the smaller frame. Colin Doeg wavered between his preference for the type of picture turned out by a

35-mm camera—great depth of field and more 'candid' shots—and the improved quality inherent in a bigger negative.

Their ideas are mostly geared to close-up photography because they are accustomed to working regularly in limited visibility. This is ideal for fish photography because a large proportion of the marine creatures you will see underwater regularly are small. The basis of their approach is two-fold: The better your camera's facility for close-ups and the less you are dependent on natural light for your illumination, the more frequently you will be able to take pictures when you go underwater.

This is expressed in the design of the underwater outfits used by all three men. Geoff Harwood is really the pioneer of these outfits. He uses a combination dubbed 'Système Harwood' and this is how he describes it:

'I like to have the best of all worlds when it comes to underwater cameras so, over the years, I evolved a system which comes fairly close to the ideal in that it can take high quality record pictures of small subjects very close to the camera and, with a mere turn of the focusing knob, can be adjusted to take scenes with a wide angle of view for pictorial shots or pictures of my fellow divers, even in murky water.

'I was never much good at holding a camera still for available light or flashbulb exposures, so for technical close-ups where definition is all-important, I use electronic flash, which is fast enough to freeze all movement. Nor was I any good at judging distances underwater, so I decided to buy an Exa single-lens reflex and convert it for underwater use so that I could focus on a ground-glass screen.

'The electronic flash unit I put in a separate box fixed to the top of the camera housing by a hinge at the front and by a sliding clamp at the back. This enables the flash to be pointed down towards the subject at especially close distances.

'It's not always easy to focus on the ground-glass, particularly if the light is poor, such as in caves or in deep water, so I have incorporated a simple device to enable me to get my close-up distances exactly right.

'A torch is installed in the flash housing in such a way that it gives a small spot of light on the subject. This, in conjunction with a scale on the sliding clamp at the back of the flash housing, works as a very accurate rangefinder for close-ups. The image of the spot of light seen through the camera ground-glass screen moves up and down the picture as the camera moves towards or away from the subject. So, by calibrating the scale on the sliding clamp to match the focusing scale on the camera lens in such a way that the light is in the centre of the picture when the image is sharp, it is possible to make quite sure that I am at exactly the right

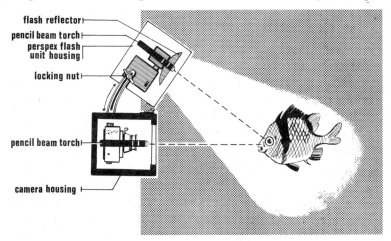

flash reflector
pencil beam torch
perspex flash unit housing
locking nut
pencil beam torch
camera housing

'Système Harwood'

distance from the subject for the lens-focus setting. The spot of light would, of course, show up on available light shots but the electronic illumination effectively drowns it in flash shots.

'If there's enough light to do without the flash then there's enough to focus normally on the ground-glass. The spotlight system is a tremendous advantage when taking photographs in dark holes or of timid subjects where you can charge in and press the shutter release at the moment the spot of light crosses the centre of the screen. The subject is usually exploding into flight by this time but, as often as not, the result is a good action shot. On the other hand, you sometimes get a lovely clear shot of the seabed, which is empty except for the tail of a fast-moving fish in one corner.

'The camera started off with an ordinary 35-mm wide-angle lens, but I wanted to be able to take really crisp close-ups of little animals as well as full-size people in the murky British water. This meant an even wider angle of view and a correction lens to improve definition. A water correction lens is a combination of single lenses which correct for the refraction effects that occur when you or the camera looks through a flat surface into the water.

'Armed with a few pieces of Perspex, 'A'-level Physics (formulae for calculating the focal lengths of lenses and all that sort of stuff), and a lathe I turned up a few correcting lenses of various curvatures and tried them out in turn in the swimming pool on a subject with a lot of fine detail—the rusty iron grid in the middle of the deep end.

'By a process of trial and error I arrived at a lens combination which gave better definition than the plain porthole and a much wider angle of view underwater into the bargain. As a bonus, the front negative element is fixed and the focusing control moves the rest. This has the effect of increasing the focusing range of the camera from infinity to 2 ft to infinity right down to 1 ft. The definition is perhaps not as crisp at the edges at long distances and wide apertures as was the ordinary lens, but for close-ups the results are a great improvement.

'The system has developed gradually over the years with refinements such as built-in exposure meter, line-of-sight viewing without the troubles or expense of a pentaprism and a little manometer depth gauge, all added as and when the ideas have occurred to me.

'Latest addition is a background-cum-effects light in the form of a little flashbulb holder on a long lead which I can trail away into the laminaria forest or around the back of a rock to give a fill-in light to the background or a dramatic backlighting effect. Initial results are quite promising—but I must get some wire that looks a bit more like seaweed!

'Final item in the complete system is the box I use to carry the camera unit around in. It is an ex-government instrument box with a fitted compartment for the camera to protect it en route to the diving site in a splashy, bouncy boat, with an extra compartment for charts, distress flares, pipe, tobacco, matches and a chocolate bar for the inner man.'

Peter Scoones and Colin Doeg have similar systems based on the Bronica. Peter has taken the light focusing arrangement a stage further by mounting two pencil-beam 'torches' on either side of the housing. The beams are adjusted so that they meet in a circle at the point at which the subject is in focus and in the centre of the negative.

The idea works well in gloomy conditions, but more powerful bulbs, possibly quartz iodine, are required if it is to be successful in brighter conditions. The big advantage, once again, is that it does away with the need to look through a viewfinder. When you want to photograph a fish you merely line up the lights on the creature as if you were following it with a torch and press the shutter release at the appropriate moment.

The device has to be used in conjunction with flash to swamp the light or with a switch in the circuit for available light shots. However, although it requires further development, the idea is most promising and is ideal for all fish photographs, particularly of fast moving specimens, because it makes the camera so much easier and quicker to operate. This is particularly useful with the larger format cameras because they tend to be heavier and more cumbersome once they are installed in a housing with a flash unit clamped on top.

One thing you have got to decide if you want a housing of this type is the direction from which you want your artificial light to come. The experts' preference is to mount the flash in such a way that its illumination simulates sunlight.

It is popular to mount flash heads on arms extending out at about 45 degrees from the housing. This is the system used on the Rolleimarin and Hasselblad, for instance. The flash units can be removed and placed in different positions or handheld, but many of the normal pictures taken by these outfits are characterised by side lighting which sometimes does not look natural.

Electronic flash is preferred by most experts because it is usually more reliable and is cheaper to run than bulbs. Furthermore, it produces a sharper result by virtue of the shorter duration of the flash. It is, however, difficult to use as 'fill-in' light.

There are two schools of thought about the best way to connect electronic flash to the camera. Certainly the simplest is a permanent waterproof connection from the flash housing to the

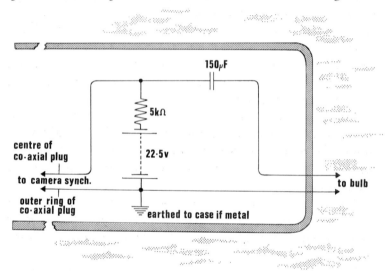

Connecting electronic flash

camera through the wall of its case. However, if this is done, you can't turn it off although you can turn the unit away from the subject when you want to use natural light.

The alternative is to operate the flash by means of a relay or a thyristor circuit. This has the advantage that you can unplug the unit when you don't want to use it and you can also fire flash bulbs from the same outlet.

To begin with you install a capacitor, resistor and $22\frac{1}{2}$-volt flash battery inside the housing, connecting it up as if it was to be used for firing flash bulbs. Wire it to a two-pin socket insulated in the wall of the housing.

The 'wet' lead which plugs into this socket goes to the flash housing where it is connected to a relay. The jolt of electricity delivered by the capacitor every time the flash contact is made in the camera is sufficient to activate the relay, which in turn fires the flash. At no time is there any electrical contact with anything that could become dangerous.

In fact, even if your flash housing did get flooded, you wouldn't come to any harm. Both Geoff Harwood and his friend Tim Glover have had leaks in flash units without any harmful effects.

As far as the flash unit itself is concerned, the small ones costing about £10 and working from penlight batteries are quite suitable. They give out the right amount of illumination for close-ups, yet are comparatively cheap.

One of the features of flashed pictures which you should try to avoid unless it is sought as a particular effect, is that of black backgrounds. This happens when the background is so far away from the flash that the sea absorbs all the light before it can reach the background.

With cameras having between-the-lens shutters you can avoid this by taking your picture mostly by the available light and using flash to paint in just sufficient illumination to crisp up the main detail and bring out the colours of the subject.

This technique of 'fill-in' flash does not work as well with a camera equipped with a focal plane shutter if you are using an electronic source. It does work as effectively, however, if you use focal plane flash bulbs which are specially designed to overcome this problem. Otherwise, you must apply so much electronic light that it provides the total illumination.

Another technique is to splash diffused light over the subject. Philip Smith, the first holder of the British Underwater Photographer of the Year title, who uses a Rolleimarin with twin flash, opts for this method. He uses particularly large bulbs behind screens of opal Perspex and produces an extremely pleasing result which closely resembles sunlight. Incidentally, Phil is also experimenting with the use of filters of various tones over his flash bulbs to add colour to the final picture. This might disturb the purists, but it can add considerable drama and impact to what, otherwise, would be a less interesting picture.

Peter Scoones has tackled the black background problem in a different way. He has installed a powerful professional flashgun in a separate housing which he carts about with him like a suitcase when he goes on a photo-safari. The flash is fired by a slave unit activated by the light from the smaller source on the camera, thus avoiding the need to trail a connecting wire all over the seabed.

Walt Deas, the famous Scots photographer now living in Australia, has mounted Mecablitz guns on either side of his Rollei SL66 housing. The flash units are small and he has retained this by relying on their nickel-cadmium batteries and direct connections to the camera. The result is an outfit that is particularly easy to handle.

Ease of handling is an important point to bear in mind not only when you design your first housing, but also when you venture into the realms of more sophisticated hardware. If you are not careful, you will end up festooned like a Christmas tree. Colin Doeg likes taking two cameras underwater with him—'and I'd take cine along as well if I had one'. But he admits that a brace of cameras can be confusing. Unless they are different makes or have the film they contain clearly indicated, there is a possibility of getting in a muddle.

The best way to work with two cameras is, for example, to load one with 400 ASA film (Tri-X) and then put 200 ASA (High Speed Ektachrome specially developed) colour film in the other. That way you only need to calculate one exposure and then open up or close down the other camera one stop, as appropriate.

An ingenious split-image camera has been constructed in America by Coles Phinzy. It is described in the May 1969 issue of *Skin Diver* magazine and has a limited application for fish photography, but it is an interesting piece of equipment. It enables him to take a picture which shows the above- and underwater scenes together on one negative.

The results are particularly attractive and are achieved by taking the photograph with a lens which has half a close-up lens on the lower part and half a neutral density filter on the upper part in order to compensate for the effects of refraction and light variation in such a way that you end up with an evenly exposed, distortion free negative showing the best of both worlds.

Basis of this camera is a Pentax single lens reflex body. Coles has built three such outfits, using either a 35- or 28-mm wide angle lens. The picture is taken through a dome shaped porthole about 8½ in. in front of the lens—it has to be this far away because otherwise the sea/air interface would produce an excessively wide band of distortion in the picture.

Coles developed this special camera by trial and error, in much the same way that Geoff Harwood produced his correction porthole. This seems to be the best way, unless you can call on the services of a computer, an optical works and a camera factory!

COLIN DOEG
GEOFF HARWOOD
PETER SCOONES

CHAPTER TEN

Accessories

Accessories which increase the range of your camera in some practical way are worth having. In this category you can list such items as close-up devices, filters, tripods and suchlike and, oddly enough, a special type of lifejacket.

The most important accessory of all is an exposure meter. Sooner or later—and the sooner the better—you should buy an exposure meter. This is unless of course you have an automatic camera. You can get a perfectly adequate exposure meter from £5 to £10 although you can pay as much as £50 for a specially designed underwater type.

Basically there are two types of meters, of which there are dozens of different makes. The type most suited for underwater use has a selenium cell which 'sees' things in much the same way as black and white and colour film.

Water absorbs various colours as you go deeper. Red is the most strongly absorbed. Then the greens disappear leaving only yellow as a recognisable colour against the blue background.

A selenium cell is not bothered by these variations, but most of the other type, which are powered by a minute battery and known as cds meters, are sufficiently affected to give inaccurate readings at some depths.

The ideal meter for underwater use is one that will give you a direct reading without requiring any knobs to be twiddled. You can then put it in a case and forget about it—as long as it is within the range of lighting conditions with which your camera and film can cope. There's no point in buying a super sensitive meter, because time exposures are not much use underwater.

For example, if you have a Nikonos, you only want to be able to cover conditions down to 1/30th at $f/2.5$ with 400 ASA film. You don't need to be able to take a reading of a black conger in a ship's hold at 200 ft because the only way to cope with that situation—apart from swimming up and away—is to use artificial light.

With this in mind go to a shop with a large selection of meters and find something suitable. There are several on the market which give direct readings. With them you pre-set the film and shutter speeds and the needle swings over to indicate the aperture to use. Other meters, including one of the Sekonic models, require only one control to do the same thing.

The easiest meter to take underwater, however, is the one which gives a direct reading without any fiddling about. To begin with you can just put it in a baby-food jar, or a Kilner jar. But mind you don't bash it on a rock.

The safest thing is to put the meter in a Perspex case, ideally one which is sufficiently buoyant to float even when the meter is inside. If you fix it to your wrist on a lanyard it will bob up out of harm's way and yet be ready for use the instant you require it.

If you already have a meter which does not give direct readings, don't despair. You can still use it by preparing a small table for each film that you use, setting out shutter speed and aperture in relation to the light value figures that are indicated by the needle, and putting that in the case as well.

The headache with most other meters is that they have a high and a low light intensity setting and most underwater work seems to fall between the two. You want the high scale for use near the surface and the low one when you get deeper. The only thing to do is to gamble on which level of readings is the most important and make a guess.

It is perhaps unkind to be too cautious about cds meters. In fact, some of the more expensive ones are colour compensated and satisfactory for underwater use. One of these is the Sekonic Marine, which is a specially designed unit, which is fully water-proofed. It costs about £50. Another is the Lunasix, which costs nearly £40 without a housing. It is a particularly sensitive instrument over a wide range of readings, but for general use it is not essential to go into this class of instrument or into that price bracket.

SOS market two selenium cell meters in cases, which each give direct readings. Both are workmanlike jobs incorporating standard meters and are well worth considering if you haven't already got a meter.

The best way to use a meter underwater is to point it from the camera position at the subject, taking care it is not directed too much at the background. Even when pointing it directly at the sun, the meter will indicate an exposure which can be relied upon to give an acceptable result.

Some people put their meter in their camera housing. This saves both the expense and bother of making a separate case, but sometimes it might mean you can't take as close or as accurate a reading as you would like.

When you buy a meter the first thing to do is to establish the accuracy of the meter and calibrate it with your camera. Load your camera with colour transparency film—this is best because it has so little latitude that you can spot the mistakes more easily. Now take several pictures of one or two different subjects. Begin by taking a careful and correct reading with your meter and set your camera accordingly. Then take pictures at settings which under- and over-expose both one and two stops on the first setting. If your camera can be adjusted more accurately, it is even worth making these exposures at half-stop intervals up to two stops.

When the film comes back from normal processing, study the results and decide which setting produces the type of result which pleases you most. You might discover, for example, that you prefer the results you get if you always over-expose by a stop or under-expose by half a stop. But at least then you know and you can eliminate one more variable.

If you want to increase the range and versatility of your camera the next accessory to buy is a close-up lens. You can either buy those which screw into the mount of your lens before you insert it into its case, or you can buy some which fit over the porthole and therefore can be put on or taken off underwater as you require them.

Both Colin Doeg and Geoff Harwood favour supplementaries which can be fitted and removed as the need arises. Peter Scoones often dives with a fixed purpose and is happy to enter the water committed to a particular type of picture no matter what else may turn up—an attitude that probably arises because much of his diving has been in areas such as the Indian Ocean where you can predict with some certainty the sort of subjects you will find.

Whichever approach you decide upon there are plenty of lenses to choose from. If you prefer to fit the supplementaries directly to your camera there are many standard ranges to choose from at a wide variety of prices. If you want to use a variety of strengths, you might find it cheaper to buy a communal holder which will accommodate unmounted supplementaries and filters.

There is a good range of slide-on close-up lenses available from SOS for both Nikonos and Calypso-Phots. From experience the one you are most likely to use is the 20 cm. They are better than screwing normal supplementaries into either the lens mount, or internal thread of the lens hood of the Nikonos, because their magnifying power is not reduced by refraction. The effect of a normal magnifying glass is greatly reduced by immersion in water unless you put a sealed air-gap either in front or behind it to maintain most of its power, which is what the SOS close-up lenses do.

But you can get quite satisfactory results by hanging a powerful magnifying glass in front of your camera porthole. Tim Glover, one of Britain's pioneer underwater photographers, tried this some years ago with a large condenser lens from a photographic enlarger bolted over the front of his Rolleimarin. With such a crude arrangement you would never think the results would be sharp, but you should look at Tim's transparencies. They are good—and the taking lens doesn't even look through the centre of the condenser.

Geoff Harwood uses an 18p magnifying glass he bought at his local chemist on the front of his Nikonos and even his pin-sharp eyes are satisfied with the results. Colin Doeg has a more expensive set-up. His lens, which is from a slide projector, cost him 63p.

Earlier on, we said it can be limiting to fit supplementaries to the camera itself. However, this is only in relation to the available visibility. Colin Doeg uses one and two diopter close-up lenses on the standard optic of his Bronica for fish portraits in limited visibility. If visibility is only 5 or 10 ft you must work to within 18 in. to $2\frac{1}{2}$ ft of your subject for good results. So fitting a lens which reduces infinity to 3 or 4 ft doesn't matter. Indeed, used in this way, supplementaries can increase the range of conditions in which you can still obtain good results.

The most difficult thing about close-up photography is to get both composition and focus correct because there is so little margin for error. If you are using a powerful close-up lens you might find that the band of sharp focus is only $\frac{1}{2}$ in. wide. In that case, for a start, you need to take the fish from the front and get the head sharp, or from the side with the camera parallel to its body. The fuzzy foreground and background can, however, be used to great advantage to create powerful pictures, which concentrate interest on the main subject.

There are several ways to tackle the composing and focusing problem. The obvious solution is to use a single lens reflex because you see your picture accurately on the viewfinder. The alternatives are to practice judging the correct distance or to use a focusing frame. You will certainly romp through film if you estimate composition and focus—even with the sideways-on technique we described earlier—but it is pleasant to cut down on the paraphernalia you have to cart about.

Focusing frames, however, do have their uses for static subjects or as a means of training your eye to learn accurate judgement of composition and focus. You can make them out of brass or stainless steel rod, but first you have to establish the area to be framed. You can do this very roughly from the leaflet accompanying a proper close-up lens or you can hold your magnifying glass or condenser lens over the front of an SLR camera borrowed from a friend to get an idea of the effect.

When you have a rough idea, put your waterproofed camera in the water-filled bath at home, fit the additional lens, lay a ruler down in front of the camera and then move a plastic bath sponge or some similar object up and down the scale taking pictures at various distances. Process the film and you will find the distance at which the moon-like surface of the sponge is sharp. From the area of the sponge on the negative you can easily work out that to be indicated by the wire frame.

If you work out the size of the frame from details on the lens manufacturer's leaflet remember that the measurements are altered by refraction and that you have to add a third to each dimension—3 in. becomes 4 in. and so on.

Focusing frames don't work with most fish—how would you like to suddenly be surrounded by a rectangle of scaffold pole as you walk down the road?—but can be useful with static subjects.

Another way to get close to your subject is by means of extension tubes—either standard ones fitted to the camera before it is inserted into its case or added to a camera like the Nikonos. They enable you to dive into the exciting realms of macro-photography —still a new sphere for fish photography. However, when you fit extension tubes it is necessary for various optical reasons to increase the indicated exposure settings and this usually necessitates the use of flash in order to obtain a sensible depth of field.

Indeed, when using most of these close-up devices it is usually desirable to introduce flash for your illumination because this allows you to use a small aperture—$f/16$ or $f/22$—and enables you to get more of the subject in sharp focus. Electronic flash also eliminates the possibility of blur from camera movement—at high magnifications even the faintest quiver of the camera will ruin definition.

A single lens reflex camera makes easy work of close-ups, but its use still requires practice. Focusing is frequently so critical that the adjustment made by turning the control knob is too coarse. The best technique is to get the focusing approximately correct and then to rock backwards and forwards—or to wriggle back-wards and forwards in caterpillar style—to make the final adjustment.

However, if you meet a close-up subject when you haven't the appropriate lens, don't despair. Provided you are loaded with a fast film, set your camera at 1/30th and the smallest aperture that the film will permit and try your luck. The small aperture—with Tri-X in shallow water you can go down to $f/16$ or $f/22$—will enable you to move about 12 in. nearer and take a semi-close-up.

Of course it is not ideal to be using 1/30th. But there is a good chance of a reasonable result if you take your picture at a moment when the subject is stationary. It's easy with sea slugs for example because they never move quickly, but it will also work with livelier fish provided you catch them at the right moment. You must be patient . . . and never again forget your close-up lens.

Filters can be another worthwhile purchase although views as to their merits are varied—even among ourselves! They can be used to create special effects or to compensate for varying conditions.

A filter which some experts believe increases the general contrast of black and white film is a yellow one. However, this filter usually requires a one stop increase in exposure and it is questionable whether it isn't easier and just as satisfactory to use a one-stop slower film or extend the development of your normal film to get the same result. Most experts disagree with each other on this topic so you had better try one for yourself and make up your own mind.

Experts also have mixed views on the need to use ultraviolet filters. General photographic advice is always that surface sea-scapes are improved by their use and, while this seems to vary from camera to camera, it is generally true. Often, however, the most useful function a uv filter can perform is to keep sea spray off the front element of the lens and stop it being scratched by sand.

Another filter which is worth experimenting with is a cyan one. Its use will probably help you reduce the black backgrounds you get in flash pictures with black and white film. It will prevent some of the warmer colours revealed by the artificial light coming back at the film so strongly that they dominate the others.

The other group of filters are those which 'correct' the colours as they are seen by colour film. This is another subject on which underwater photographers have mixed views. Some believe you should show the underwater scene as it really is, green cast and all. Others use various filters to put back into the subject some of the colours which would otherwise not be visible because they are absorbed by the water.

In our view, these filters have a definite application for general photographic work, particularly cine, but their use is wrong for marine biological illustrations. Technical illustrations should be accurate. They should be made accurate either by the use of artificial light to restore the missing rays of the spectrum or by giving an unfiltered, diver's eye view of the subject.

However, let us assume you are more interested in enhancing the general appearance of your transparencies or film. In this case it is well worth experimenting with colour-correcting filters. But first you have to decide the actual colour of the sea before you can determine the filtration to use—red, magenta or even blue.

The best way to do this is to stand somewhere which enables you to look down through about 6 to 10 ft of water to a sandy seabed. Ask yourself, 'Does it look blue like a swimming pool, or green like grass or a bluey-green?' When you do this make sure that you look straight down into the water. Otherwise all you will really see is the reflection of the blue sky—if you are lucky— and you will draw a false conclusion.

Generally you will find a Colour Correcting Red (CCR) filter is suitable for blue or blue-green water, but a Magenta (CCM) one is more effective in particularly green conditions. You need greater skill and experience, however, if you propose to use a CCM. If you overfilter with red the results will be 'sunsety' but not too unpleasant. A mistake with the strength of a magenta filter will turn everything puce. And you too, probably, if it is an important shot!

The most universal application for colour correcting filters is to even up the backgrounds of your cine footage so that they all look as if they have been taken in similar conditions. If you are going to work in 5 ft of coastal water begin with a CCR 20. If you are going deeper down to 30 or 40 ft fit a CCR 40. If you are going deeper still don't bother because everything will be greyish-green anyway unless you introduce artificial light.

Both the colour-correcting range and other filters can be bought in gelatine sheets. This way they only cost a few pence. The easiest way to fit them to a camera with a removable lens is to stick them to the mount surrounding the rear element of the optic. A few tiny dabs of Evostik are all that is needed.

This is the best way to fit them to a Nikonos. Cut out a circle of gelatine and push it inside the rim of the lens mount. It can be held in place either by a few dabs of silicone grease, Vaseline or Evostik. But keep the lubricant or adhesive off the lens and don't scratch it either.

There is only one accurate way to judge exposure with a filter. Put another piece of the same gelatine filter over the window of the exposure meter. No further compensation is necessary.

In addition to those accessories we have already mentioned for the Nikonos, there are many others, mainly from American sources. The most interesting are mini-housings, which enable you to fit either a fish-eye lens or an extremely wide angle lens.

Maybe the fish-eye effect is not everyone's choice, but the lens has a number of practical applications as well as being a worthwhile creative tool. One of its great values is as a means of obtaining a picture in conditions which would beat any other lens.

Flip Shulke, the American photographer who developed these accessories and now markets them, was able to squeeze the shape of a whole killer whale on to his negative by means of the fish-eye. Nothing else would have covered the length of the fish within the limits of visibility and lighting that were prevailing at the time. Give the fish-eye another thought. After all, how better to portray fish than through another fish-eye?

Lenses with as short a focal length as 20-mm can be incorporated in another Shulke housing. They are ideal for photographing large fish or large shoals of fish where, despite refraction, you want to get a lot on a small negative and/or take the picture from as close as possible.

These mini-housings incorporate domes, which are now coming into general use on housings in place of flat portholes. They overcome the effects of refraction, restoring the lens to its normal field of view and therefore greatly improving picture quality. The theory behind the use of domes underwater is delightfully simple. Light passing from water into air does not suffer refraction if it passes through at right angles to the surface. With a flat porthole this applies only to the centre of the picture. But, if we make the porthole a transparent dome and if the camera lens is at its centre of curvature, then all light rays will pass through at right angles no matter how wide the lens angle.

Until recently it has been difficult and expensive to obtain a dome of sufficient optical quality for this purpose. But plastics manufacturers have discovered that if Perspex is carefully heated to an accurately controlled temperature and held in a special jig the flat sheet can be blown by compressed air to form a dome of near perfect optical quality at a satisfactorily low price.

The dome acts like a concave lens and, therefore, the camera lens has to be made 'short-sighted' to see clearly out through it. This is done by adding a supplementary lens—best worked out by trial and error—or using extension tubes to bring it into the 'close-up' range. Better still, use lenses which themselves will focus sufficiently close.

The 20-mm Flektagon, for example, focuses down to about 6 in. which is ideal when combined with a $3\frac{1}{2}$ in. dome. The focus/dome ratio is easily calculated. Infinity will be at about two-and-a-half times the diameter of the dome. This means that, with the 20-mm Flektagon, it will appear to be about $9\frac{3}{4}$ in. away.

Is a lifejacket a photographic accessory? Expert underwater photographers think so. They have used Fenzys for nearly five years and consider they are worth every penny of their £30-odd. Other makes of these compressed-air inflated jackets are now on the market.

This type of lifejacket is a working tool as far as the serious photographer is concerned, particularly if he dives with an aqualung. It means that he can dive in greater safety even when considerably overweighted with extra lead and other equipment. They can be used as an emergency air supply for a short period. They can be inflated and used to sit in at your ease on the surface for a rest or you can partially inflate them and make the swim back to shore that much easier.

One thing to avoid when you use these compressed-air life-jackets however, is having heavy cameras such as a Rolleimarin slung round your neck. Its weight will partially deflate the jacket. A heavy camera should be carried on a loop in the crook of your arm or secured by a safety line to one of the D-rings on the side of the life jacket.

£30-odd seems a large price to pay for a lifejacket. But you'll never regret the expense once you have used one for a few dives. In fact, in many ways, you should regard it as important a piece of diving equipment as your fins.

Last item on our list of accessories is a tripod—and you'll certainly need a Fenzy to help you cart a large one about. However, as underwater photographers are becoming more imaginative, there is increasing scope for the use of a tripod. It can be a distinct help if you are trying to compose very accurately a close-up shot. It also helps to keep the camera reasonably steady amid wave surge, especially if the tripod is festooned with about 12 to 16 lb of lead.

A tripod can also improve the quality of cine films where one of the most common faults is that the camera is not kept sufficiently steady, but waved about during shooting. It also can have its uses for time-lapse sequences where the camera is set up and then left to work automatically. You will probably not have the equipment to do this, but there could be merit in leaving your weighted tripod at a particular location so that you can return and mount your camera in that precise position again.

Obviously it doesn't do a tripod a lot of good to be immersed in the sea. However, a good quality alloy one with girder section legs won't come to a lot of harm if you always wash it thoroughly and immediately in fresh water when you come out of the sea. Dry it carefully—even using meths—and lubricate it each time. An alternative is to buy a surveying tripod from a surplus store. It will need some modification, but is cheaper and is mostly made of wood so that it doesn't need as much care.

Table top tripods can be extremely useful. They are small, but often give just the right amount of extra height to improve a close-up. If you look around you will be able to find one made either of stainless steel, or brass or steel coated in chrome. Don't forget to give it a good wash in fresh water after each dive in order to slow down corrosion.

The idea of mounting a camera on a tripod and then firing it by remote control has not yet been exploited, but it has considerable potential for fish photography. Colin Doeg still tells (with anguish) the tale of the mullet he saw nuzzling about within a few feet of Swanage Pier in shallow water. He had finished his day's diving and had packed up all his gear. But the opportunity was irresistible. So he unpacked everything, loaded fresh film in his camera and stealthily slid into the water.

As soon as the tip of his fin touched the water, the mullet vanished. As if pulled by a piece of string, it reappeared as soon as Colin walked away. The fun went on for over $1\frac{1}{2}$ hours. The moment Colin gave up and left the sea the mullet cheekily nosed its way back inshore. At one point Colin left his Nikonos on the seabed to mark the area favoured by the fish. As soon as he reached the pier, the mullet reappeared and began nuzzling the camera.

If it had been possible to mount the Nikonos on a tripod and fire it by remote control it would no doubt have been possible to obtain some excellent pictures. As it was, Colin returned home many hours later than he intended—without mullet pictures!

COLIN DOEG
GEOFF HARWOOD
PETER SCOONES

Appendices

Appendix 1

WHERE TO LEARN TO DIVE
Branches of the British Sub-Aqua Club

As long as you are a reasonable surface swimmer, the British Sub-Aqua Club will teach you to dive. All you have to do is to contact your local branch and apply for membership. Entrance fee is £2, which is really a payment for the Club's excellent Diving Manual, and the annual subscription is £4 (with reductions for junior members).

If you need any further details write to: The Director, The British Sub-Aqua Club, 160 Great Portland Street, London, W1N 5TB.

Ordinary branches in the United Kingdom, open to the general public

ABERDEEN (67): J. B. Gray, 20 Cairnory Road, Aberdeen.
ALDERSHOT (60): Miss H. Mackenzie, 52 Kingsway, Aldershot, Hants.
ALFRETON (302): I. Warhurst, 9 Dale Avenue, Riddings, Derby.
BARNSLEY (95): W. A. Burton, 398 Burton Road, Monk Bretton, Barnsley, Yorks.
BATH (33): Miss P. A. Molyneux, 'Conifers,' Hoopers Pool, Southwick, Trowbridge, Wilts.
BEDFORD (89): Mrs G. S. Potter, 11 Griffin Street, Rushden, Northants.
BELFAST (30): P. A. M. Paice, BA, 63 Glenholm Park, Belfast, BT8 41Q.
BERMONDSEY (42): F. H. White, 14 Brookehouse Road, London, SE6.
BIRMINGHAM (25): R. M. Leveton, 65 Burford Road, Birmingham 22C.
BLACKHEATH (188): M. Lovegrove, 102 Brampton Road, Bexley Heath, Kent.
BLACKPOOL (4): C. J. Walmsley, 10 Cumberland Avenue, Blackpool.
BOLTON (84): G. Diggle, 19 Top O'th Gorses, Darcy Lever, Bolton, Lancs.
BOURNEMOUTH (6): R. Smith, 15 Wickfield Avenue, Christchurch, Hants.
BRADFORD (44): Miss W. G. Walton, Barnsley Cottage, Charlestown, Baildon, Yorks.
BRIGHTON & WORTHING (7): J. F. MacMahon, 3 Leigh Road, Broadwater, Worthing.
BRISTOL (3): K. Hicks, 7 Eaton Close, Fishponds, Bristol, Somerset.
BROMLEY (26): M. Inch, 8 Alton Close, Bexley, Kent.
BURNLEY (143): D. Wakefield, Prudential Buildings, Manchester Road, Burnley, Lancs.
BURTON-ON-TRENT (296): G. G. Crofts, 29 Park Road, Stanton, Burton-on-Trent, Staffs.
CAMBRIDGE (240): M. J. Wilson, 5 Pettits Close, Fulbourne, Cambs.
CANTERBURY (326): J. R. Oaten, 6 Chequers Park, Wye, Nr Ashford, Kent.
CHAPLETON (256): M. Hobson, 106 Potters Gate, High Green, Sheffield.
CHELSEA (45): Miss Lilian Stokes, 82 Urmstone Drive, London, SW19.

APPENDIX 1

CHORLEY (304): A. Hardman, 42 Brown Street, Chorley, Lancs.
COTSWOLD (332): Mrs E. Birch, 16 Ashton Hill, Corston, Nr Bath, Somerset.
COVENTRY (58): Mrs J. McDonagh, 'Welcome,' Birmingham Road, Warwick.
CRAWLEY (148): Mrs C. J. Bramson, Wallace Lane, Crawley Down, Sussex.
CROYDON (23): R. S. Frankham, 38 Farley Road, Selsdon, Surrey.
DARWEN (47): A. Smith, 23 Thornhill Road, Chorley, Lancs.
DEPTFORD (M7) (236): R. Palmier, 42 Wrickle-Marsh Road, Blackheath, SE3.
DERBY (72): R. D. Price, 7 Howe Street, Derby.
DONCASTER (75): K. Rucastle, 'Ke-Bar,' 6 Conisburgh Road, Edenthorpe, Doncaster.
DUNDEE (334): J. Reilly, 83 Murrayfield Court, Dundee.
DURHAM CITY (104): C. R. Wells, 86 Moor Cross, Giles Gate Moor, Durham.
EAST ANGLIA (11): M. D. C. Maltby, c/o Anglia Television Ltd, Anglia House, Norwich.
EAST CHESHIRE (100): Mrs S. Hamer, Brooklyn Cottage, Holly Vale, Mill Brow, Marple Bridge, Cheshire.
EAST LANCS (2): Mrs P. A. Winterbotham, 5 Wilson Crescent, Ashton-under-Lyne, Lancs.
EAST LONDON (15): J. H. Simpson, 15 Colvin Gardens, Chingford, London, E4.
EAST YORKS (176): J. B. Forrest, 3 Morgan Street, Scarborough, Yorks.
EDINBURGH (21): Dr D. W. Green, 22 Priestfield Avenue, Edinburgh 9, Scotland.
EXETER (62): R. Ritchie, 36 Beacon Heath, Exeter, Devon.
FALMOUTH (214): G. Nicholls, 6 Mayfield Road, Falmouth, Cornwall.
FLINTSHIRE (167): R. J. Parke, 105 Barkhill Road, Vicars Cross, Chester.
FOLKESTONE (303): Mrs P. Wright, Upper Winterage Farm, Acrise, Nr Folkestone, Kent.
FURNESS (61): E. Lowther, 36 Foundry Street, Barrow-in-Furness, Lancs.
GRANTHAM (209): K. R. Mayes, 44 Belvoir Gardens, Great Gonerby, Grantham, Lincs.
GRIMSBY (37): M. C. Downs, Flat 83, Floor 14, Garibaldi House, Albion Street, Grimsby, Lincs.
GUILDFORD (53): M. Douglas, Leander, Manor Road, Farnborough, Hants.
GWYNEDD (71): Miss I. R. Beamer, 23 Llwyn Onn, Rhos-on-Sea, Colwyn Bay, N Wales.
HALIFAX (48): Mrs J. M. Cowan, Middle Hallershelf Farm, Luddenden Foot, Nr Halifax.
HAMPSTEAD (179): K. A. White, 125 Highfield Way, Chorleywood, Rickmansworth, Herts.
HARLOW (141): D. Johnson, 68 The Maples, Harlow, Essex.
HARROGATE (39): S. Clarke, 21 Castle Close, Killinghall, Nr Harrogate, Yorks.
HIGH WYCOMBE (293): E. Secker, 40 Princes Street, Piddington, Nr High Wycombe, Bucks.
HOLBORN (130): Miss E. J. Bryan, Flat 1, 88 Church Road, Lowther Parade, Barnes, London, SW13.
HOUNSLOW (55): R. C. S. Grove, 30 Forest Road, Kew, Surrey.
HUDDERSFIELD (18): K. Flinders, 15 Red Doles Road, Fartown, Huddersfield, Yorks.
HULL (14): P. McMullen, 12 Eden Rise, Ellerker Rise, Willerby, Hull, Yorkshire.
ILFORD (49): Mrs T. Lightfoot, 5 Macclesfield House, Dagnam Park Drive, Harold Hill, Romford, Essex.
ILFRACOMBE (86): N. Hutchinson, 27 Heanton Street, Braunton, N Devon.
INVERNESS (346): Mrs A. Aitken, 35 Greig Street, Inverness.
IPSWICH (32): A. R. Todd, 66 Beechcroft Road, Ipswich, Suffolk.
ISLE OF MAN (76): Mrs J. P. Colby, Bay View, Central Promenade, Douglas, IOM.
ISLINGTON (333): P. J. Kingston, 77 Knollys Road, London, SW16.
KEIGHLEY (117): Miss C. A. Woods, 9 Raeburn Drive, Buttershaw, Bradford 6, Yorks.
KINGSTON (17): J. Stanton, 5 Minerva Road, Kingston, Surrey.
LEAMINGTON & WARWICK (217): Miss J. M. Drabble, 33 Dugard Place, Barford, Warks.
LEEDS (115): BS-AC Sec, 65 Hall Lane, Leeds 12, Yorks.
LEICESTER CLUB DEL MAR (312): J. M. Collard, 3 Churchill Drive, Leicester Forest East, Leicester.
LEICESTER UW EXPLORATION (321): Mrs M. Mitchell, 191 Wicklow Drive, Leicester.
LINCOLN (109): A. C. Temperton, 29 Minster Drive, Cathedral View, Cherry Willingham, Lincoln.
LONDON (1): Mrs. M. Prendergast, 64 Elgin Mansions, Elgin Avenue, London, W9.
LUNESDALE (138): W. Torrance, Jnr Clenafton, 43 Worwood Drive, Torrisholme, Morecambe, Lancs.

LUTON (105): J. Austin, 9A Marsh Road, Luton, Beds.

MARGATE (106): Mrs V. J. Windridge, 'Rosedene,' 38 Price's Avenue, Cliftonville, Margate, Kent.

MATLOCK (121): P. A. Morley, 18 Warner Street, Mickleover, Derby.

MEDWAY (59): M. J. Varney-Burgh, 76 Townley Road, Bexley Heath, Kent.

MERSEYSIDE (5): Miss N. Cavanagh, 44 Meadow Lane, Willaston, Wirral.

MEXBOROUGH (41): J. Hardcastle, 73 School Street, Darfield, Nr Barnsley, Yorks.

NEWHAM (168): T. F. Barwick, 2 Markhams, Stanford-le-Hope, Essex.

NEWPORT & CARDIFF (35): Mrs V. Barlow, 28 Commercial Street, Newport, Mon, Wales.

NORTH EAST ESSEX (54): Mrs M. Long, 'Dornhurst,' 63 Colchester Road, Halstead, Essex.

NORTH OXFORDSHIRE (74): T. T. Winkless, 10 Park Road, Banbury, Oxon.

NORTHAMPTON (13): Mrs A. P. Shepherdson, 126 Beech Avenue, Northampton.

NORTH GLOUCESTERSHIRE (80): D. Rockett, 10 Cherry Avenue, Charlton Kings, Cheltenham, Glos.

NORTH STAFFS (12): W. J. B. White, Hilltop, 9 Liverpool Road E, Church Lawton, Stoke-on-Trent.

NORTH WARWICKSHIRE (315): R. J. Veasey, 71 Holyhead Road, Coventry.

NOTTINGHAM (16): D. J. Townsend 'Nerys,' Church Road, Boughton, Nr Newark, Notts.

OXFORD (34): Miss A. Symons, Bramblefinch, Boults Lane, Old Marston, Oxford.

PENNINE (323): Mrs J. V. Greenwood, 5 Hebden Terrace, Midgehole, Hebden Bridge, Yorks.

PENZANCE (116): R. H. Trethowan, 26 William Street, Camborne, Cornwall.

PERTH (218): D. L. Trail, 3 Abbey Road, Scone, Perthshire.

PETERBOROUGH (297): Miss L. Coates, 9 Elmfield Road, Peterborough, Northants.

PLYMOUTH SOUND (164): G. Jensen, 34 Fairview Avenue, Laira, Plymouth.

PONTEFRACT (190): Mrs P. Hudson, 30 Baden Powell Crescent, Pontefract, Yorks.

READING (28): R. J. Wilson, 33 Malone Road, Woodley, Reading, Berks.

REDDITCH (248): M. G. Odell, 25 Sherwell Drive, Alcester, Warks.

RHONDDA (282): E. G. Thomas, 47 Ely Street, Tonypandy, Rhondda, Glam.

ST ALBANS (311): V. R. Jones, 15 Alma Road, St Albans, Herts.

SCARBOROUGH (83): The Secretary, Scarborough Branch, British Sub Aqua Club, 25 St Mary's Street, Scarborough, Yorks.

SHEFFIELD (36): M. G. Plater, 32 Beechwood Road, Dronfield, Sheffield, Yorks.

SOLIHULL (264): R. A. Shale, 100 Richmond Road, Olton, Solihull, War.

SOUTHAMPTON (139): D. J. Millard, 25 Shaggs Meadow, Lyndhurst, Hants.

SOUTHEND (22): Mrs C. Hall, 'Rustana,' Lancaster Road, Rayleigh, Essex.

SOUTHPORT (278): R. Olive, 77 Cornwall Way, Ainsdale, Southport, Lancs.

SOUTHSEA (9): H. G. Yelf, 36 Carlisle Road, Southsea, Hants.

SWANSEA (99): C. D. Withey, 48 Meol Emrys, Swansea, Glam.

SWINDON (46): J. E. Hamilton, 11 Springfield Road, Swindon Old Town, Wilts.

TAMWORTH (137): E. S. George, 13 Borough Road, Tamworth, Staffs.

TAUNTON (10): A. C. Charlton, 'Lorien,' 11 Stoke Road, Taunton, Somerset.

TEES-SIDE (43): J. A. Sturrock, 13 Blackfriars, Yarm-on-Tees, Yorks.

THORNTON HEATH (210): P. Mann, 30 Springfield Road, Thornton Heath, Surrey.

THURSO (119): D. Mackay, 4 Sigurd Road, Thurso, Caithness.

TORBAY (8): E. A. Collins, 20 Sherwell Lane, Torquay, Devon.

TUNBRIDGE WELLS (149): Miss L. Gamlyn, Swan Hotel Garage, London Road, Tunbridge Wells, Kent.

TYNESIDE (114): H. Harvey, 40 Hulne Avenue, Tynemouth, Northumberland.

WAKEFIELD (77): S. Webb, 14 St Richards Road, Otley, Yorks.

WEST BROMWICH (151): F. J. Collier, 198 Frederick Road, Aston, Birmingham 6.

WEST CUMBERLAND (94): E. C. Carnhall, 71 Gosforth Road, Seascale, Cumberland.

WEST LANCS (153): N. Wall, 35 Finsbury Avenue, Blackpool SS, Lancs.

WESTMINSTER (159): L. Zanelli, 81 Long Lane, London, N3.

WESTRAY ORKNEY (340): W. F. Brown, Myrtle Cottage, Westray, Orkney.

YORK (50): R. C. Scaling, 'Ryedale,' Hull Road, Wilberfoss, York.

APPENDIX 1

Spearfishing branches

Spearfishing only, no Breathing Apparatus used

HOME COUNTIES (285): D. M. C. Rosemeyer, 87 Cambridge Road, New Malden, Surrey.
IPSWICH UNIVERSAL DIVERS (291): A. J. B. Beckerleg, 101 Claygate Lane, Ipswich, Suffolk.
SOUTHSEA BUBBLES (295): Mrs R. C. Pearce, 26 Stockheath Road, Leigh Park, Havant, Hants.
SPEARFISHING CLUB OF G.B., PLYMOUTH (286): A. Rendle, 24 Shaldon Crescent, Honick-nowle, Plymouth, Devon.
SUSSEX SPEARFISHING CLUB (289): J. P. Weedon, The Sussex Spearfishing Club, 'The Cricketers,' The Green, Southwick, Sussex.
WEYMOUTH ASSOCIATED DIVERS (269): R. J. Ford, 8 Reforne Close, Easton, Portland, Dorset.

Ordinary branches overseas

BARBADOS (310): Mrs S. K. Hendy, 'Barhill,' Elizabeth Drive, Pine Gardens, Bridgetown, Barbados.
BLANTYRE (243): W. A. L. Apps, PO Box 393, Blantyre, Malawi, Central Africa.
BS-AC DE PANAMA (262): J. H. Willis, Sn, PO Box 62, Coco Solo, Canal Zone, Panama, USA.
DURBAN ASSOC DIVERS (200): The Secretary, Associated Divers, PO Box 3396, Durban, South Africa.
INDIANAPOLIS-1ST USA (154): T. T. Haver, 6001 Compton, Indianapolis 20, Indiana, USA.
JAMAICA (51): The Secretary, Jamaica Sub Aqua Club, PO Box 215, Mona, Kingston 7, Jamaica, WI.
LIMASOL, CYPRUS (258): B. J. Leek, SCAF Supply Wing, RAF Akrotiri, BFPO 53.
MONTEGO BAY, JAMAICA (192): Miss D. Titterington, c/o Montego Bay High School for Girls, Union Street, Montego Bay, Jamaica, WI.
NAPIER NZ PACIFIC DIVERS (244): Miss R. A. Smith, Main Road, Clive Hawkes Bay, New Zealand.
NEE SOON (228): Q/Pte C. Orton, 32 Coy RAMC BMH c/o PO Singapore.
NEW JERSEY (220): F. A. Vogel, 1557 Deer Run Drive, Manasquan NJ 08736, USA.
NICOSIA MEROUS (147): Secretary, Nicosia Merous Sub-Aqua Club, c/o American Embassy, Nicosia, Cyprus.
RHODE ISLAND (284): Mrs W. S. R. Russell, 5 Porter Road, Middletown, Rhode Island, USA.
SALISBURY-RHODESIA (63): The Secretary, Salisbury R. Branch, BS-AC, PO Box 3532, Salisbury, Rhodesia.
TRINIDAD (129): A. Oliver, c/o Myerson Mouldings Ltd, PO Box 111, Port of Spain BWI.

Special branches—Home and Overseas

Membership confined to those who are members of the other organisations listed

ABERDEEN UNIVERSITY (314): R. B. Smith, Wavel House, Hill Head Halls of Residence, Don Street, Aberdeen, Scotland.
AQUATIC GROUP (180): Mrs D. R. Shiers, 11 Epping Way, London, E4.
ASTON UNIVERSITY (241): K. B. Higgs, 65 Wooton Cres., St. Annes, Bristol 4.
AWALI (261): R. C. Dickinson, Box 247, Awali, Bahrain, Arabian Gulf.
BARNARD CASTLE GARRISON (341): L/Cpl Gilduff, D., 5 OFP Stainton Camp, Barnard Castle, Co Durham.
BEA SILVER WINGS (146): Miss S. E. Savage, 21a Northdown Close, Ruislip, Middlesex.
BERLIN INF BRIG GROUP (203): 23802231 Sgt Oates, W. J., 247 Prov Coy RMP BFPO 45.
BOAC SPEEDBIRD (337): J. B. Wood, 159 Brabazon Road, Heston, Middx.
BOROUGH POLYTECHNIC (186): D. F. W. Hawes, 79 Tarnwood Park, Court Road, London, SW9.
BOSTON & HORNCASTLE SCHOOL (215): Secretary, Sub-Aqua Club, Boston & Horncastle Grammar School, Boston, Lincs.

APPENDIX 1

BP LLANDARCY (331): M. Thornbery, c/o BP Refinery (Llandarcy Ltd), Britannic House, Llandarcy, Neath, Glam.

BP MEADHURST (181): R. J. Fulleylove, Flat 2, Lordsbridge House, High Street, Shepperton, Middx.

BRADFORD CITY POLICE (195): R. Holt, Central Police Office, York House, Upper Piccadilly, Bradford 1.

BRISTOL AEROPLANE (88): N. Besant, 3 Bromley Drive, Downend, Nr Bristol.

BRISTOL UNIVERSITY (276): P. G. Baker, 9 Nugent Hill, Cotham, Bristol 6.

CAMBRIDGE UNIVERSITY (52): C. J. Wakefield, Trinity Hall, Cambridge.

CARNEGIE COLLEGE (287): K. S. Watson, Fairfax Hall, CLCC Backetts Park, Leeds, 6.

CASTERTON SCHOOL (335): Miss H. Jones, Vincent House, Casterton School, Bycarnforth, Lancs.

CHELSEA AND SIR JOHN CASS COLLEGES (123): Miss March, c/o Chelsea College SAC, Chelsea College, Manresa Road, London, SW3.

CITY UNIVERSITY (70): British Sub-Aqua Club, City University Union, St John Street, London, EC1.

29 COMMANDO LIGHT REGIMENT RA (268): Capt J. A. Cook, RAPC, 29 Commando Light Regt RA Dieppe Barracks, FAFB (FE) BFPO 164.

CRESTA QUAY (339): J. N. H. Stansbie, Devonshire House, Mrabat Street, Sliema, Malta, GC.

CROYDON TECHNICAL COLLEGE (187): M. K. Todd, 23 Hillcrest Road, Orpington, Kent.

DE HAVILLAND-BOLTON (101): A. Beddows, 129 Turton Road, Bradshaw, Nr Bolton, Lancs.

DHEKELIA (120): Cpl J. Wilson, RMP Provost Unit, Dhekelia, BFPO 53.

EBBW VALE SWIMMING CLUB (263): Brian Druce, 57 Stonebridge Road, Rassau, Beaufort, Monmouthshire.

EKON (234): E. E. Hutchings, 8 Fairview Drive, Watford, Herts.

EPISCOPI JS (150): Flt Lt S. J. Blower, Station Medical Centre, RAF Akrotiri, BFPO 53.

ETON COLLEGE (279): E. G. Lock, c/o R. H. Parry, Eton College, Windsor, Berks.

EXETER UNIVERSITY (246): M. D. Bailey, Brendon House, Birks' Grange, New North Road, Exeter, Devon.

EXUL (320): Miss E. P. Owen, 3/4 Balfour Place, London, W1.

FAMAGUSTA SERVICES (267): S/Sgt R. A. Jones, R. Signals, 9th Signal Regiment, BFPO 53.

FARELF (152): WO1 E. A. Kavanagh, c/o 40 Command Workshop, c/o GPO Singapore.

FIFTY-NINE CLUB (292): M. D. Elliott, 'Rosaburn,' Ivy Mill Lane, Godstone, Surrey.

1ST BN THE SHERWOOD FORESTERS (257): The Secretary Sub Aqua Club, LAD REME 1 Forresters, BFPO 57.

FORD MOTORS (227): M. Wakeling, 51 Windermere Avenue, Elm Park, Hornchurch, Essex.

4TH DIVISIONAL ENGINEERS (313): Lt B. N. Wilks, RE, 44 FD SP SQN, RE, BFPO 16.

GRANADA AQUANAUTS (253): P. B. Schofield, 17 King Street South, Rochdale, Lancashire.

HARROGATE ARMY APPRENTICES COLLEGE (350): Capt R. P. D. Brook, Army Apprentices College, Harrogate, Yorks.

HINCKLEY GRAMMAR SCHOOL (325): Hinckley Grammar School Sub Aqua Club, Hinckley Grammar School, Forrest View, Butt Lane, Hinckley, Leics.

HMS MAURITIUS (322): Porrel C. Cordwell, Senior Rates Mess, HMS Mauritius, BFPO 161.

HULL UNIVERSITY (245): The Secretary, Underwater Club, c/o The Union, University of Hull, East Yorkshire.

ILFORD FILMS (177): R. Simmons, 3 Railway Square, Brentwood, Essex.

ILFORD YOUTH WING (345): M. Ibbotson, Youth Tutor, Ifield Youth Wing, Crawley, Sussex.

IMPERIAL COLLEGE (64): The Secretary, IC Underwater Club, Imperial College, Union, Prince Consort Road, London, SW7.

JOINT HQ RHEINDALEN (277): Capt R. L. Thompson, RAMC, JHQ Rheindalen Sub-Aqua Club, c/o HQ BAOR (Med), BFPO 40.

JUNIOR PARACHUTE COY (342): WO11 A. Richer, Junior Parachute Coy, Browning Barracks, Aldershot, Hants.

JUNIOR SAPPERS (309): CSMI Dolphin, D., Jnr Ldrs Regt, Royal Engineers, Old Park Barracks, Dover, Kent.

LATHOL SPECIAL (306): P. Schofield, Swimming and Sub-Aqua Section, Billet Lane, Stanford-Le-Hope, Essex.

LEEDS UNIVERSITY UNION (124): The Secretary, Leeds University Union Sub-Aqua Club, c/o Leeds University Union, Leeds.

LIVERPOOL UNIVERSITY (280): The Secretary, Liverpool University Sub-Aqua Club, University Sports Centre, Bedford Street North, Liverpool, 3.

LONDON ARMY (328): Capt S. E. Roberts, RMP Lon Dist Pro Coy, RMP Kensington Palace Barracks, Church Street, Kensington, London, W8.

LONDON FIRE BRIGADE (250): B. Keane, 12 Maple Court, Winton Way, London, SW16.

LONDON HOSPITALS (254): M. J. Osborne, St Thomas's House, Lambeth Palace Road, London, SE1.

LONDON INTER-VARSITY CLUB (208): Miss H. F. A. Sewell, 39 The Riding, Woking, Surrey.

LONDON SCOUTS (20): W Best, 57 Henry Wise House, 53 Vauxhall Bridge Road, London, SW1.

LONDON UNIVERSITY (69): J. D. Harrison, Secretary, Sub-Aqua Club, University of London Union, Malet Street, London, WC1.

LOUGHBOROUGH COLLEGE (165): The Secretary, (BS-AC) Loughborough College Branch, c/o Mr Millard, 74 Holt Drive, Loughborough, Leicestershire.

LOUGHBOROUGH UNIVERSITY (238): M. E. Holden, Students Union, The Edward Herbert Building, Ashby Road, Loughborough, Leics.

MCMILLAN, BLOEDEL & NELSON (349): D. Kitson, c/o McMillan Bloedel Cont Ltd, Edward Street, Nelson, Lancs.

MARCONI BASILDON (219): S. J. Fawkes, c/o The Chairman, Basildon Marconi Branch BS-AC, c/o The Marconi Co Ltd, Christopher Martin Road, Basildon, Essex.

MARFA RIDGE MALTA USAF (351): Chester C. Craven Jr, Olympic Hotel, Paceville, Malta.

NAC-SAC (NAVAL AIR COMMAND SUB-AQUA CLUB) (66): R. W. Crocker, 51 Mongleath Avenue, Falmouth, Cornwall.

NEWBIGGIN SEA CENTRE (348): T. E. Wilson, 67 Northumberland Avenue, Newbiggin-by-Sea, Northumberland.

NEWCASTLE UNIVERSITY (249): Miss S. Duncombe, University of Newcastle.

NEW CROSS INSTITUTE (102): P. R. Hudson, 47A Lewisham Hill, SE13.

OTIS SPECIAL (301): P. McGivern, 45 Sandon Road, Walton, Liverpool 9.

OXFORD UNIVERSITY (169): David Squire, University College, Oxford OXL 4BH.

PENANG SWIMMING CLUB (225): The Secretary, Penang Swimming Club, 517 Tanjong Bungah, Penang, Malaysia.

RAAF BUTTERWORTH (230): The Secretary, BSAC, RAAF, Sub Aqua Club, RAAF Base Butterworth c/o Penang, Malaysia.

RAF AKROTIRI (107): 506528 Sqn Ldr Ashley, K. F., TPM, RAF Hospital Akrotiri, Cyprus, BFPO 53.

RAF BENSON (156): M. A. Leese, 1 Chipmunk Road, RAF Benson, Oxon.

RAF BINBROOK (224): Secretary, Sub-Aqua Club, RAF Binbrook, Lincoln.

RAF BRIZE NORTON (318): The Secretary, Sub-Aqua Club, RAF Brize Norton, Oxon.

RAF CHANGI (265): The Secretary, Changi Sub-Aqua Club, RAF Changi, c/o GPO, Singapore.

RAF CHIVENOR (329): Sac Miller, G., 'B' Flt 1 Sqdn, RAF Chivenor, Barnstaple, Devon.

RAF COLLEGE (193): Flt Cd C. J. Long, Junior Mess, RAF College, Cranwell, Sleaford, Lincolnshire.

RAF DEBDEN (274): Mrs S. Cass, 94 Debden Drive, Debden, Saffron Walden, Essex.

RAF EL ADEM (201): The Secretary, RAF El Adem Sub-Aqua Club, BFPO 56.

RAF FINNINGLY (211): Officer-in-Charge, Sub-Aqua Club, RAF Finningly, Doncaster, Yorkshire.

RAF GAN (126): Officer-in-Charge Sub-Aqua Club, Officers' Mess, RAF Gan, BFPO 180.

RAF GIBRALTAR (317): Flt Lt S. Brayshaw, Officer in Charge, Sub-Aqua Club, RAF Gibraltar.

RAF GUTERSLOH (221): K0689105 Cpl McGaw, A. M., 4 Sqn, RAF Gutersloh, BFPO 47.

RAF HALTON (247): Cpl Steward, G., 87 Longecroft Avenue, RAF Halton, Nr Aylesbury, Bucks.

RAF KAI TAK (344): Cpl P. Patterson, RAF Commcen, Hong Kong, RAF Kai Tak, BFPO 1.

RAF LEACONFIELD (307): The Secretary, RAF Leaconfield Sub-Aqua Club, Station Post Office, RAF Leaconfield, Beverley, Yorks.

RAF LEEMING (298): 1937745 SAC Todd, D. C., GRSF, RAF Leeming, Northallerton, Yorks.

RAF LYNEHAM (231): Flt Lt Warren, T. N., 15 Hungerford Road, Calne, Wilts.

RAF MALTA (213): The Secretary, RAF Malta SAC, RAF Luqa, BFPO 51.

RAF MARHAM (171): Fg Off M. S. Dean, 130 Sandringham Avenue, RAF Marham, King's Lynn, Norfolk.

RAF MUHARRAQ (242): RAF Muharraq, Sub-Aqua Club c/o PSI, RAF Muharraq, Bahrain, BFPO 63.

RAF NEWTON (255): Secretary, Sub-Aqua Club, RAF Newton, Nottinghamshire.

RAF NICOSIA (216): Cpl R. A. Sharp, ESS, RAF Nicosia, BFPO 53.

RAF NORTH LUFFENHAM (273): T4275075 Cpl Llewell, R. G., RAF North Luffenham, Oakham, Rutland.

RAF NORTHUMBRIA (324): D. A. Hewitt, Sgts Mess, RAF Acklington, Morpeth, Northumberland.

RAF ST ATHAN (281): 3508585 Flt Lt Martin, J. A., Officers Mess, RAF St Athan, Glamorgan, Wales.

RAF ST MAWGAN (288): Sgt D. Stevens, 83 Trelogean Road, Newquay, Cornwall.

RAF SCAMPTON (189): Secretary, Sub-Aqua Club, RAF Scampton, Lincoln.

RAF SELETAR (98): Secretary, Sub-Aqua Club, RAF Seletar, c/o GPO, Singapore.

RAF SHARJAH (270): E. A. White, PO Box 8, Sharjah, Arabian Gulf.

RAF STAFFORD (252): P4266869 SAC Beamish, W., c/o Transportation, No 16 MU, Stafford.

RAF TENGAH (134): The Secretary, Tengah Sub-Aqua Club, c/o Station Post Office, RAF Tengah, Singapore.

RAF TOPCLIFFE (319): V0684586 Sgt Hurst, D. G., 25 Chestnut Avenue, RAF Topcliffe, Thirsk, Yorks.

RAF VALLEY (308): Flt Lt 608372 Longdon, D. C., Officers Mess, RAF Valley, Anglesey, North Wales.

RAF WADDINGTON (251): Mrs A. B. Benfield, 24 Wellington Square, Waddington, Lincoln.

RAF WATTISHAM (299): E0588914 Sgt Maguire, J. J., MSS, RAF Wattisham, Ipswich, Suffolk.

RAF WILDENRATH (207): Mrs J. V. Edington, c/o D1948463 SAC Edington, J. M., ASF, RAF Wildenrath, BFPO 42.

RAF WITTERING (305): Secretary, Sub-Aqua Club, c/o RAF Wittering, Peterborough.

RAF WYTON (161): Secretary, BS-AC, Sgts Mess, RAF Wyton, Huntingdon.

RMA SANDHURST (202): The Secretary, Sub-Aqua Club, RMA Sandhurst.

2 ROYAL IRISH REG (343): L/Cpl Thompson, REME, 7 Beuna Vista, MSQ Gibraltar

RSASRG (91): P. M. Brosniham, 4 Gilson Way, Salisbury, Rhodesia.

RUISLIP & NORTHWOOD SWIMMING CLUB (206): Dr S. Laing, 10 Burwell Avenue, Greenford, Middx.

22 SPECIAL AIR SERVICE REGIMENT (327): Cpl W. Holden, 22 Special Air Service Regt, Bradbury Lines, Hertford.

SECOND DIVISION SIGNAL REGT (290): L/Cpl M. Goatley, 'B' Troop, 3 Sqn, 2 Division Sig. Regt. BFPO 22.

SELO BRENTWOOD (237): J. E. Sweetingham, 72 Fernbank Avenue, Elm Park, Hornchurch, Essex.

SEREMBAN GARRISON (259): Capt T. M. Pleyman, Seremban Garrison Sub-Aqua Club, 17 Div/Malaya Dist Pro Coy RMP, c/o GPO Seremban, Malaysia.

SHELL QATAR (336): S. R. H. Johnson, Shell Qatar SAC, The Shell Co of Qatar Ltd, PO Box 47, Doha, Qatar, Arabian Gulf.

7TH SIGNAL REGT (266): 483934 2/Lt Hughes, B. J., c/o Officers Mess, 7th Signal Regt, BFPO 15.

SOUTH SHIELDS VOLUNTEER LIFEGUARD (222): R. D. Osborne, 205 Stanhope Road, South Shields, Co. Durham.

STC BASILDON (204): Miss M. South, 14 Beehive Lane, Basildon, Essex.

ST ANDREWS UNIVERSITY (300): Miss R. L. Briggs, 12 Kilymont Road, St Andrews, Fife, Scotland.

ST JOHN'S SINGAPORE (223): J. Haddy, 131 Queens Avenue, Singapore 27.

SUNDERLAND TECHNICAL COLLEGE (275): Secretary, Sub-Aqua Club, Students Union, Sunderland Technical College, Sunderland, Co Durham.

TIDWORTH GARRISON (294): Major G. Rushby, 3 Div Pro Unit RMP, Tidworth, Hants.

TRIALS ESTABLISHMENT (338): Cpl J. D. Muscat, REME Wing, Ter Ty Croes Camp, Anglesey.

UNIVERSITY OF SURREY (316): R. A. Furneaux, 3 Ash Grove, Guildford, Surrey.

WALTON LIVERPOOL TECHNICAL COLLEGE (260): Miss P. L. Hassell, Flat 6, Larcherly Road, Fairfield, Liverpool 7.

WESTLAND (352): E. Smith, 32 Bucklers Mead Road, Yeovil, Somerset.

WILMOT BREEDEN (330): M. Waite, 46 Dagnall Road, Acocks Green, Birmingham 27.

WOOLWICH RI (162): T. H. Simms, 347 Old Farm Avenue, Sidcup, Kent.

WYCLIFFE COLLEGE (68): C. Ellis, No 7 Queen's Road, Stonehouse, Glos.

ZOOLOGY DEPT UC SWANSEA (239): Dr J. Moyse, Zoology Dept, University College of Swansea, Glamorgan, Wales.

THE BRITISH SOCIETY OF UNDERWATER
PHOTOGRAPHERS

All the authors of this book are members of the British Society of Underwater Photographers—and all the serious underwater photographers in Britain belong too.

The Society was formed in 1967 to form a central clearing house for all information about underwater photography and to enable members to meet and discuss their own particular techniques. This spread of knowledge has in fact saved members hours of experimental underwater photographic work and opened up the experts' 'secrets' to the complete beginner.

A comprehensive technical advisory service is available to all members. Regular meetings are held and a newsletter is circulated.

The Society is now concerned in the organisation of many of the major underwater photographic competitions in this country and members give lectures to any organisation or group of divers on request.

The annual subscription is £3.15.

For further information, write to: Geoff Harwood, The Secretary, The British Society of Underwater Photographers, 47 Dudley Gardens, Harrow, Middlesex.

EQUIPMENT SUPPLIERS AND MAKERS
OF HOUSINGS

Any good shop that sells diving equipment or any good photographic dealer can get the amphibious cameras for you and will have little difficulty in getting the better-known makes of housings.

But if your needs are more specialised the following sources will be of use to you:

AQUASNAP, 158 Oulton Road, Stone, Staffs. Have an amazing range of housings and will also build one specially for your camera (still or cine). This firm also sells controls etc. for those building their own housings. Write for their comprehensive catalogue.

TONY DIXON, 503A Gale Street, Dagenham, Essex. Will supply a standard range of cases as well as building one specially for you.

TIM GLOVER, 73 Platts Lane, London, N.W.3. A specialist in custom-built housings for cameras, electronic flash, exposure meters and TV cameras.

BIBLIOGRAPHY

1 Books on the art of diving

Note: You cannot learn to dive from books and must take a proper training course (*see* Appendix 1).
British-Sub Aqua Club Diving Manual
(from Club offices at 25 Orchard Road, Kingston-on-Thames, Surrey)
Atkinson, J., *Skin Diving With Snorkel and Aqualung*. Foulsham, 1968.
Balder, A. P., *Complete Manual of Skindiving*. Collier-Macmillan, 1968.
Busuttili, M., *Underwater Swimming*. Newnes, 1968.
Carrier, B. & R., *Dive*. Kaye, 1963.
Matkin R. B. and Brookes, G. F., *Scuba Diver*. Macdonald, 1963.
—— and ——, *Snorkel Diver*. Macdonald, 1961.
Poulet, G., *Complete Guide to Underwater Swimming*. Newnes, 1964.
Terrell, E., *The Principles of Diving*. Paul, 1965.
Zanelli, L., *Underwater Swimming*. E.U.P., 1967.
——, *Underwater Swimming, Advanced Handbook*. E.U.P., 1969.

2 Books on underwater photography

(Many of these are American and these are indicated by US after the publisher.)
Dobbs, H. E., *Camera Underwater*. Focal Press, 1962.
Frey, H. and Tzimoulis, P., *Camera Below*. Association Press (US), 1968.
John, D. H. O., *Photography on Expeditions*. Focal Press, 1965.
Rebikoff, D., and Cherney, P., *Guide to Underwater Photography*. Chilton (US), 1965.
Schneck, H. and Kendall, H. W., *Underwater Photography*. Cornell Maritime Press (US), 1957.

3 **Books for fish and marine mammal reference**

Alpers., A., *Dolphins*. Murray, 1963.

Burnaud, T., *Fishes*. Hamlyn, 1966.

Cooper, A., *Fishes of the World*. Hamlyn, 1969.

Croft, J., *Life in the Sea*. Hamlyn, 1969.

Danois, E. R., *Marine Life of Coastal Waters, Western Europe*. Harrap, 1957.

DeHaas, W. and Knorr, F., *Marine Life*. Burke, 1966.

Fishing News Ltd, *Multilingual Dictionary of Fish and Fish Products*. 1968.

Hardy, A. C., *The Open Sea: Fish and Fisheries*. Collins, 2 vols: I, 1956; II, 1958.

Heuvelmans, B., *In the Wake of the Sea-Serpents*. Hart-Davis, 1969.

Jenkins, J. T., *Fishes of the British Isles*. Warne, 1936.

Kenyon, L., *Discovering the Undersea World*. U.L.P., 1962.

Kosch, A., *Seashore*. Burke, 1963.

Lilly, J., *Man and Dolphin*. Gollancz, 1963.

Luther and Fiedler, *Die Unterwasserfauna der Mittelmeerküsten*. Paul Parey; also a Spanish ed.

Lythgoe, J. N. and Lythgoe, G. I., *Fishes of the Sea*. Blandford, 1971.

McCormick, H. W. and Allen, T., *Shadows in the Sea (Sharks, Skates and Rays)*. Sidgwick and Jackson, 1964.

Marshall, N. B., *The Life of Fishes*. Weidenfeld and Nicolson, 1965.

Ommonney, F. D., *The Fishes*. Time Life International, 1963.

Ray, C., and Ciampi, E., *Underwater Guide to Marine Life*. Kaye 1958.

Stenuit, R., *Dolphin, Cousin to Man*. Dent, 1969.

Theodor, *Mediterranée Vivante*. Payot.

Wells, A. L., *Observer's Book of Sea Fishes*. Warne, 1958.

Wheeler, A., *The Fishes of the British Isles and N.-W. Europe*. Macmillan, 1969.

4 **Books of general interest relating to fish and/or underwater photography**

Butterfield, A. and Greenberg, J., *The Coral Reef*. Hamlyn, 1965.

Carson, R., *The Sea Around Us*. Panther, 1969.

——, *The Edge of the Sea*. Panther, 1965.

Carson, R., *Under the Sea-Wind*. Panther, 1965.

Cousteau, J-Y., *The Silent World*. Hamish Hamilton, 1953.

——, *The Living Sea*. Hamish Hamilton, 1963.

Cropp, B., *Shark Hunters*. Angus and Robertson, 1965.

——, *Whale of a Shark*. Angus and Robertson, 1969.

Dugan, J., *World Beneath the Sea*. National Geographic, 1967.

Eibl-Eibesfeldt, I., *Land of a Thousand Atolls*. Macgibbon and Kee, 1965.

Gillett, K., *The Australian Great Barrier Reef*. Reed, 1969.

Hass, H., *We Come from the Sea*. Jarrolds, 1958.

——, *Expedition into the Unknown*. Hutchinson, 1965.

Hull, S., *The Bountiful Sea*. Sidgwick and Jackson, 1966.

Lorenz, K. Z., *On Aggression*. Methuen, 1966.

Lurie, R., *Under the Great Barrier Reef*. Jarrolds, 1966.

McDonald, K., *The Underwater Book*. Pelham, 1968.

——, *The Second Underwater Book*. Pelham, 1970.

——, *More than Skin Deep*. Pelham, 1971.

——, *How to get more fun from your boat*. Pelham, 1970.

McKee, A., *Farming the Sea*. Souvenir, 1967.

Monkman, N., *Quest of the Curly-Tailed Horses*. Angus and Robertson, 1963.

Shroeder, R. E., *Something Rich and Strange*. Allen and Unwin, 1967.

Slosky, B. and Walker, A., *Guide to the Underwater*. Oak Tree, 1966.

Straughan, R. P. L., *Exploring the Reef*. Kaye and Ward, 1968.

Woods, J. D. and Lythgoe, J. N., *Underwater Science*. O.U.P., 1971.

Index

1311 H · 5/5 ·